Hellions

Pop Culture's Women Rebels

Maria Raha

SEAL PRESS

Hellions
Pop Culture's Women Rebels

Published by Seal Press
A Member of the Perseus Books Group
1700 Fourth Street
Berkeley, CA 94710

Library of Congress Cataloging-in-Publication Data
Raha, Maria.
  Hellions : pop culture's women rebels / by Maria Raha.
    p. cm.
  Includes bibliographical references.
  ISBN-13: 978-1-58005-240-5
  ISBN-10: 1-58005-240-1
  1. Women in popular culture--United States. 2. Sex role--United
States. 3. Feminism--United States. I. Title.
  HQ1410.R34 2008
  305.420973--dc22
                        2008018646

Cover design by Tabitha Lahr
Interior design by Tabitha Lahr
Printed in the United States of America
Distributed by Publishers Group West

Dedicated to the feminist super-renegades of the 1970s
and all women
who have eased the way

Epigraph

It is useless to go to the great men writers for help, however much one may go to them for pleasure. Lamb, Browne, Thackeray, Newman, Sterne, Dickens, De Quincey—whoever it may be—never helped a woman yet, though she may have learnt a few tricks of them and adapted them to her use.

—Virginia Woolf, *A Room of One's Own*

contents

introduction ● 1

chapter 1 ● The Rebel Curve 10

chapter 2 ● Crime and Punishment 46

chapter 3 ● Cherry Bombs 85

chapter 4 ● The Political Gets Personal 122

chapter 5 ● The Taming of the Shrew 151

chapter 6 ● Angels, Aliens, and Ass Kicking 185

chapter 7 ● Uneasy Riders 218

conclusion ● 243

notes ● 249

works cited ● 263

introduction

"You mustn't give your heart to a wild thing. The more you do, the stronger they get, until they're strong enough to run into the woods or fly into a tree. And then to a higher tree and then to the sky."[1]

—Holly Golightly, *Breakfast at Tiffany's*

Rebels have always populated my life. When I was young, mostly fictional outcasts fought for elbow room in my thoughts, on my overstuffed bookshelf, and in the prime-time television companionship I cherished when I was too young to know better. Many of the women and girls whose audacity I admired were questionable rebels at best, but they all somehow went against the cultural grain, informed my own rebellious sensibility, engaged and emboldened my spirit, and propelled me to search for more marginalized stories, characters, authors, and images as I grew up. Among others, there was Jo Polniaczek on the sitcom *The Facts of Life* and *Little Women's* Jo Marsh. There was the gum-cracking, rock 'n' roll cool of Pinky and Leather Tuscadero on *Happy Days;* Rizzo in *Grease;* a vengeful Carrie White; Cyndi Lauper; Pat Benatar; the quiet and confused opposition of the characters Judy Blume created; a shorn-haired Helen Slater running for her life in *The Legend of Billie Jean;* the outcast girls of John Hughes's films; and Nellie Oleson on the TV version of *Little House on the Prairie.*

I always favored pop culture's rebellious characters, whether sneaky, snide, or sassy—no matter what the medium or how badly they behaved. Any female character who couldn't keep me laughing, reading, or rapt instantly lost my attention. I cringed at the transformation of an apathetic, goth Ally Sheedy into a pearls-and-lace "pretty girl" in *The Breakfast Club,* and delighted in the insolent frown of blond-haired, blue-eyed Nellie Oleson. I was perfectly content with the way all these individualistic characters clamored to inform my definition of girlhood and womanhood, and what kind of woman I wanted to be. I found kindred spirits in fictional outcasts, sympathized with acts of willfulness that I didn't see in reality, and witnessed bravery greater than any I'd found in traditional leading women or mainstream pop stars. Rebel girls and brats inspired me, made me feel less alone, and allowed me to smile at my own impertinence and at the seemingly unlimited possibilities of being a young girl and, later, a young woman. With an inner sneer, an outer temper, and a bent toward mischief good and bad, I was utterly possessed by girls who were far from sugar and spice and everything nice. They legitimized me.

When I was twelve, something else came along. I saw *Rebel Without a Cause* for the first time, and was hooked faster than I could mutter, "Sayonara, Rizzo." Maybe I needed the complexity (and sensuality) of James Dean's Jim Stark as I grew into a more complicated and rebellious girl. I began watching *Rebel Without a Cause* at least once a week, forgoing reruns of movies and television shows populated with the varied characters I was raised with through the '70s. Although I watched *Rebel* countless times, I have no memory of how I felt about Natalie Wood's conflicted and angst-ridden Judy. All I remember is Jim, slumped over and brooding, as he suffered through and resisted the dysfunction of '50s middle-class culture.

Later, as I became consumed with the counterculture that defined the 1950s and '60s, I started reading Jack Kerouac, Tom Wolfe's *The Electric Kool-Aid Acid Test,* and Hunter S. Thompson, and listening to Jimi Hendrix and the Doors, wishing I could write and live the way they did. Though the classic rebel image excluded bad girls, such as the characters who had formerly resounded with me, I slipped uncomfortably into romanticizing countercultural rebels without a thought to where the women around them lived or how they loved. Lacking easy access to female rebels who evolved with my own resistance and cultural sensibility, I threw myself wholeheartedly into classic American-male rebellion. At the time—as all of the women rebels I'd witnessed as a girl slunk off the air or offscreen, or became victims of cultural amnesia—no other option seemed quite as appealing.

I willed myself to ignore the fact that mid-twentieth-century American rebel men were still the standard for cultural images of rebellion, and that women, on the whole, were denied the right to enjoy similar renegade status. Instead, they were relegated to merely decorating the edges of men's lives and art, or serving as folly between men's travels, or plotting to foil male wanderers' plans. And I didn't think twice about why the presence of the women I saw as rebels and outcasts during my childhood were fleeting, while the male characters and icons—along with Marilyn Monroe straddling a subway grate and Lucy Ricardo whining to her husband, Ricky—long outlasted the zeitgeist from whence they came.

There's nothing inherently wrong with wanting to follow the trails blazed by loner rebel males. Beneath the surface and beyond the formula, though, there are many ways in which to rebel, live creatively, and be an individual. The girls of every decade who are restless enough to want to follow the call of the road, and who aren't satisfied with mainstream culture's limited examples of female defiance, end up adoring the very heroes who would relegate them to the back seat of rebellion. The Beat Generation's fixation on movement and spontaneity meant favoring new experiences no matter whom they left in their dust. Neal Cassady—Kerouac's and Ginsberg's mythic muse, a legend of the generation to younger fans, and the man on whom the enigmatic Dean Moriarty is based in *On the Road*—bounced from wife to lover and back to wife again. In 1950, he took a jaunt to Mexico, intending to get a divorce from his wife, Carolyn. After leaving Mexico, he headed to New York, married another woman, and got her pregnant without having divorced Carolyn.[2] Later, he returned to Carolyn and then left her again. It wasn't as if women were only a passing thought, either—Kerouac kept lists of the women he'd slept with and when, and Cassady sent letters to his friends detailing his conquests.[3]

The women involved in the Beat movement also wrote furiously, but without landing the acclaim granted to Jack Kerouac, William

Burroughs, and Allen Ginsberg. Diane di Prima, for example, has written forty-three books and has been praised by her male peers, yet she is hardly as synonymous with the Beat movement's influence as the aforementioned men. Given all the old trappings of what we as a culture consider attractive and culturally legitimate when it comes to women—and given target-marketed cultural products' recent return to extreme gender specificity—most girls will dream only of dating a rebel, not of actually becoming one. The former dream seems safer and more accessible, if we measure it based on the ways in which active female artists often seem ill-fated and undermined, versus the fame and comfort that many male artists' wives and girlfriends enjoy. It certainly has a history of more tangible social success than rebellion itself does.

Our most iconic, earlier images of male rebellion captured the imagination as powerfully as they did in the 1950s and '60s because, in an era when domesticity reigned, they symbolized courage, possibility, and liberation from the stranglehold of governmental authority and the status quo. But male rebellion also repeatedly whispers the limits women and girls represent to wandering American masculinity. As we sift through popular American rebel culture, we will find accommodating femininity in movies like *The Wild One;* nonconforming women who renege on their rebellion (as in *Breakfast at Tiffany's*); or women punished by others or by themselves for their difference (as in the cases of writers Sylvia Plath and Dorothy Parker). Exposed to repeated messages of what attracts the loner rebels they admire and what generally happens if they themselves rebel, as well as to the veneration of breathy and compliant female celebrities like Marilyn Monroe, young girls and women haven't been given many examples of how they can be simultaneously attractive, restless, roaming, and appealing in the same way that male icons are. In capturing the pop-culture imagination, our female legends' claims to fame are usually limited to one of these characteristics—which makes their allure predictable and uninspired compared with the ever-present enigma that their male counterparts represent.

We worship certain men and women merely for their reinforcement, their embodiment, of the most hardened and pure aspects of traditional gender roles—Brando oozed machismo; Monroe was steeped in submissiveness. What I didn't realize as a young woman was that iconic images also have certain hidden layers that deepen their meaning—underpinnings that our culture has forgotten or ignored, but that could be discovered by scratching their surface.

For instance, there are ways to read beyond the romanticization of Sylvia Plath's desperation and Virginia Woolf's despair, just as there are darker sides to the energetic bounce of the Beat movement. There are women whose insubordination we've largely forgotten, such as Mae West, and visionary women we might not consider subversive, like Susan B. Anthony. While the men we've come to know as touch-stones for rebellious imagery actually reinforce white masculinity, the women we deem immortal reveal how we as a culture view women who stand out. Marginalized outlaws who didn't make the cut for the rebellion canon may not appear intriguing on the surface, but in reality, the backlashes of people of color, the queer community, and white women have always presented greater risks than those of culturally sanctioned male rebels. Questioning the narrow definitions we've allowed for our pop-culture rebels also makes room for examining and revering other, more interesting men and women.

The truth that may appear too late (or for some girls may never appear at all) is that women can be angry and restless and still appealing as women—and that we can be so without the complete social rejection we're taught comes with rebellion.

Unfortunately, because we're presented with such limited options of womanhood, we tend to downplay our differences, as pop culture's examples have urged us to do, in order to remain acceptable and attractive in mainstream culture. Without having robust models of revolt that mainstream culture embraces, young girls are far less likely to explore their own self-defined, diverging paths.

*E*mbodying rebellion or denying it tends to be an either/or proposition for female icons. James Dean in *Rebel Without a Cause* can appear alternately angry, frightened, sad, sexy, and tough. Women who exist outside of the traditional leading-lady role or the virgin/whore divide are usually quirky (like Edie Sedgwick) or evil (like Joan Crawford or Bette Davis). And the good, wholesome, loyal leading ladies don't generally have a voracious sex drive or occasional wanderlust. Few female characters embody complex sexuality, rebelliousness, and kindness all at once. A woman who abandons a traditional female role or her family the same way men do, by easily hopping on her bike and leaving town, is considered cruel—a role saved for the vamp or the villain.

Images like these, which lean on stereotyping even while bucking it, appear paired with today's Hollywood celebrities. The escapades of Kate Moss, Lindsay Lohan, and Paris Hilton have made them the real-life representations of *Sex and the City*'s sexually rabid Samantha Jones—wealthy, notorious, and hopelessly self-indulgent—and these young women garner media attention for merely indulging themselves. If these are our culture's "bad girls," have we really evolved from last century's symbols, whose cultural contributions were, at the very least, tangible? With women like these becoming more infamous and celebrated, how do women rebel, roam, and retain their sexuality? When our media markets shift from one celebrity sex scandal to another, and physical attractiveness is the most important feature on offer for teenage girls, what image will they be drawn to? Surely it won't be Peter Fonda in *Easy Rider,* or even the eventually lonely and conflicted Holly Golightly in *Breakfast at Tiffany's.*

In the stilted version of womanhood our culture touts, there is no love for outcast or wayward women. The underlying message remains the same: Rebellion rarely comes with love; if a rebel loves, she gives up her ability to be a rebel. There is no additional consideration for a woman's love for the world around her, or for the autonomy that indicates self-love. As a result, what passes for female rebellion upholds the status quo, rather than breaking new ground. This pattern leaves real rebellion underrecognized and ignored by a culture that refuses to acknowledge that women experience the same restlessness as men do—and are naturally curious about and long for alternate paths of resistance.

What I learned as I delved into the cast of memorable and pioneering women nestled in these pages is that each of these women's lives and personalities contain relevant, insightful stories that can help inform and enrich our own identities as strong, powerful women. From Sylvia's and Virginia's discipline to Marilyn's and Janis's disappointments; Bettie Page's sexual liberation; Mae West's biting wit; Angela Davis's, Jane Fonda's, and Eleanor Roosevelt's optimistic drive;

Pam Grier's gun-toting vigilantism; Susan B. Anthony's determination; and Cindy Sheehan's confrontational and public righteousness, each of these women have something inspiring and empowering to offer us—even when our culture remembers them less than fondly. They can propel us toward our own individual rebellions and can conjure the same contagious excitement and intellectual stimulation that male rebellions have provided decade after decade. Given the relative lack of freedom and the public criticism female icons face, our "other" rebels have more to offer us than the much-lauded rebel-male movement.

I know how bored I would have been as a young girl if pop culture's quasi-rebels hadn't filled my head, my bedroom, and my imagination. I want girls and young women to see themselves in our most influential public figures, and to be filled with a sense of possibility, rather than the isolation, inadequacy, or self-deprivation that we witness women inflicting on themselves in pop culture. I'd like to think these women could make our souls soar. And I can't imagine what a dull world it would be if, as adults, we merely tiptoed the same slight tightropes as those whom we lionize. Only when we elect collectively to relish a broader range of emotion, intellect, humor, and misbehavior in the women we idolize will the general population of Western women accept their own broad range of flaws and strengths. And only then will others embrace us for flaunting those qualities.

chapter 1
The Rebel Curve

"Hey, Johnny, what are you rebelling against?"
"What've you got?"[1]
—The Wild One

Brooding and cool, slumped over and sneering, rebels have been a cultural landmark for each generation since the beginning of the twentieth century. In the 1931 film *The Public Enemy*, for instance, James Cagney's Tom Powers perched at his breakfast table, perusing the paper and gorging on breakfast as he sat beside Kitty (Mae Clarke). A stereotypical early-twentieth-century gangster moll—anxious, gum-chewing, and cutesy—Kitty hounded him in her high-pitched voice.

Just as Kitty's predictable cuteness and nagging misrepresented real womanhood, Cagney's character was far from being the societal threat the film billed him as. The infamous outburst in which Powers, fed up with Kitty and her incessant squealing, ground a half-moon of grapefruit into her confused, crumpled face, should have made his character infinitely less likable. But instead of remaining a public enemy, his frustrated persona became a classic Hollywood image, and his resistance pumped blood into the portraits of angst-ridden men as time went on.

The classic rebel formula keeps rearing its macho head, proving that its popularity hasn't faded. Fast-forward to 1980 and *Raging Bull's* initial depiction of prizefighter Jake La Motta's family life as he sat at home, eating and talking to his brother, Joey. In the first of many incensed moments that characterized Jake's relationships in the biopic, he abruptly upended the kitchen table as his wife hurried into another room to the soundtrack of his death threats: "You break anything in there, and I'm gonna kill ya! I swear to God, I'm gonna come in there and I'm gonna kill ya!"[2] The brutish reactions of both La Motta and Powers to these women were conveyed as "acceptable" emotion in male antiheroes. They also painted a dark picture of the rebels' need to disrupt the domestic lives that suffocated them.

Beginning in the mid- to late 1990s and persisting today, many of the most successful rappers have promoted the themes of gangsta rap—once a subgenre of a larger, more politically and socially oriented hip-hop movement—from a place of ordained authority: 50 Cent brags about his multiple gunshot wounds, and the lifestyle of the hustler is routinely glorified, most notably in Snoop Dogg's cartoonish, recent incarnation as a cane-wielding, slyly self-satisfied "pimp." The 2005 film *Hustle & Flow* took a compassionate stance toward poverty and desperation but also deified its incarcerated bad-boy protagonist and received an Academy Award for 36 Mafia's hit "It's Hard Out Here for a Pimp." And consider the anger simmering in Eminem, who, before his rhymes focused on his celebrity status, wrote "Kim," the story of a man drowning his trunk-trapped wife while his daughter witnessed her murder.

Although it's too soon to know whether today's rebels will outlast their generational popularity in the same way the post–World War II American renegades did, the popularity of someone like 50 Cent— whose 2003 mainstream debut album, *Get Rich or Die Tryin,* sold more than eight hundred thousand copies in its first four days, and whose follow-up album, *The Massacre,* sold 1.14 million in the same stretch of time—indicates that some of these rebels are destined to become legends.[3]

Since the male rebels we dote on treat women with such contempt, we need our own antiheroic cachet. That's precisely why female rebels are so essential to growing up in this crazy country. When I say "crazy," I'm referring to the hands-down maddening mixed messages we're bombarded with when we're young: We're told that courage involves doing the right thing, being ourselves, thinking our own thoughts, and sticking by our developing ideals and those instilled in us. We are educated about the American Revolution and the revolt against authority that developed the United States. We're taught that freedom, liberty, and our historical rebellion against an oppressive authority are the cornerstones of American life. We learn about the value of difference—but only enough to retain that old "melting pot" moniker. And we're expected to conform enough to succeed in school and obey the law.

Then we become young women who are expected to avoid getting too fat, too loud, too inquisitive—no matter who we are, what our backgrounds are, or whether or not we're receiving other, more accepting messages at the same time. We should hold ourselves out there for young boys to see, but retain our virginity for as long as we can. Look, but don't touch. Indulge, but not too much. Love ourselves, but with limits. We're told to avoid being too angry or unhappy, yet we're also taught that we should never be satisfied with ourselves: We should constantly seek self-improvement through wearing what the media tells us is the "right" clothing, makeup, and accessories, and through avoiding typically masculine behavior. We shouldn't be too aggressive (though assertiveness occasionally makes a comeback). For women, having "enough" self-love translates into caring for ourselves in the way traditional beauty standards and the industries relying on those standards require, but not enough to inspire an all-out rejection of them.

Perhaps the most powerful societal message of all is an idea that's imposed on us starting from the time we're old enough to harbor memories: We're bamboozled by the idea of marriage and true love as the ultimate life-success story. And even as the number of single women in the nation grows, we're told that if we don't marry by a certain age, we've done something wrong. We're told that our wedding day is the biggest day of our lives—next to having a baby, of course. We're often pitied or reviled for valuing our careers over our children, our minds over our bodies, or wanderlust over suburban stability.

Pressure to conform to these traditional ideas about womanhood can negatively affect wandering, wondering, questioning women when we try to explain our lives to uncomprehending family members, friends, and even strangers. We begin to doubt ourselves. The looks and the questions can make us feel undervalued, unworthy, or unwomanly. We become oddities and rebels, alienated from ourselves—and often lonely. When we become aware of the expectation to rein in our zestful girlhood dreams as we get older, that knowledge can deaden our former passion and foster resentment of other women who can represent the female ideal easily.

Sorting out that conflict can lead young women to become consumed with being desirable, especially at a time when social rejection is a daily fear. But when we begin resisting our true spirit— as layered human beings who don't always want to eat, do, wear, or say the "right" thing—the sense of mischief that seems so present in childhood slips away. Instead of embracing our complexity and imperfections and questioning the physical and behavioral standards set for us, we end up turning for inspiration to the examples we're inundated with on television, in new media, and in our daily lives.

To complicate matters, the media landscape that influences our ideas about femininity and encourages us to display overt sexuality is increasingly vast, technologically complicated, and individualistic. We have access to more diverse depictions of women, many of which fill the representational gaps that existed in the past. But how many of those are prevalent enough to drown out the narrower view of womanhood lurking in publications like *Cosmopolitan,* on television shows like *Desperate Housewives,* or in the menagerie of backstabbing, emotionally damaged women found in gossip magazines or on almost any "reality" television show today? The most accessible and repetitive presentations of women, those traveling through the pop-culture pipeline, become the most resounding messages young girls receive about what kind of women gain cultural attention, and what kind of women young girls should become. Unsurprisingly and unfortunately, the most ubiquitous images of women are usually the most ridiculously self-indulgent, greedy, and debased—and least interesting and complex—ones readily available to the general public. We see Victoria's Secret ad campaigns; *America's Next Top Model, Rock of Love,* and *The Real Housewives of Orange County;* a host of hopelessly mediocre sitcoms; MTV's parade of shallow programming and video vixens; blockbuster Hollywood comedies full of boring or witless beauties; vicious, violent, lonely, or corrupt women (most recently glorified in *Notes on a Scandal*); and the even less engaging army of stock characters retread in romantic comedies, often highlighted by the toothy, white-bread smile of a non-threatening, multimillionaire actress such as Julia Roberts.

As a woman who doesn't meet mainstream beauty standards; who has never had enough money to even consider indulging in material overconsumption (another expectation for women); who questions too much and is too loud, too angry, and too unhappy with the world around her much of the time, I know the most important thing to me during some of the most challenging times in my life has been cultural images commemorating women who pick up, move on, and stare down convention like a time-tested enemy. As American culture continues to overvalue beauty and wealth—as in our continuing fascination with Hollywood's cadre of rich, young, and socially irresponsible women—it abandons women who don't slip easily into the very narrow roles we prescribe, and makes affirming our own worth seem impossible. Young girls are surrounded with the message that being underweight, privileged, and fairly ignorant is the primary way to hold society's attention. Relishing female rebellion and widely permitting women to be as "cool" as the boys, on the other hand, allows other, less prominent rebellious females to love themselves.

Amid such pitiful fare, culturally prominent female rebellion becomes increasingly important in battling the broken, battered, bruised images we're subjected to as women. Rebel women fill the holes, inhabit empty spaces, and help American girls seeking more engaging, attainable images feel less lonely and less insane. They certainly make America seem less crazymaking and less alienating. For those reasons alone, female images are worth reevaluating—and female rebellion is worth celebrating.

*T*hroughout our pop cultural history, we have occasionally celebrated acts of female bravery—such as those of Rosa Parks or Florence Nightingale—and we *admire* many women for it. We do not, however, make such women as seductive or as glorified in film or in print, or grant them as much mystique and power as we do pop culture's American rebel male. Our stories of female rebellion, both fictional and true, are tempered by self-destruction (Janis Joplin), desperate isolation (Sylvia Plath), or political or social abandonment (Cindy Sheehan). When women have spoken out, instead of honoring them, we memorialize the ways in which female rebels have been maligned, burned, driven to destruction, reduced to physicality alone, or, worst of all, forgotten and neglected. The moral of the conventional story is rarely that a woman who fights the good fight will win—or even survive.

Women certainly deserve to be remembered for fighting the good fight and taking risks. We have been suffragists like Susan B. Anthony;

feminists like Gloria Steinem; and courageous groundbreakers like the girls of the Little Rock Nine, who desegregated Central High in 1957, despite the presence of an irate Arkansas governor and the National Guard. We have been Italian immigrants protesting unsafe working conditions in New York City's Greenwich Village in the early twentieth century; women who formed the reactionary New York City and Washington, DC, dyke marches in 1993. We have fought for birth control, abortion, sexual freedom, job safety and security, childcare, women's safety, and gender, racial, and class equality. We have spoken out against war, nuclear weapons, and global oppression; we have died for more causes than one woman can list. We continue to be leaders, resistance fighters, political prisoners, soldiers, and activists. In other words, women have always actively contributed to progressive rebellion. When these movements haven't wanted us in their ranks, we've shrugged our shoulders, mobilized, and struck out on our own. Privately and individually, we rebel by assessing cultural messages and choosing which ones we will walk away from, which ones we'll publicly critique, and which ones we'll accept. Whenever we're empowered or inspired by another woman's courage, we demonstrate the necessity of diverse, widely recognized images of and stories about rebellious women.

Giving voice to our dissatisfaction galvanizes support, facilitates change, and provides comfort for outcasts. Female artists have always been defiant in a culture that legitimizes male pursuits in music, literature, and all forms of visual art far more than it does works produced by women. In 1928, Radclyffe Hall published the controversial novel *The Well of Loneliness,* which laid bare the struggle and secrecy associated with being a lesbian, and sparked censorship debate and a 1928 trial in London.[4] In 1963, Betty Friedan's *The Feminine Mystique* explained how damaged suburban housewives were and sparked the feminist revolution of the late 1960s and '70s. Punk rock and its most revered female progenitor, Patti Smith, sprouted dozens of women of her generation who looked, acted, and thought differently than most other popular female musicians did, affecting the way women performed rock music across all styles and expanding female musical self-expression. These and other landmark female artists sparked new movements, articulated women's unexpressed, repressed desires, and validated female misbehavior.

Real-life women rebels are necessary for progress—not only to sustain the vitality and vibrancy that individuality brings to the world, but also because they improve our general quality of life. Without rebels, we'd be pioneer women procreating and cooking with only the exception of spinsterhood to save us. Slavery would still be legal. Our schools, restaurants, and transportation systems would still be segregated. We wouldn't pay tribute to (or have access to) black culture's contributions—except for what white culture has appropriated. Minorities wouldn't be able to vote. In life, in politics, and in society, rebels have always paved the road for the majority's acceptance of progress. The unpopular, often mocked positions that rebels push for eventually affect the mainstream mindset, and sometimes even the law.

As we learn in school, rebellion generates revolution. But beyond simplified classroom examples of the civil rights movement and the American Revolution, we don't ever clearly define exactly what a rebel is. There is no single standard for rebellion, but rebels are first. They break ground, and they make our lives easier through their example and by struggling against the blowback that visionaries suffer in a culture commandeered by conformity—which is why the notion of what rebellion actually is changes for every generation.

Once I uncovered it, real rebellion resonated more deeply with me than its fictional versions did. I admire the rebels who question everything, whose actions have compassionately, creatively changed the course of American reality, and who have repeatedly impelled many others to action through their thoughtful willingness to fight— or at least to try. The rebels who have inspired me plunge into causes they've never encountered before and muddle their way through, learning from their mistakes. They accept difference in themselves and in others. They don't capitulate when their opinions are vilified, or when their lives are disrupted because they've taken a stand. Sometimes they laugh in the face of oppression or repression, and encourage their audiences to do the same. They live brashly (as long as no one gets hurt). They believe in equality for all. And they have often kept me hopeful and feeling alive.

But real rebellion nestles uncomfortably next to fictional, mainstream representations thereof. Pop culture romanticizes fictional rebels even as it ignores or avoids real-life resistance. In the 1950s, for example, James Dean questioned authority in his movies and stood for excitement and possibility—a foreshadowing of the upheaval lurking ahead in the turbulent '60s. Meanwhile, in real life, and in direct opposition to Dean's entertaining and accessible portrayal, the police rooted out homosexuals for illegal sexual behavior, and the House Un-American Activities Committee weeded out the nation's suspected communists.

Rebellion in reality, then, wasn't welcome at all, even as the fictional version marked the youthful spirit of the decade, and the fictionalized version is what stuck. Furthermore, it has exacerbated the challenge of excavating instances of female rebellion from the dominant image of the American rebel as white and male. In many cases, fictional representations of rebellion, in films such as *Rebel Without a Cause* and in novels like Jack Kerouac's *On the Road*, have become intertwined with the men creating the characters. In the cases of James Dean and Marlon Brando, for example, the cool they exhibited onscreen was folded into their celebrity personae. Whether or not they actually embodied machismo (Dean didn't) became irrelevant as cultural legend sprang up around them. Their perfected false sense of masculinity and their simplified rebellion transformed Dean's and Brando's images into acceptable, desirable versions of hypermasculinity. Our cultural icons today are often sculpted into rebels through these time-tested perceptions of rebellion, and through their similarity to older versions of pop culture–defined rebels. For men to perpetuate these legends' power, they have to ape the same old masculine formula, often including out-and-out rejecting women around them. Real rebellion is overshadowed by an overblown portrayal of cool in mass culture.

No matter how each generation lives vicariously through the antiheroes it worships, lashing out at what pop culture's women have come to symbolize—the taming of wild men, a safe place in which to prove dominance, and the dashed dreams of the wanderer—is a repetitive mainstream idea that underscores the rebellion of male characters. We have a bounty of historical outcasts that could enable us to redefine "real men" and how to identify their power (not to mention redefining who *has* the power), but U.S. popular culture happily relies on the tried and true to do so. Despite our having divergent inspiration in the form of mobs of rockers, politicos swaggering on the far left, transgendered performers, experimental visual and noise artists, the whole of the 1960s, punk culture, the black liberation movement, the women's liberation movement, the gay rights movement, radical activists, and pacifists for diverging inspiration, the traditional male still owns the rebellious image.

The ubiquity of our male rebel icons reinforces our collective captivation with masculinity, and provides poor examples of manhood to emulate. The very masculine ideals attached to them prevent women from being anything more than the "other." Unless we're copying conventional masculinity ourselves, we're the antirebel by default. Worse, while we're portrayed as a collective obstacle to movement and change, most glorified male rebels don't actually stand for progress or change at all.

Besides being the most widely disseminated image of rebellion, Hollywood's cinematic rebel is created from a fairly simple and predictable recipe: Take one part lonesome drifter, one part enigma, and add emotional detachment. He doesn't speak much. When he does, it's not to utter anything revelatory, but to sound and appear less vulnerable. Hollywood's rebel usually exudes sex appeal, avoids eye contact (preferring to stare loftily toward the horizon), is somehow embroiled in illegal or unnamed activities, and is prone to anger or violence. He typically treats his motorcycle or his car more reverentially than he does people, and the vehicle becomes a part of his roaming physical identity. The rebel stares down his nose at the women fawning at his feet, and usually leaves them behind as he rides off to another small town to inflict the same pathology and seduction on another overly intrigued population. He dresses differently than the people he encounters and regards almost everyone with disdain or merely silence. Overall, he is unpopular, the underdog, and misunderstood. The women he encounters exist to feed his image and affirm how seductive his emotional distance can be.

Besides being lonesome, misunderstood, brooding, and male, the rebel's characteristics depend upon the particulars of each new youth generation or aesthetic movement. What constitutes rebellion eventually becomes acceptable to the mainstream, and new outlaw ideals must therefore expand in order to infuse new characters with power. Cinematic culture has traveled from Brando to Dean to Steve McQueen; to Peter Fonda and Bruce Dern in *The Wild Angels;* and to Peter Fonda and Dennis Hopper in *Easy Rider,* and then abandoned the open road for dark characters such as those found in Martin Scorsese films like *Taxi Driver* and *Raging Bull* or in *Dirty Harry;* Quentin Tarantino's parade of underdog criminals; the aimless young addicts in Gus Van Sant's *Drugstore Cowboy;* Blaxploitation heroes such as Shaft; and the many so-called heroes of post-1980 action films, including the *Road Warrior* series and *Die Hard*'s John McClane. Rebellious music has moved from rock 'n' roll sensuality to improvisational jazz, an articulation of the black struggle found in 1960s and '70s soul, from psychedelic rock to garage, from punk to hip-hop to techno and noise.

Regardless of generational change, the most frequently referenced images of rebellion are built on a few key images of the 1950s postwar period: Rock 'n' roll, James Dean's mystique, Marlon Brando's hypermachismo, and Jack Kerouac's *On the Road* all converged on the culture at a time when the United States was fixated on the traditional, white nuclear family as the "dream" of the nation. These countercultural elements paved the way for later interpretations of rebellion, helped lay the groundwork for the social revolt of the mid- to late 1960s, and continue to inform our cultural definition of the rebel as a macho, wandering, loner male who needs no one but himself.

The oppressive attitudes against which rebels struggled were displayed abundantly in 1950s television programming. Families included happy-go-lucky, shellacked, inevitably white children and teens spawned by inevitably toothy, doting, ever-stylish mothers and hardworking, chipper, well-mannered fathers (as in the frighteningly mild *Leave It to Beaver*). Houses were immaculate. Families, it was assumed, always had enough money and were never broken by infidelity or alcohol. When families like *The Honeymooners'* Kramdens struggled financially, it became a classic recipe for comedy. And a rigorously chaste love always prevailed—all in the miraculous span of a mere thirty minutes. Such shiny, homespun comedies certainly didn't leave room for any rebellion, let alone that of the female variety. Since television's family portraits were rigidly stable and suburban, women were relegated to roles as happily attentive housewives who didn't give a thought to the possibility of restlessness.

Hollywood usually followed in the same simplistic "happy ending" vein as television. No matter what happened between the opening and closing credits, Hollywood's profitable and canned entertainment reflected television's candy-coated narratives: Nice guys finished first and married their girls, and happiness wasn't only promised; it was guaranteed. As if the message wasn't broadcast often enough in prime time, a major sign of the saccharine times was the screen musical. Musicals were at their peak in the 1950s: *Singin' in the Rain* (1952), *Oklahoma* (1955), *Guys and Dolls* (1955)[5], *Kiss Me, Kate* (1953), *Annie Get Your Gun* (1950), *Gentlemen Prefer Blondes* (1953), and *Showboat* (1951) were all released during this era, and most were powerful moneymakers for Hollywood. When it came to clean, feel-good endings, nothing could wrap up two gleeful, light hours and send them off into the sunset like a musical. As with television's smiling families, the musicals sang primarily of love, marriage, and the eventuality of children, and insisted on the middle-class, suburban dream as their happy ending. But alongside pop culture's repressed and narrow images of the alleged good life, the reality of vicious racism, homophobia, and the anticommunist McCarthy witch hunts made rebellion in the 1950s fairly easy. There was a lot to revolt against, and rebels didn't have to stray very far from the mainstream to shrug off the iron fist on their collar.

Still, when it came to character development and plotlines, '50s Hollywood had a bit more elbow room than the staid suburbia television offered. While Beaver Cleaver sweetened television with his high-pitched innocence, psychological intricacies surfaced in Academy Award Best Picture nominees like *A Streetcar Named Desire* (1951) and *On the Waterfront* (1954). Both films starred a restless, sullen Marlon Brando, who in *Streetcar* portrayed the downtrodden Stanley Kowalski, prone to rage and violence toward women. In *On the Waterfront,* Brando's Terry Malloy struggled against a corrupt dockworkers' union, wrestled with his own code of ethics, and sorted out his life's failures. Kowalski's and Malloy's complexities, along with Brando's exceptional acting and sensuality, brought a roiling sensibility to an otherwise simplistic Hollywood, and Brando quickly became the epitome of the consumable rebel.

Hollywood's complex women were not rewarded with the same accolades. Instead, they were punished if they rebelled, and rewarded if they swooned over their men at the end of the film. Only rarely did a film, such as 1949's *Casablanca,* allow a leading lady (in this case, Ingrid Bergman's Ilsa) to win out and leave her costar and lost love (Rick, played by Humphrey Bogart) behind. Rick was bewitched by this elusive, unattainable woman who wandered in and out of his life. She was almost otherworldly—ethereal, mysterious, and presented in the period's soft-focus aesthetic—and she exhibited conflicting emotions and exuded the qualities of an untouchable idol. She whispered breathily, alternately clinging to Rick and pulling away— an exquisitely rendered object of torture to him. The push-and-pull nature of their relationship allowed Rick to be the long-suffering jilted lover—a role that wasn't necessarily macho, but that did reinforce the idea of woman as man's downfall—although he eventually became the heroic one, sacrificing his love for the good of victory during World War II.

Another unconventional woman appeared in 1952's *Sudden Fear.* Joan Crawford played an independent, successful playwright swindled by a new husband who was interested only in her money. After marrying him, she uncovered a plot he and his partner had hatched to kill her for the money she'd willed to him. Crawford deftly deceived both of them and ended up saving only her own life. It was an intense role: a woman who plotted alone and prioritized herself over love. There was also the smart, curious, and courageous Grace Kelly investigating the apartment of a possible murderer in *Rear Window.* But any role in which women rose to the top, without love being the focus or the film's eventual ending, made for unusual plot twists in 1950s Hollywood. And a film that starred an atypically beautiful woman like Crawford was even rarer than one featuring happily single women.

Other mainstream roles for women in the 1950s were less complex. Women were perky sidekicks, like Debbie Reynolds in *Singin' in the Rain,* or marriage-obsessed dimwits, such as the burlesque blond Vivian Blaine played in *Guys and Dolls.* Love stories abounded, such as *Love Is a Many-Splendored Thing, From Here to Eternity, Sabrina,* and *The African Queen.* Any curves thrown were mostly in body alone: Women focused solely on men and how to trap them in comedies like *How to Marry a Millionaire* and *Gentlemen Prefer Blondes.* They were overwhelmingly reduced to roles as love interests or objects lacking character depth; psychologically conflicted roles like Brando's and Dean's were beyond their reach.

The early-1950s rebel was encapsulated in 1953's *The Wild One,* starring Marlon Brando. While the movie's campy, klutzy dialogue is unimpressive, the drifting main character is imprinted on our cultural consciousness. Brando's sneering, leering, leather-clad Johnny Strabler was also a walking checklist for his rebellious descendants to follow. Like mysterious and unwelcome cowboys sidling up to saloons, Johnny and his gang rode into a small town at the beginning of the film, quickly confounding its population. The film itself centered on the disruption the gang caused in the town, but its underlying focus was Johnny's apathy and rejection of the stable "American" way of life. Throughout *The Wild One,* the gang's nomadic lifestyle was embedded in the dialogue ad nauseam. When the group made its grand, roaring entrance, two bystanders kicked off the following exchange:

> *"Where's that bunch from?"*
> *"I don't know—everywhere."*
> *"I don't even think they know where they're goin'."*[6]

Regardless of Brando's later eccentricities, the cool and mysterious aura he conveyed in films like *The Wild One* managed to color his entire life. In Brando's *New York Times* obituary, Rick Lyman summed up his cultural significance in the 1950s:

> *To American audiences who first saw him in the late '40s, what was most apparent about Mr. Brando was that compared with other actors of the period, he was brooding, muscular, and intense. Detractors called him a slob. He appeared in tight blue jeans and torn T-shirts, grimy with sweat, alternately slack-jawed with stupidity and alive with feral cunning. And he was more openly sexual—in an animal way—than the actors who immediately preceded him.[7]*

Even when the women playing opposite Brando exhibited more complexity than his characters, he outshone them with his animal attraction. In *A Streetcar Named Desire,* for example, Brando's sensuality rippled beneath ripped T-shirts and exploded intermittently in rage. Although the film was not an independent product of postwar rebellion—it was based on a Tennessee Williams play—Brando also played Stanley Kowalski in *Streetcar's* stage production, and thus bound his image permanently to the character Kowalski. The furious, frustrated, alienated Stanley was the role that first widely showcased his talent and demonstrated his onscreen virility.

Vivian Leigh, most famous for her role as Scarlett O'Hara in *Gone with the Wind,* played Blanche, the sister of Kowalski's wife. Blanche was a degenerated, debauched debutante, an aging, desperate woman, and was much more mysterious, manipulative, and complicated than other roles for 1950s actresses—and infinitely more intricate than Stanley. In fact, the *New York Times* review of *Streetcar* described Blanche as "lonely," "brave," and "defiant"—yet the role didn't permanently romanticize her, or Leigh, as a rebel. Her beauty diluted the public's receptiveness to her defiance: A nod to Leigh's "beautifully molded face" kicked off an extremely positive review of her performance,[8] whereas Brando's equally appealing body wasn't noted at all.

Although Leigh delivered an outstanding, multilayered, and unique performance, Brando still surfaced as the film's centerpiece. Kowalski was hardly heroic—his rape of the fragile Blanche sent her over the psychological edge. Brando, who didn't win the Oscar, while the two leading actresses did, is still more renowned for *Streetcar* than either Leigh or Kim Hunter (who played Stella, his wife). The legendary articulation of Stanley's rage relied on his having Stella and Blanche as unlucky sounding boards and punching bags. It also involved Brando in one of the most memorable moments in mid-twentieth-century cinema: the infamous, guttural calls for "Stella!" from a desperate Stanley on the street after a violent argument. Even for those who hadn't seen the film, the reference was instantly recognizable and forever linked to Brando's macho reputation. Blanche ended up unwound, terrified, traumatized, alone—and nowhere near as widely referenced as Stanley was in cinematic history.

Brando's combination of "slack-jawed stupidity" and "feral cunning" also reflected the ideals of Kerouac and the other prominent and early members of the Beat Generation—William Burroughs, Allen Ginsberg, and Neal Cassady—even though that definitive Beat novel *On the Road* wouldn't be published until six years after *A Streetcar Named Desire* was released. "When [*On the Road*] finally appeared in 1957," stated Kerouac's obituary in *The New York Times,* "it immediately became a basic text for youth who found their country claustrophobic and oppressive."[9] The main character, Dean Moriarty, who was based on Cassady, came to embody the same qualities Brando conjured: a sexually charged, independent-thinking, enigmatic, itinerant outsider.

Beat culture blatantly opposed the reinforcement of American middle-class values and introduced the larger culture to the questions that would become the subcultural fabric of 1960s social turmoil. *On the Road,* now considered a cornerstone of American literature, energetically advocated for spiritual change via the nation's cultural underbelly: a hyperkinetic celebration of jazz culture (which, however politically naive, was a rare and public white homage to black culture); a lack of regard for employment; the urgency of fleeting experiences; and an unquenchable desire for physical movement and psychic change.[10] In the novel, Kerouac famously wrote of a jaunt from New York to California, "We were all delighted, we all realized we were leaving confusion and nonsense behind and performing our one and noble function of the time, *move.*"[11]

Diane di Prima, one of the most recognized female poets associated with the Beat Generation, eloquently summarized Beat rebellion when she wrote:

> *To be an outcast, outrider, was to be eternally innocent of the inflicting of pain. Scornful, contemptuous, and beyond the concern for appearance. And yet our obsession with innocence remained. It kept us outside of what we saw as the truly criminal—the respectable world around us. . . .*
>
> *. . . To be artist: outcast, outrider, and explorer. Pushing the*

bounds of the mind, of imagination. Of the humanly possible, the shape of a human life. "Continual allegory." Of a woman's life, pushing the limits. Opening endlessly to the image, words. The rhythm or pattern, sound—the vector swiftly drawn in the dark. And fleeting as lightning.[12]

Regardless of the work of Di Prima and of other female Beat writers, such as Joyce Johnson, Anne Waldman, and Elise Cowen, the works hailed as American classics and the writers who produced them were male. Certainly, fewer women than men were generating Beat work, but women were most strongly connected to the movement as muses and lovers. In Kerouac's case, he did experience the life he recounted in *On the Road,* but he also oversimplified his behavior. In the book, the aunt he relied on financially was a far cry from his mother in real life, with whom he had a close and submissive relationship. And like Sal Paradise, his fictional counterpart in *On the Road,* Kerouac rebelled against steady work—a hallmark of the "American dream"—but counted on going back to his family in between trips and borrowing money from his mother when the traveling life became unbearable. The seemingly impulsive and nomadic Kerouac, rather than being free to roam, lived with his mother on and off, and then mostly on, before his death in 1969.[13] If this were the popular belief about Kerouac outside of his most ardent fans and literary circles, it would emasculate his image and the power of his resistance, and his masculine rambling would be seen as it actually was: transient, short-lived, and less extraordinary.

Kerouac also elevated Dean Moriarty's character—which he based on Cassady precisely because of Cassady's insistence on freedom—while managing to neatly sidestep Cassady's affair with Allen Ginsberg[14] when he described a period of maniacal bed-hopping in *On the Road*.[15] And quintessential teen rebel James Dean is now widely believed to have had same-sex affairs. From the audience's seats, an idealized masculinity hovers around these rebels, even as they failed to embody it and embraced sexual adventure instead. Meanwhile, because women were presented with much more limited life choices within 1950s culture, when they chose their own paths, questioning and exploring their own unique sexuality and writing about it (as di Prima recounted in *Memoirs of a Beatnik*), their progressive endeavors were even more potent, more interesting, and much more loaded with risk than the men who gained mainstream acclaim were.

On the Road is still revered for having mobilized a generation; in 2007 and 2008, the New York Public Library staged an expansive exhibit entitled *Beatific Soul: Jack Kerouac on the Road*. Kerouac's books are still dog-eared, devoured, and the subjects of word-of-mouth acclaim from young and questioning readers. The technique of *On the Road*, which favored rapid-fire accounts over traditionally heralded storytelling and literary construction, is what marks its significance in literature. In reality, the excitement for the reader isn't in the technique alone, though, the "go now!" attitude of that era, and Kerouac's rebellion, are what reverberate. Still, fictional rebellion trumped reality once again: Kerouac was much more politically conservative than his work led readers to believe, and was never as anti-American as the 1960s outlaws he helped to spawn. As he became associated with '60s hostility toward zealous patriotism, Kerouac became more volatile about how his own belief system differed from that of his radical fans. In the late '60s, he separated himself from the groups of people reading, worshipping, and citing him as inspiration as they radically mobilized. In fact, he wrote an article in which he publicly distanced himself from the radical political Left, which was stoked by peers like Ginsberg. In it, he stated, "I'm pro-American and the radical political involvements seem to tend elsewhere. . . . This country gave my Canadian family a good break, more or less, and we see no reason to demean said country."[16] Writing separately about youth movements, and particularly about liberals, he asked with contempt, ". . . [W]hy is it that the type of young men and women who are drawn to 'youth movements' are always more or less sexually unattractive, completely unathletic and physically deficient, and on the whole, somewhat repulsive in their loud, graceless, unyouthful manners and bearing?" He went on to call "liberals" failures in family life—the exact failure that made heroes of the On the Road characters—and signed the article from "a rebel reactionary."[17]

On the Road's Sal and Dean weren't as obviously emotionally detached as their contemporaries. They were excited and excitable; they exhibited a contagious passion for living, in contrast with most iconic loners. The road-tripping, maniacal Dean Moriarty impulsively indulged his desires by alternating between various wives, lovers, and mistresses throughout his life, leaving behind a trail of pain in favor of soaking up more jazz, gulping more drugs, and falling over more adventures on the road. Cassady's reality mirrored his fictional counterpart's activities, and Kerouac's and Cassady's cultural representations were conflated with their fictional personae. Kerouac did acknowledge having moments of extreme loneliness in the book, but they hardly compared with its lengthy sections of manic joy and the moments in which Paradise and Moriarty clearly felt that there was no other place to be and no other moment in which to live. Sal and

Dean's fun and chaos dwarfed their lifestyle's eventual isolation and the great pain undoubtedly inflicted on loved ones by their repeated, unpredictable abandonment.

Propping up the status quo ever more, the Beat rebellion, the countercultural film *Easy Rider,* and the 1960s radical Left willfully refused to acknowledge women's autonomous desires even as they demanded more freedom for men. Kerouac, while traveling through bohemian culture, must have come across rebellious women (like di Prima, whom he met in New York), but instead highlighted the maleness of his experience through the omission of outsider women from *On the Road,* despite the unlikelihood that every radical person Sal and Dean met was male. Instead, the women who littered the book's roads and towns, buses and byways were housewives, alcoholics, or mere respite for the wandering men. By omitting women's potential for acting out, and by presenting them as little more than sexual conquests, Kerouac and Cassady empowered themselves to seem like much more fully realized and unique individuals—which also revealed how they devalued women. The book is packed with lengthy descriptions of other Beat writers, like fictional renderings of Burroughs and Ginsberg, while the women's importance is limited to their looks, their lovemaking ability, and their potential to support the boys' ecstatic whims. Regardless of Kerouac's expressed joy concerning different viewpoints, female rebellion wasn't even suggested in *On the Road,* let alone recorded.

While the Beats were pushing the boundaries of the dreaded "respectable world," they were confined to the urban underbellies of San Francisco, Mexico, and New York. Until the public reception to

On the Road in 1957, and until print journalism's eventual fascination with the Beats, mainstream America could easily write them off. The overall implications of rock 'n' roll, with its ties to black culture as well as to sexuality, however, left white, middle-class parents reeling. Rock 'n' roll shifted sexuality from the back seats of cars parked at the drive-in to primetime, and eventually, granted it a permanent place in mainstream culture. And no one in rock 'n' roll exuded sexuality more publicly than Elvis Presley. Or, as Lester Bangs stated in *The Village Voice* in 1977, " . . . Elvis kicked 'How Much Is That Doggie in the Window' *out* the window and replaced it with 'Let's fuck.' The rest of us are still reeling from the impact. Sexual chaos reigns currently, but out of chaos may flow true understanding and harmony, and either way Elvis almost single-handedly opened the floodgates."[18] By giving American teenagers a sexually driven rallying cry that caused parents to clutch their pearls, rock 'n' roll pitted them against the older generation. The impact of Elvis was, of course, the culture's most profound touchstone for rebellion.

Rock 'n' roll's rebel stance was also built on the back of an unacknowledged and poor black population— and white parents' violent reaction intimated that desegregation was what white culture *really* feared. Like most cultural products that become typical versions of rebellion, rock 'n' roll relied on the existing power structure and an underclass to legitimize itself and solidify its place in pop culture. Although rock 'n' roll owed a tremendous debt to the black culture it was quietly exploiting, white men built their uprising on the work of fringe and then-unrecognized black folk music for content. Women were the objects of rebel desire, and rock 'n' roll's legions of screaming girl fans were the yardstick by which its popularity was measured.

In other words, marginal groups were essential to rock 'n' roll's white, male success—and were instrumental in forming white men's rebellious identities.

Aside from country crooners like Patsy Cline, June Carter, and Loretta Lynn, women were rarely onstage. Young girls and women may have been the classic rock 'n' roll audience, but they were not the representation of the genre itself. Classic footage of Elvis, for example, is framed by cutaway shots of screaming, young, specifically female fans. They swooned, fainted, chased their idols, and bought stacks of records and merchandise. Wanda Jackson, a female rock 'n' roll anomaly who wailed rockabilly-style, played guitar, and occasionally toured with Elvis Presley, never gained the acclaim of men who did the same. She did, however, record such songs as "Big Iron Skillet," in which she explained how she'd use her skillet to beat her man. Jackson is virtually the only prominent female from the '60s with a forceful and specifically feminine viewpoint, a traditional rock sound, and a definitive cult following. (Unfortunately, she has since reneged on her earlier rebelliousness by turning to devout Christianity.)

James Dean solidified the specifically teenage rebel icon at the onset of rock 'n' roll's chart in 1955. *Rebel Without a Cause*, coincidentally, was released the same year a popularity rock 'n' roll single ("Rock Around the Clock," by Bill Haley and His Comets) spent nineteen weeks on Billboard's Top Ten.[19] *Rebel Without a Cause* was a hit, too—no doubt in part because Dean died just before the film's release.[20] Like the lasting impressions Brando and Kerouac made, *Rebel Without a Cause* was recently remembered as "a bible of masculinity" in *The Boston Globe*: "Even people who have never seen him and don't know his name do James Dean without knowing it, influenced by posturing, glowering avatars."[21]

Not all rebels scowled the way Dean did, nor did they conjure signature rebel characteristics in the same way. Most male rebels also had no home, were separated from their families, or both. In fact, a closer look at Hollywood's portrayal of the male rebel reveals that most were also physically or emotionally fatherless. *Rebel Without a Cause* broke from the notion of the tranquil traditional family through the story of three disaffected teenagers who experienced varying levels of familial detachment. Unlike their picture-perfect television counterparts, Dean (Jim) and his costars, Natalie Wood (Judy) and Sal Mineo (Plato), portrayed emotionally conflicted and unstable suburban teens. Jim struggled with his passive father, and Plato and Judy searched ardently for attachment to father figures. While *The Wild One's* Johnny Strabler came from a nebulous nowhere and disappeared back into it, the desperation of *Rebel's* Jim Stark was amplified, and originated, at home.

Although *Rebel* focused largely on Jim's struggle with society and his family, Natalie Wood's Judy was a different kind of rebel. She ran with the "cool" kids at the beginning of the film and hid behind a good-time-bad-girl front, but she struggled with her increasingly estranged relationship with her emotionally distant father. Judy and Jim eventually found solace in each other, and united against the society feeding their angst in favor of their mutual longing for love, community, honesty, and belonging. While Jim desired strength from his emasculated father, Judy longed for familial tenderness. Wood created a caring and soulful rebel female—but one who remained the love interest of the true rebel of the film. While the plot culminated in their friend Plato's death, Jim and Judy also fell in love by the end of the film, and the 1950s Hollywood formulaic wrap-up of leads in love thus prevailed.

In the same way in which Kerouac was much more straitlaced than *On the Road* implied, Jim's defiance in *Rebel* was just as misleading. Jim angled for truth from his parents, frustrated that his father was completely submissive to his mother—evidenced not so subtly in one scene that featured Frank Stark (Jim Bacchus) making dinner in a flowered apron and visibly embarrassing Jim. Not only did Jim feel misunderstood by his father, but his angst also stemmed from his father's lack of traditional masculinity, against which Jim lashed out consistently throughout the film. As Peter Biskind pointed out in *Seeing Is Believing,* Jim may have appeared to resist authority, but his anger and conflict indicated a lack of traditional gender roles at home, and what unraveled when a man turned his back on being rigorously masculine.[22]

Familial distance makes the rebel more mysterious and confounding and helps construct the romanticized "free" masculine life, one without the middle-class responsibilities of employment, children, or a wife. In this universe, women are prevented from expe riencing the same restlessness men do, and from enjoying the same amount of freedom. Kathie Bleeker, Johnny's love interest in *The Wild One,* begged Johnny to rescue her from the town and take her on the road with him—even after he tried to assault her. In the end, Kathie watched Johnny ride off without her. *On the Road* was littered with women left to raise children and mend broken households— amid the tornado of Sal's and Dean's indecision, travel plans, and short attention spans—while male curiosities were sated. Wandering was the hallmark of what was "different" about these men and their behavior, while abandoned, immobile women symbolized the stagnancy of domesticity and a home base for the rebel's resentment, rather than gaining the ability to rebel. Pauline Kael made a similar comment in a 1996 *Atlantic Monthly* missive on Brando when she described his onscreen relationships with his female costars: "In the case of Brando, the most powerful ladies were especially virulent because they were obviously part of what he was rebelling against. . . . "[23]

*E*asy *Rider*'s true-to-form characters don't have homes or even call each other by name. Originally titled *The Loners*,[24] *Easy Rider* connoted an older generation of rebel cowboys in the characters' names, Wyatt (after Wyatt Earp) and Billy (after Billy the Kid).[25] In a moment of genius or supreme artistic pretension—but most likely somewhere between the two—an inordinate amount of time passed in *Easy Rider* before either character uttered a word. A quick jaunt to Mexico for a cocaine purchase and its resale to a wealthy American provided them with the money to hit the road. The entire sequence occurred without any dialogue. The two then wordlessly hopped on their bikes and began their adventure, free of whatever ambiguous lives they had left behind. Fonda is quoted as having said during production, "Captain America [Wyatt] don't have no fuckin' parents, man. He sprung forth, just the way you see him."[26] Except for Fonda's mentioning his mother during an acid trip, the feeling of spontaneous existence, of springing forth, is complete from beginning to end.

Women fared no better in *Easy Rider* than they did in other postwar road stories. Implausibly, as Billy and Wyatt cruised through the country, taste-testing the nation's various lifestyles and liberties, the film managed to dismiss racial struggles and the civil rights movement altogether, even though both were critical elements of 1950s and '60s social movements and the *exact* movements out of which white radicalism grew. Very few people of color populate the film, outside of its Mardi Gras sequence and the possibly Latina farmer's wife with whom Billy and Wyatt share a meal.

Once again, art was imitating life. In reality, the rebellious Left couldn't stomach women's revolt as a part of its own. Take '60s revolutionary Angela Davis's point of view—although speaking directly to her experience with the L.A. Student Nonviolent Coordinating Committee at the end of the '60s, accounts like hers litter stories of the decade's insurgency. In her autobiography, she described her own struggles with certain factions of the black nationalist movement and radical men's insistence on remaining dominant over their female peers, even though, she asserted, "some of them were politically mature enough to understand the reactionary nature of these trends."[27]

In the '60s, rebels were actively resisting change, rather than embracing it. If marginalization has not been forced upon someone by virtue of their race, class, or gender, outsider status can be romanticized, because it never has to be a permanent state of being, indicate a supposed weakness, or possess undesirable qualities that threaten or alienate social power. Willfully resisting the new is also how pop culture manages to embrace rebellion: erasing or refusing what is truly revolutionary and identifying only with its nonthreatening elements. *Choosing* to be marginalized is the only acceptable safety net, and the only rebellion that can embrace commanding masculinity while remaining in opposition, however slightly, to the status quo.

You're pulled inside. You're gettin' a little distant, man, you're gettin' a little distant.[28]

—Billy to Wyatt, *Easy Rider*

*F*amilial disconnection and rejecting domesticity intensified the mid-century, classic male rebel's loner status and protected him from emasculation—but never as much as the rebel's emotional detachment did. In the mainstream cinematic version of rebellion, repressed emotions, a monotone delivery of lines, sarcasm, and a general unresponsiveness to stressful or upsetting situations dominate the characters' dialogue and develop their individual mystiques. Only a distinct, tragic anomaly tends to add depth to these antiheroes' general stoicism, while any other emotion (usually frustration) is expressed through physical aggression (usually callously inflicted)— the exact emotional reaction that larger culture continues to expect of "real men."

Under the shadow of his perpetually furrowed brow, Clint Eastwood's Dirty Harry fed deadpan wisecracks in an annoyingly gruff, muted, melodramatic voice that laid the groundwork for his trademark acting style. Marlon Brando's Terry Malloy unknowingly led informant Joey Doyle to his death at the start of *On the Waterfront*. He muttered subtly as he witnessed the rooftop death, "I figured the worst they was gonna do was lean on him a little bit. . . . He wasn't a bad kid, that Joey."[29] When infamous characters like these are the ultimate masculine ideal, men in general begin to dread expressing emotion or attachment more than they already do. The ensuing emotional repression, then, only perpetuates American men's most socially reinforced behaviors. The only resistance such emotionally stiff individuals share is another refusal of change: the refusal to be seen as soft. The rebellion itself is often less important than the cool, collected way they glare at restrictive forces working against them.

As the decades have progressed, the rebel's evolution has been as unchanging as his emotional range, even while culture and women evolve around him. In 1970s cinema, for example, male domination of women became more brutal and overt. Rebels weren't just abandoning their families or partners anymore—their dialogue was battering, even if their actions weren't. Once the rebel was established as powerfully seductive in the 1950s, he was free to fulfill the macho fantasy of turning women down; of not being submissive to his feelings about women; and, eventually, of acting out violence on, or in the name of, women—as in films about violent solitary figures, such as Scorsese's *Taxi Driver*.

Predictable emotional stoicism wasn't enough to prove masculinity, apparently. New, younger rebels relied on their forebears' cachet to exhibit and verify their own ultramale traits. A young Presley, Peter Guralnick noted, bore "the hurt, truculent expression we had seen before in Marlon Brando's motorcycle epic, *The Wild One*."[30] In a 1968 television comeback performance, Presley wore head-to-toe leather,[31] both recalling Brando in *The Wild One* and invoking Jim Morrison, the more feminine and modern rebel icon. In (quasi-)fiction, *Raging Bull* (1980) revived Brando's infamous "I could've been a contender" speech from *On the Waterfront,* and William Plummer described Kerouac as "the brain behind Presley's pelvis and Brando's sneer" in *The Holy Goof,* his biography of Neal Cassady.[32] Jim Morrison was also compared to Kerouac's Beat hero Neal Cassady.[33] In Oliver Stone's biopic *The Doors,*

Jim mentioned wanting to make his own version of *Easy Rider*. This exchange of pop-culture references builds and banks on the established collateral of the rebel male that audiences recognize. But offering something familiar and palatable resuscitates the old masculinity and lessens the power of rebellion existing outside of it, thereby limiting the development of progressive, reality-based rebellion.

*T*he unifying factor in all of these images is the male rebel's struggle against a force larger than himself. Aloofness or misogyny aside, each performer, writer, filmmaker, or film character meets clearly defined opposition: *Rebel Without a Cause's* Jim Stark fought against his family's dysfunction and struggled with notions of masculinity, and Elvis was subjected to racial, religious, and parental criticism. Being black in America and raised in New York ghettos, 50 Cent and Jay-Z beat the odds by becoming record-company gold. But all these men are valued for something other than actual revolt. In fact, it's often the technical or aesthetic qualities of their work that confer legitimate rebellious status upon them—such as Kerouac's rattling, startling, new, and musical prose, or Scorsese's portrayal of homegrown grit and his uncompromising personal vision.

Rebel women faced high, strict, pervasive cultural standards that they could refuse to comply with. Long before male rebellion became a formula for Hollywood, a woman's wearing a pair of pants was the ultimate Hollywood transgression. Katherine Hepburn made film fans shudder when she wore pants in the 1930s. Screen icon Marlene Dietrich slipped in and out of sexually aggressive, and occasionally predatory, identities. She dressed in drag, yet she is viewed as equally seductive as her more "feminine" peers, like Greta Garbo. In literature,

Dorothy Parker crafted snide and resentful portraits of 1920s New York society, and wrote self-deprecating and humorous poetry that often criticized male behavior. Though she was much more famous in Mexico, Frida Kahlo's self-revelatory, gut-wrenching paintings rendered pain and sorrow and intimate female experiences, such as miscarriage. Her self-portraiture revealed a woman with a powerful, accusatory stare that, consciously or not, combated the submissive female portrait subjects that mark modern art history.

*T*he twentieth century was certainly thick with testosterone. Since women can't rely on a long legacy of sulking, slouching, and shrugging off love, female rebellion contains more elements of surprise. For instance, Madonna is an unquestionable icon, one who strongly opposed a restricted role for women in music and has broken pop-music boundaries throughout her career by integrating liberal political and social commentary into her work. She depicted a biracial relationship against a backdrop of burning crosses in 1989's "Like a Prayer." She also displayed gay male make-out sessions during the musical documentary *Truth or Dare*. But Madonna first-gained attention by rebelling sexually, which is the most widespread and predictable tactic groundbreaking women are remembered for. Initially, she wasn't the aggressive, crotch-grabbing Madonna we see in the "Express Yourself" video. She was a virgin bride rolling around on the altar of the MTV Video Music Awards. Exaggerating distinctly heterosexual, submissive female sexual behavior isn't really controversial at all. It's actually the most typical rebellion for women that exists.

When women are honored for stepping off the pedestal of female iconography in rebellious ways, their acclaim is sparing, rarely lasts more than a decade, and seems to occur in a cultural vacuum—as if a psychologically complex woman is an image so rare that it doesn't take hold in mainstream culture and the rebel canon. The 1970s movies that featured more complex female roles (such as Scorsese's *Alice Doesn't Live Here Anymore* or *Norma Rae*) gave way comfortably to typical romantic comedies, such as *When Harry Met Sally,* in the '80s and '90s—barring Thelma and Louise's crashing of the male rebel club.

Rock's rebel females—with the exception of those with longer shelf lives, such as Tina Turner, Joan Jett, and Madonna, whose enigmatic allure has persisted—rarely outlast their generations and become legends on the scale of men like Elvis, Jim Morrison, or Jimi Hendrix. Even though mainstream female rock bands and women such as the Go-Go's, Pat Benatar, and the Bangles thrived in the '80s, they've since either faded into novelty or become co-opted by the music industry and promoted as acceptable versions of male fantasy, as was the fate of Blondie's Debbie Harry. Renowned females continue to battle society's persistent habit of reducing them to and defining them by their sexuality. We need look only as far as *Playboy* magazine for proof that Marilyn Monroe continues to indulge male fantasies: The publication printed transcripts of her therapy sessions in 2005.[34] Predictably, the published portion revealed Monroe's alleged sexual secrets, including her supposed affair with Joan Crawford.

It's time to recast our collective definition of rebellion, and time to look at these hopelessly white, haplessly male figures and permanently reinvent whom we hold up as truly brave. The iconic rebel has always faced a much simpler struggle than men of color and women, whose social subversions are rarely played out and praised in the classic identity doled out so freely to men who don't have to risk as much to be defiant. White male rebellion can be accepted as openly and enthusiastically as it is precisely because it upholds the current power structure, as well as the power structure of the audience for which it was initially intended (read: other white men).

In Hollywood and mainstream entertainment, women are forced to swoon and suffer while men do all the swaggering. The conventional rebel image, perpetuated most often by Hollywood films, once represented the hope and the vision of something different: a solitary underdog kicking at conformity and hinting at progress, change, and possibility. But underneath their surface, fictional rebel men deprive women of the same qualities mainstream culture generally denies us: attainable representations of females; a sense of autonomy; and happiness presented without inevitable disappointment or punishment for our acts of freedom attached. Given the real rebellion women have been engaged in against our own oppression, we need to seek out female role models who encourage us to be strong and brave, rather than wallowing in martyrdom and falling victim to voiceless and beautiful immortality.

chapter 2
Crime and Punishment

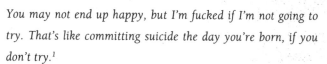

You may not end up happy, but I'm fucked if I'm not going to try. That's like committing suicide the day you're born, if you don't try.[1]

—Janis Joplin

Society has a habit of casting female icons' legacies in an entirely different mold than their male counterparts'. Rather than being memorialized as brooding images, leaning against a motorcycle or regarding love with a sneer, our heroines are more likely to be remembered for their untimely deaths or other downfalls that make them appear to have surrendered to alienation, instead of moodily resisting it. Yet self-destructive male rebels landed in exactly the same place as women who are recollected largely for harming themselves, such as Sylvia Plath or Billie Holiday: Jack Kerouac, Neal Cassady, Elvis Presley, Jim Morrison, and Jimi Hendrix all overdosed or died of complications stemming from substance abuse. Their tragic ends rendered them no weaker or less autonomous in the public mind, nor did their self-imposed loss tarnish their public image. Immortalized for their cool, male rebels are hardly ever punished for their behavior, and they aren't routinely analyzed by the press for the tortured way they live or die. Women's suffering, though, can significantly impact our memories of them.

Pop culture's women, like our heroines in the dramatic finale of *Thelma & Louise,* careen over cliffs of all kinds. From early-twentieth-century writer Virginia Woolf to '60s blues singer Janis Joplin, prominent rebellious women are less known for their brash ways and trailblazing than they are infamous for their self-destruction. The truth for some women rebels, unfortunately, is that their vibrant, visionary, vital lives are recalled as merely stark, lonely, desolate, or desperate. When a woman's legacy manages to survive for multiple generations, the not-so-subtle mainstream focus is ultimately on her downfall or death, which generally occurs "before her time." Whether or not women rebels' mystique is driven by characteristics similar to men's, their memory is shrouded in sadness, rather than in the mystery so insistently draped upon men who may or may not deserve the romanticization. Often, it seems, the underlying appeal of female rebellion is its passing.

For it needs little skill in psychology to be sure that a highly gifted
girl who had tried to use her gift for poetry would have been so

thwarted and hindered by other people, so tortured and pulled
asunder by her own contrary instincts, that she might have lost
her health and sanity to a certainty.[2]

       —Virginia Woolf, *A Room of One's Own*

Woolf was writing about the sixteenth century, but her words apply almost as well to the twentieth and twenty-first. In 1929, she published *A Room of One's Own*, the lengthy speech (virtually a rant) she crafted for delivery at Cambridge in England. Fiery, irreverent, and revolutionary, Woolf's text—which argued for an annual 500 English pounds and a room of their own in which women could write fiction—has been studied, taught, and referenced in the United States since it was published. Now a feminist classic, *A Room of One's Own* was also a landmark for the flood of feminist works published since the best-selling and revolutionary *The Feminine Mystique* in 1963. In the book, Woolf described the educational limitations placed on women in the early sixteenth century, presenting a hypothetical situation in which she tried to find a place where she could first contemplate, and then research, the issue of women and fiction. She matter-of-factly presented the impossible dilemma of being denied access to the well-protected study and research spaces provided for men—and, after finally being granted entry, discovering the dearth of work about women written by women. Ultimately, she refused to capitulate to the difficulties of becoming an educated woman, writing, "Lock up your libraries if you like; but there is no gate, no lock, no bolt you can set upon the freedom of my mind."[3] In *A Room of One's Own,* her most radical idea is her simple, steadfast, unapologetic belief that women *deserve* to be educated, independent, and academically legitimate.

Woolf also wrote *A Room of One's Own* with a levity that her fictional works did not convey. *A Room of One's Own* and her diaries are her most exuberant texts—yet her zeal for life, literature, and academic equality are often superseded by compulsory references to her troubled past, which continues to dim the brightness in her work. In her extensive biography of Woolf, Hermione Lee recalled the questions she inevitably fielded during her research:

> *Positions have been taken, myths have been made. I have noticed that in the course of any conversation about this book, I would, without fail, be asked one or more of the same four questions: Is it true that she was sexually abused as a child? What was her madness and why did she kill herself? Was Leonard a good or wicked husband? Wasn't she the most terrible snob?*[4]

But Woolf's dark and loaded history are only part of a much larger story, one that should highlight courage and discipline instead of her struggle. While she did have bouts of serious depression and mental illness throughout her life, she also resisted giving in to them, and produced a voluminous catalog of work that swells with life and passion. In listing her resolutions for the new year at the onset of 1931, she wrote, "Here are my resolutions for the next 3 months; the next lap of the year. First, to have none. Not to be tied."[5] And in her April 21, 1932, diary entry she confided, " . . . [N]ow that I'm grey haired & well through with life I suppose I like the vital, the flourish in the face of death."[6]

Beyond the rebellion so plainly packed into the pages of *A Room of One's Own,* Woolf's fictional work offered insight into deeper, more complicated female characters than the shallow portrayals in fiction written by men. *Orlando,* published in 1928, presented an androgynous character that encompassed both male and female viewpoints, a quality Woolf insisted writers must be able to invoke to fully represent both genders in literature. Halfway through the book, nobleman Orlando wakes up one morning in the body of a woman. The experience of seeing the world as both man and woman created a character with a profound wisdom about his/her time—not to mention one who adapted to change surprisingly well, considering his/her unexpected and instantaneous sex change. But Orlando didn't remain startled for very long. Slipping out of the male gender, the character lived life fully— adventurous and smart, inquisitive and brave; a being who searched for something much deeper than the limitations of either gender presented in literature. Once he became a woman, he found himself able to see men's faults quite clearly with his new, female body:

> . . . *"To fall from a masthead," she thought, "because you see a woman's ankles; to dress up like a Guy Fawkes and parade the streets, so that women may praise you; to deny a woman teaching lest she laugh at you; to be the slave of the frailest chit in petticoats, and yet to go about as if you were the Lords of creation. Heavens!" she thought. "What fools they make of us— what fools we are!"*[7]

Orlando's revelation about the differences between the two genders revealed the foolishness of constructed sex roles for men and women alike. Rather than blaming women for having been roundly painted as frivolous by virtue of their sex, the character mused on and revealed society's superficiality. Orlando nimbly moved between society's expectations of men and women while capably playing both the forward-thinking hero and heroine. His/her deft identity transitions shifted gender roles from being biologically inherent to being imposed by society. Woolf herself was courageous enough to trust that her readers could suspend their disbelief to relate to a character that existed in complete fantasy, and she deemed the book a fictional "biography." *Orlando* was a proto-sci-fi novel, a mystical adventure in which the hero trips over his/her own fate and slips in and out of personae beautifully and gracefully, without losing either a sense of humanity or the readers' sympathy.

But Virginia wasn't as adaptable as Orlando. She drowned herself in 1941, at the age of fifty-nine. The suicide note she left to her husband, Leonard, read, "I have the feeling that I shall go mad and cannot go on any longer in these terrible times. I hear voices and cannot concentrate on my work. I have fought against it, but cannot fight any longer. I owe all my happiness in life to you. You have been so perfectly good. I cannot go on and spoil your life."[8] While her work was a way to combat the illness she lived with, Woolf's disappearance and drowning often usurp cultural perceptions of her as a vibrant, dedicated, and socially active woman far ahead of her time—one who ran Hogarth Press with Leonard, entertained Britain's cadre of writers and artists (including American T. S. Eliot), and was at the crux of British intellectual life during the early twentieth century. It's important to remember what allowed her to produce as prolifically as she did, however: She came from a privileged background and had the distinct advantage of time, money, a supportive husband—*and* a room of her own in which to work.

Woolf's writing is commonly referred to as dense and depressing—but rarely is it either. It is the world seen through a new lens, one that is both critical of the author's culture and imbued with repeated romantic notions of nature and time.[9] Her work was also revelatory for its representations of divergent women in British literature, particularly when it gave voice to women's dissatisfaction with their place in the world, as it did in *Mrs. Dalloway*.

The Hours, a 2002 film adapted from Michael Cunningham's novel of the same name, was a modern account of *Mrs. Dalloway*. Both the book and the film include the plot of *Mrs. Dalloway* and a limited interpretation of Woolf herself. For audiences new to Woolf's work or unfamiliar with her biographical details, *The Hours* lent credence to common misconceptions about her. Woolf (played by Nicole Kidman, who won an Oscar for her performance) is portrayed as an entirely internal, misanthropic, quirky woman who was tortured by her own mind. She spoke just above a whisper, often to herself, with a glazed-over and intense stare seeming to border on maniacal. The film managed to reduce a lively intellectual to someone who was maddeningly incapable of clear verbal communication longer than a sentence, and who was perpetually unpredictable and insane (which, by most accounts, including Woolf's own diary, was not the case). And Woolf's effervescent irreverence sailed offscreen quicker than the film's opening credits.

While Woolf's words jump off the page and enliven the room in which one reads them—and although her work was revolutionary, and her attitude freethinking—the mention of her name tends to call forth the odd character *The Hours* presented. The passionate beliefs she expressed throughout her intellectual and personal life are overshadowed by the image of a severe, studious, and highly antisocial creature churning out page after serious page during an austere life. More important, the popular conception of Woolf offers us her academic complexity without her humanity, and ignores the idea that women's lives and minds can be simultaneously steeped in profound discipline, beauty, and bravery while fluctuating between happiness, madness, and sadness.

Where lightness has been politely tucked away from Woolf's legacy, it's been ripped with one ferocious yank from Sylvia Plath. A mid-twentieth-century, U.S.-born poet and author, Plath was known for her crisp language and stark poetic style. One volume of poetry, *The Colossus*, as well as her infamous novel *The Bell Jar,* was published before her death in 1963. Numerous volumes of work were also released posthumously, including *Ariel* and *The Collected Poems.*[10] Her unabridged journals were first published in 2000.

Plath's suicide—which occurred when she was thirty and had been recently abandoned by her husband, British poet laureate Ted Hughes—has been the major focus of writings about her life and her work. It continues to color interpretations of her work, characterizing her early death as the inevitable outcome of her well-honed dissatisfaction. As Katha Pollitt once wondered, "Has more nonsense been written about Sylvia Plath than about other modern poets, or does it just seem that way?"[11] Part of such "nonsense" is the lack of wit with which Plath's work is read. Her writing can be discomforting, mostly for the fierce simplicity of her brutal confessions, but her journals revealed a zeal for life, food, nature, her husband, and her work. A conversational, cynical drawl snaked through all but the most highly depressive of her entries. Signs of her willingness to confront her restlessness as a woman are evident, too. For example, she confided, as an eighteen-year-old, in 1951:

> I am jealous of men—a dangerous and subtle envy which can corrode, I imagine, any relationship. It is an envy born of the desire to be active and doing, not passive and listening . . . . I can pretend to forget my envy; no matter, it is there, insidious, malignant, latent.[12]

There is also the confessional and autobiographical intimacy of *The Bell Jar*, the novel for which Plath is most widely known. The book was published in Britain a few weeks prior to the author's death,[13] and in the United States in 1971. *The Bell Jar*'s narrator was Esther Greenwood, a young collegiate woman faced with the possibilities of her forthcoming adult life. Esther was far too smart to ignore the dissatisfaction she knew she would feel if she were solely a housewife: She stared through a myopic lens at a future of marriage or at the singular, dreaded alternative: mid-twentieth-century "spinsterhood." As Esther's life unfolded in her mind, she became paralyzed by having to choose one path, knowing that for women, doing so meant giving up the other one. Her confusion pushed her toward a breakdown, one that Plath documented candidly. She also highlighted the frustrating plight of young, middle-class women in the 1950s and elucidated how women's rebellion was far more socially risky than that of men during the same time period—if women felt free enough to rebel at all, that is. Plath likened Esther's life choices to a fig tree: It branched out into numerous options, but she couldn't choose one, "starving to death" while the figs shriveled up and fell around her motionless body at the base of the tree.[14]

Unlike the fresh-faced, happy teenage girls and eagerly servile wives of the '50s, Esther had a bluntly expressed disdain for men, who were criticized harshly throughout the book. Buddy Willard, a Yale student who pursued Esther before the time period the book covered, stripped naked in front of her. Her reaction was hardly one of adoration: "The only thing I could think of was turkey neck and turkey gizzards and I felt very depressed."[15] Esther also recognized marriage as the prison it was (and remains) for many. She knew that a woman might be charmed by a man while she dated him, but was also certain that "what he secretly wanted when the wedding service ended was for her to flatten out underneath his feet. . . . "[16] Esther's sarcasm and wit are found in her descriptions of her institutionalized peers, as well as in the book's opening, in which she flounders through an internship at a women's magazine in New York.

For women in literature at the time—whether characters or writers—this kind of audacious female honesty and cynicism was sporadic at best. The Bell Jar loudly articulated its protagonist's inner conflict about the main feature of mid-twentieth-century woman-hood: its lack of choice. Plath opened the door for discussion of these issues, no doubt creating solace for similarly troubled female readers. She also revealed inner truths about women, rather than propagating the delicate, marriage-crazed ideal that other forms of popular culture upheld. Where rock 'n' roll's rebellion barely allowed women recognition outside of lyrical objectification and screaming teenage fandom, and while women's magazines relied on sterile domesticity for content, The Bell Jar confronted the toll women's limited options took on them.

Plath not only made traditional femininity's shortcomings visible, but also made the implications of such a confining lifestyle quite clear: Without choice, women went mad—and not because they were, as society suggested, simply emotionally or mentally frailer than men, or prone to breakdowns and hysteria. Like Woolf, Esther simply believed there was a life for her that focused on something more stimulating than a compulsively sought-after husband. Part of her mental paralysis—though implied, not stated directly—stemmed from her feeling unable to seek out a life of her own design.

The press indulged itself with the grim facts of Plath's death. *The New York Times* described her as having "gassed herself and passed into myth" in its 1971 review of *The Bell Jar*.[17] *Time* magazine's review rightly described the first part of the book as "hilarious"—but not without including this paragraph:

> *She was 30 when she died, an exhausted, mad mother of two, estranged from her poet husband, Ted Hughes. A typically American-looking blonde, she was much admired in English critical circles; half of literary London blamed itself for her death. Yet* The Bell Jar, *like the late poems, makes that tragedy seem a pathetic inevitability.*[18]

Esther's story, on the other hand, was one of survival, not of "pathetic inevitability." As Esther attended the funeral of Joan, a friend of hers who committed suicide, Plath laid bare a plain truth about Esther's ability to face her friend's death, and her own capacity for survival, with two hopeful sentences: "I took a deep breath and listened to the old brag of my heart. I am, I am, I am."[19] Esther eventually began to heal, but *The Bell Jar* ended ambiguously. Plath had planned on continuing the story in its next volume, one that, according to her mother, would have portrayed Esther living healthily.[20] Plath's suicide, however, which occurred soon after the book's publication in Britain, left only the impression that Esther's future, inside or outside of the asylum, was unresolved, and definitively punctuated Esther's potential for recovery.

More than thirty-five years later, the 2003 film *Sylvia* did nothing to combat the existing image of her. The film gave an account of her relationship with Ted Hughes, and portrayed a sparkling and intelligent Plath (Gwyneth Paltrow) who permanently unraveled as she uncovered Hughes's infidelity. Her journals, which never lacked intimacy, don't reveal quite so immediate a breakdown.[21] In fact, Plath's May 19, 1958, journal entry revealed her suspicion about Hughes's involvement with a female student. She was understandably angry and insecure, but also wrote, "No, I won't jump out of a window . . . or slit my wrists and lie in the bath. . . . [T]here are the various—and few—people I love a little. And my own dogged and inexplicable sense of dignity, integrity that must be kept."[22] *Sylvia* completely plucked the fighting spirit out of Plath; it homed in on her periods of writer's block and her terrible rages about Hughes's indiscretions, allowing the breadth of her personality and ideas to be reduced to her relationship with her husband (a tactic that Plath probably would have resented) and her eventual madness. The movie's characters were simplified versions of the couple, with Hughes playing an innocent victim to Plath's eternally humorless shrew, leaving the plot entirely deaf to the brave "old brag" of Sylvia's heart. It's no wonder the Associated Press bought into the myth and simplistically referred to it as "a bummer biography of depressed poet Sylvia Plath" upon the film's release.[23]

*T*he scope of rebellious women in literature has widened considerably since *The Bell Jar,* which has also gained mainstream acclaim and had a lasting impact. Among others, Rita Mae Brown's *Rubyfruit Jungle* was the first widely read lesbian novel of the latter twentieth century, and Toni Morrison's *Beloved* told the story of a woman rebuilding her life in the wake of slavery. Both books have become part of college curricula (as have *The Bell Jar* and *A Room of One's Own*). We have popular, best-selling novels, such as Dorothy Allison's *Bastard out of Carolina,* about women's poverty and abuse; Katherine Dunn's *Geek Love,* an epic about the socially, physically misfit daughter of a carnival family and her search for belonging; and *Middlesex,* by Jeffrey Eugenides, which traced the history of a Greek American family, starting with their immigration from Greece to the United States, from the early settlers to the central character and narrator, Calliope, a hermaphrodite who was raised as a girl and later opted to live as a man.

Calliope's confiding and personal qualities showcased a truly outcast character with little control over her biological oddity. *Middlesex* was the natural progression of *Orlando:* Told over generations, by one narrator, it outlined Detroit's twentieth-century history and dealt with Calliope's and the nation's shifting gender roles. Calliope was rebellious from the outset, urinating on the priest during her baptism,[24] struggling for self-discovery, familial acceptance, and self-acceptance, and eventually deciding to live as a male. During the Detroit riots of 1967, while her father attempted to protect the family business, a seven-year-old Calliope hopped on her bike and headed toward the heart of the riots and in between army tanks while her family hid out at home. As she made the decision to brave the tumultuous streets, she mused about her younger brother's characteristic lack of heroism and then, her own potential for it:

> *I did what any loving, loyal daughter would have done who had been raised on a diet of Hercules movies. In that instant, I decided to find my father, to save him, if necessary, or at least to tell him to come home.*[25]

At the end of the book, mirroring *Orlando's* explicit self-realizations of gender roles, the male Calliope, Cal, realized another uncontrollable variable of his new, privileged experience:

> *When I was little, street-corner dudes like that would sometimes lower their shades to wink, keen on getting a rise out of the white girl in the backseat passing by. But now the dude gave me a different look altogether. He didn't lower his sunglasses, but his mouth, his flared nostrils, and the tilt of his head communicated defiance and even hate. That was when I realized a shocking thing. I couldn't become a man without becoming The Man. Even if I didn't want to.*[26]

While Plath and Woolf and their characters might have suffered for their confessions, each laid the groundwork for a robust lineage of women's self-exploration in which the literary rebel, renewed or reborn, meets an uplifting end. The newer rebels, like Calliope, are more extreme from the outset. In both *Geek Love* and *Middlesex*, the narrators are born misfits, and thereby possess what could be a tragic, alienating quality dictated by society (such as early-twentieth-century womanhood). Instead, Dunn and Eugenides both provide enlightening, engrossing, and full glorifications of the female viewpoint within their pages. These days, the outsider, while tortured by loneliness and crises of identity beyond those plaguing a character such as Esther Greenwood, can finally discover a place in the world.

Billie Holiday, one of the most popular and influential vocalists of the early to mid-twentieth century, is also usually remembered for her drug addiction, rather than for the dogged survival instinct she so often demonstrated. Following a Baltimore childhood spent hustling and scrubbing steps, Holiday made her way to Harlem, where she gained acclaim as one of the most influential jazz vocalists of the twentieth century. In a 1958 issue of *Ebony* magazine, Frank Sinatra said, "It is Billie Holiday who was, and still remains, the greatest single musical influence on me."[27]

While *On the Road* idealized the same world Holiday inhabited— that of both jazz and larger black culture—Holiday's experiences offered insights Kerouac couldn't possibly have idealized. As she said in her ghostwritten autobiography, "Don't tell me about those pioneer chicks hitting the trail in those slip-covered wagons with the hills full of redskins. I'm the girl who went West in 1937 with sixteen white cats, Artie Shaw, and his Rolls Royce—and the hills were full of white crackers."[28] Often, Holiday had to wait on the bus and have band members bring food out to her after their meals.[29] On tour with bandleader Artie Shaw in 1938, Holiday recalled a confused St. Louis performance-hall manager when he noticed her presence, wondering aloud why there was a "nigger" in his establishment when he hadn't hired any to clean.[30] Holiday also traveled with the Count Basie Orchestra in 1937,[31] and when performing in Detroit, she was asked to wear blackface in order to avoid confusion about her race.[32] On the same tour, she had to either wait for an appropriate bathroom (which were few and far between) or relieve herself on the side of the road.[33] The American ability to wander with abandon obviously belonged strictly to privileged white men. Minorities on the road certainly weren't celebrating the liberation showered on the Beats.

Holiday's hallmark song is "Strange Fruit," a haunting, achingly slow and graphic anti-lynching ballad first recorded in 1939. After singing popular standards, which (as is predictable for popular music of any decade) were mainly about love, Holiday could point to her performance of "Strange Fruit" as a turning point in her catalog and in her popular image. As Angela Davis noted in *Blues Legacies and Black Feminism*:

> The felt impact of Holiday's performance of "Strange Fruit" is as powerful today as it was in the 1940s. By placing this song at the center of her repertoire, Holiday firmly established the place of protest in the black popular musical tradition. Her use of this work in her career helped dismantle the opposition, firmly entrenched until her singing of this song, between fame and commercial success on the on hand and social consciousness in music on the other.[34]

As for any black woman openly asserting her anger, singing "Strange Fruit" was a major gamble for Holiday. Being black in

America, she was aware of the implications of its message and the loss she could suffer by expressing her frustration. So was Columbia Records. True to cultural form, the corporate entity that would later cash in on rock's rebellion was fearful of releasing the song.[35]

"Strange Fruit" may have been the most public and tangible example of her resistance, but she was a rebel throughout her life. As Artie Shaw bassist Sid Weiss's wife, Mae, who traveled with her, once recalled, "She was living 'black is beautiful' before it was fashionable. Her whole stature and the way she carried herself is what you see today, the pride in being black. She did it before she even knew what it was; that's the way she lived."[36] Barney Josephson, owner of the integrated Café Society nightclub where Billie played, mentioned one incident when Billie had a particular dislike for her audience and lifted her dress to expose her backside. "[The audience] gasped, aghast. . . . But that was one time a black person said, 'Kiss my ass' and showed it. I told her never to do that again. She said, 'Fuck 'em.'"[37]

Her music seems to reveal a much different Holiday than the woman who told an audience to kiss her ass. Her lyrics were often interpreted as submissive or romantic. Her saddest songs, save for "Strange Fruit," are infused with a clear and lilting, almost insistently positive and bemused voice, which some argue can alter the music's mood from sadness or pure spun sugar to light and salty satire.[38] While nicknamed Lady, and often depicted as possessing a saintly delicacy, Holiday was also known to voice her opposition to racism and loudly defend herself, and was given to tantrums and unpredictable anger. Holiday was hardly resigned to racism. She was open within her own circles about her bisexuality, too, sometimes passing women off to male musicians, and often taking them home herself.[39]

Despite her insistence on her rightful due, and her indignation, individuality, and strength, Billie Holiday's life was rife with marital conflict, physical abuse, arrests, and years of heroin abuse. As a result, she's been documented repeatedly as breakable and utterly defenseless. In the foreword to her autobiography, David Ritz referred to her as "our wounded angel"[40]—reducing Holiday to a childlike or sainted figure and begging the question of who, exactly, owns her. This kind of worshipful claim negates her complex womanhood and the enormous struggle that went with it, martyring her for her pain— and, selfishly, for our loss of her artistry—instead. Blind adulation, and the image of a Holiday who can do no wrong, recasts her as a victim helpless to her own destruction and excess; it prohibits her anger, dissatisfaction, and disillusionment; and it prevents her from being seen as anything other than a perfect female being. It also minimizes the great cultural weight of "Strange Fruit": If Billie was as lamb-innocent as her image, then white culture can be exonerated of inflicting the pain that inspired the song. "Strange Fruit" made the protest song popular again, while Holiday's addiction both raised her to the status of willing victim and made her a spectacle before she died of neglected cirrhosis in 1959.

As an untouchable anomaly, Holiday also prevents women from thinking of such idealized females as equals—and when an "angel" is attached to a misleading sense of emotional simplicity and "senseless" self-destruction, who would want to? Peers referred to Holiday repeatedly as authentic and down-to-earth—which was not necessarily unlikely in jazz, but was surprising for the candy-coated pop singers that dominated mainstream music throughout the 1930s, '40s, and early '50s. Instead of welcoming Holiday's genuineness and identifying with the struggles that her personality engendered, we have glossed over the individual depth that informed the artistry for which she was famous, and aligned her with the saccharine and socially constructed pop stars of her era.

Janis Joplin might have embodied a more joyfully flawed individualism if her death—which happened when she was alone in a hotel room in 1970, the result of a dose of strong heroin—weren't so tragic. Joplin, who was equally infamous for her wailing vocal strength, her ever-present bottle of Southern Comfort, and her membership in the 27 Club (which includes other rock stars, such as Kurt Cobain, Jimi Hendrix, and Jim Morrison, who all died at age twenty-seven), publicly defended and epitomized late-'60s youth rebellion. Along with Grace Slick of Jefferson Airplane, she became one of the only female rock superstars of that era. Both Joplin and Slick hovered somewhere between femininity and masculinity. Neither seduced audiences with the traditional female sexuality that was considered necessary at the time for captivating male audience members. Still, Janis was well known for her long parade of lovers, both male and female (though she never publicly copped to being bisexual), and for seeking lovers in her audiences. In 1973, *Time* called her "the only female star to become a sex symbol on the order of Mick Jagger or Jim Morrison."[41] She rarely wore makeup, and flailed herself through her songs in a style that completely captivated her audience: She bared all her emotions and yet so entranced her male fans that they submitted to her, rather than making her physically submissive to them—reversing the singular role women had been playing in music (and all of pop culture) for most of the century. Aside from Joplin,

Slick, and Maureen Tucker, the Velvet Underground's nontraditional drummer, a physical and artistic rejection of femininity would not become widespread until Patti Smith gained infamy for her androgyny in the early to mid-1970s.

Joplin's voice wailed and warbled and crept and wept and screamed; it was a tool for expressing the exploding emotion the cool male stance denied so blatantly. Joplin also chose to humble herself before her obvious blues influences, rather than remaining silent, taking the credit, and hoarding her profits. (Big Mama Thornton, who publicly complained to *The New York Times* about Presley's neglect, was paid royalties by Joplin and asked permission to use the song "Ball and Chain."[42]) And it was Joplin's utter fearlessness of being herself—a single, wild, uncontrollable, unapologetic woman in a pressure-cooker culture wincing at authentic difference—that made her contribution so startling and confrontational, and simultaneously such a challenge for her in her personal life.

"Janis's fame had revealed the limits of the 'San Francisco free thing,'" wrote Alice Echols in *Scars of Sweet Paradise,* "but her real sin was in being a ballsy broad, a chick with acne who took up too much space in the boys' club of late-sixties rock 'n' roll."[43] In her attempts to upend this boys' club, Joplin met with resistance within her own circles. In two separate exemplary events, she broke a bottle over Jim Morrison's head[44] and got ready to hit rock 'n' roll performer Jerry Lee Lewis when he insulted her.[45] Janis battled the male musical rebellion directly oppressing her as a woman, and as a musician as she battled mainstream conformity. Because of her strong personality, as well as the press's general exploitation of the counterculture, Joplin infused the dialogue with unconventional ideas and shifted the boundaries of outcast women's acceptable public behavior. In a 1970 interview with Dick Cavett, she openly criticized what she saw as men's typical treatment of women.

> **Janis:** *I wrote the first tune, the one we just did. It's, um, it's about men.*
>
> **Dick:** *It's about men. . . .*
>
> **Janis:** *. . . It's about—did you ever see those mule carts? They, uh, there's a dumb mule up there, right, and a long stick, with a string and a carrot hanging there. And they hang this thing out in front of the mule's nose, and he runs after it all day long.*
>
> **Dick:** *Who's the man in this parable: the mule or the person holding the carrot?*
>
> **Janis:** *The woman is . . . the mule, chasing something that someone's always chasing her with.*
>
> **Dick:** *And . . . constantly chasing a man who always eludes her.*
>
> **Janis:** *Well, they just always holdin' up something more than they're prepared to give.*
>
> **Dick:** *I have to defend my entire sex, ladies and gentlemen. The burden of the defense.*
>
> **Janis:** *Go right ahead.*[46]

Like Holiday, Joplin became a spectacle for her excess, which she celebrated openly in the press and onstage. Rock 'n' roll offered a lot more license for boundary-breaking than jazz ever did, and Janis used her widened berth to take advantage of her audience's voyeuristic captivity: to seduce them with the qualities that caused the press and the public to gawk and gasp. Instead of being recalled by the culture at large as a woman who cultivated her own personality and shocked the public with her openness, Joplin is usually remembered more for her death than for being the outsider, outrider woman she was in life. She, Hendrix, and Morrison represented the dark side of hedonism that the '60s generation practiced so brazenly. In accounts of the '60s, the three are consistently referred to as trailblazers and geniuses, but their deaths, which occurred within a year of one another, are pinpointed as cultural moments when the optimistic fire of the decade was extinguished. "Janis Joplin. Jimi Hendrix Jim Morrison. Burnt-out martyrs to the cause, done in by drugs and alcohol. The nobility of their nihilism is, today, a nightmare, the dark side of the force set free in the '60s," wrote *Time* in 1989.[47] As recently as 2006, *Blender* listed "the age of 27" as one of the top ten worst things to happen to music.[48] The idea was also overreported after Kurt Cobain's death in 1994, and again when Heath Ledger died in 2008. For all Joplin's bucking of tradition and her musical gender bending, she's more overwhelmingly known as a "tragic heroine."[49]

While we as a culture tend to raise outcasts to hero status, it is no small thing to be a hero when reverence is fickle and never on time. True rebels pay the price of isolation and misinterpretation. The burden of being a marginalized woman in the public eye—different enough to be culturally significant, but not so much so that she is unacceptable; and working twice as hard to be taken half as seriously by her male colleagues and society at large—is dropped from the cultural conversation about why such women are lonely and tend to self-destruct.

A peek at Holiday's mainstream press is quite telling about the resistance she was up against. It wasn't always overly kind, and in this case, it was flagrantly cruel. When *Time* reported the release of "Strange Fruit"—which the publication described as "a prime piece of musical propaganda"—the message of the song was diluted by the writer's myopic beauty standards: "Billie Holiday is a roly-poly young colored woman with a hump in her voice. . . . She does not care enough about her figure to watch her diet, but she loves to sing."[50]

Another unappealing quality for female audiences envisioning these women as admirable rebels is their dreaded solitude. When female icons are isolated, or suffering from abuse or self-destruction, those circumstances are generally thought to be by-products of being alone and misunderstood—not because they have chosen a less traveled, more free lifestyle, or because they simply cannot live up to the culture's impossible artistic and societal demands. For women, aloneness has never been equated with the freedom granted to male rebels; it's viewed instead as an inevitable corollary to their self-destruction.

The true nature of these tragedies is overlooked in favor of casting these women as simplified "angels" or "heroines" who died before their time. The cases of Holiday, Joplin, and Plath all point to the excruciating pain of being a woman who refuses to play the part already written for her. It's because of the sparse cultural reference points for women who seek more than they are given that these three artists are so often misconstrued as hapless idols on paths of self-destruction, rather than as the renegades they truly were. Since the pop-culture female fantasy never truly changes shape, these artists often spent their time trying to get beyond stereotypical assumptions or enduring having their unconventional exploits repeatedly marveled at and recounted.

Because pop culture's version of rebellion is propped up by the notion that women, rebellious or not, rely on men, these female celebrities' fragility and need to be "rescued" are far more pleasant fodder for the male imagination than what might lie beneath their suffering. Furthermore, these qualities dutifully reinforce both traditional masculinity and femininity. Rock journalist Ellen Willis once wrote of Joplin:

> Janis sang out of her pain as a woman, and men dug it. Yet it was men who caused the pain, and if they stopped causing it they would not have her to dig. In a way, their adulation was the cruelest insult of all. And Janis's response—to sing harder, get higher, be worshiped more—was rebellious, acquiescent, bewildered all at once.[51]

Something similar happened to Holiday following her 1948 release from spending nearly a year in prison for drug possession. Holiday biographer Donald Clarke asserted that she was conscious of herself as a spectacle for audiences, and that playing the role of the destructive woman was one to which she was partially accustomed.[52] As Holiday and Joplin became conscious of audiences that flocked to performances to gawk, their awareness of voyeuristic packed houses and fans agape must have been frustrating and hurtful. Their pain had become a more valuable commodity than their music, and that caused them to turn on themselves even more, rather than carving out a new niche for themselves and for future generations of women.

The overarching message is that no life chosen outside of the current female norm will end happily. What if *The Hours* focused on another Virginia Woolf—one who felt accomplished and was socially engaged in the world? What if, in the same way Kerouac's mystique lives on through his work, the ebullience found in *A Room of One's Own* became Woolf's primary legacy? What would happen to "our wounded angel" if Holiday were praised for her antiracism efforts and the pain of fighting her way through life? If women were able to steer their own public images and interpretations of their lives and their work, they would not be construed as oversimplified martyrs. And if their individual rebellions were honored more emphatically, the whispers of early death as the fate of all questioning women might not be so prevalent or so linked to the male-fantasy construct of the damsel in distress.

*T*hough Hollywood and syrupy endings go hand in hand, cinematic accounts of female rebellion haven't fared much better than the real thing. It's as if mainstream culture is dipping its toe in a pool of ice-cold water but can't commit to diving all the way in. Hollywood *wants* to believe in the existence of the female rebel, and occasionally *tries* to celebrate her, but usually manages to upend any hope that the character will walk away clean. It's probably a decent reflection of how difference has historically been handled in the United States, but it's also a grim message for outsiders, especially outsider women. Although women occasionally enjoy social-justice victories over corporate corruption, such as in *Erin Brockovich* and *Norma Rae,* many of the typical films portraying female rebels are biopics that end in death, such as *Silkwood, Monster, Boys Don't Cry,* and *Bonnie and Clyde,* and only reinforce the dangerous nature of female resistance with hard and dramatic proof of its fate. The repetition of such images also allows Hollywood's sore lack of imagination to shine through: It's as if a female rebel complicated by something other than sexuality is unimaginable. It's doubtful that martyr biopics and "chick flicks" are the only scripts about women beefing up the studios' submissions piles, but they're the ones the studios love to make, decade in and decade out.

Strictly fictional films heap on mixed messages in the same way biopics do. In 1961, the Lillian Hellman play *The Children's Hour* was adapted for the screen by director William Wyler and starred Audrey Hepburn and Shirley MacLaine. Hepburn and MacLaine played Karen and Martha, respectively, two single friends and schoolteachers who opened their own school. The film began by clearly expressing the emotional satisfaction they gained from running the school, instead of from relationships and domesticity, but turned from an example of happy singlehood to doom when a cantankerous student spread a rumor that the two women were lovers. The falsehood destroyed their reputations, closed the school, and eventually caused Martha to confront her own homosexuality and then commit suicide.

The Children's Hour was a study in paranoia's triumph over acceptance. It criticized the 1950s anticommunist witch hunt, as well as addressing the nation's puritanical attitude toward homosexuality and its backward view of single women. Unfortunately, the film's only overtly rebellious element was Mary, the tomboy and class tyrant who started the rumor that ruined the women's career.

Karen and Martha did uphold some of the post–World War II mentality about femininity, however: Hepburn's Karen was more traditionally feminine-looking than MacLaine's Martha and was engaged, while Martha was perpetually single. Although Martha's homosexuality was revealed at the end of the film, her character was predominantly that of a wisecracking, homelier sidekick whose main purpose was to react to her more classically beautiful friend's life. Without knowing her sexuality, the audience witnesses Martha's constant sacrifices for Karen, and what seems like stereotypical spinsterlike jealousy of Karen's relationship with Joe (James Garner). But at least the film challenged the expected plotline with original twists.

On other levels, though, Karen was unconventional. She was hesitant to marry Joe, and more focused on the school's success than on the possibility of marriage and children, while the 1950s and early '60s favored females more eager for marriage than their male counterparts were. Her decision to maintain her career while married was one step ahead of the housewives' disaffection that Betty Friedan documented in *The Feminine Mystique,* published in 1963. But Martha and Karen's assumed rebellion, which was actually a nonexistent and misunderstood relationship, was what they were eventually punished for. Their real sin lay in valuing their work and each other over the traditional marriage trail—and that was threatening enough to ruin them.

Karen and Martha's dramatic sense of fear about their futures and the town's homophobia portrayed just how dangerous it was to be a lesbian at the time. The film could have further challenged stereotypes about lesbians by casting Hepburn, the more established Hollywood leading female, as gay, but alas, options were limited in an industry that was blind to the beginnings of the '60s rights movements. After the two women were left cowering at home, ostracized and ridiculed, Martha admitted her love to Karen. The movie's subject matter alone was revolutionary, but to include a coming-out monologue from

Martha was unheard of in mainstream cinema at the time. Monologues are a regular device of playwriting, but Hollywood's usual practice was to allude to "deviant" behavior without explicitly stating it. The overtly gay content may have been allowed because Martha didn't recognize her homosexuality until she was accused of being a lesbian, but it was more likely permitted because the monologue was amply self-hating.

> It's funny; it's all mixed up and there's something in you, and you don't know anything about it, because you don't know it's there. . . . I can't stand to have you touch me! I can't stand to have you look at me! Oh, it's all my fault—I've ruined your life, and I've ruined my own! I swear I didn't know it! I didn't mean it! Oh, I feel so sick and dirty, I can't stand it anymore![53]

Unpredictably, Karen didn't ostracize Martha for coming out. She tried to convince her to make a fresh start by fleeing with her and Joe. Instead, Martha hung herself. Karen buried her friend at the end of the film, walking gracefully out of the cemetery and off on her own—without Joe. Karen might have been exonerated and free to begin her life again, but Martha, the true outcast, was tortured enough by her difference to end her life. *The Children's Hour* was a potent statement about fear and power in America, communicating that unavoidable—and unrepentant—differences in women and minorities were unforgivable.

Thirty-eight years after the release of *The Children's Hour*, homophobia's continuing and weighty cultural presence was unpacked again in *Boys Don't Cry*, the 1999 film depicting the true story of Brandon

Teena, a biological woman (born as Teena Brandon) living as a transgendered man who was killed in 1993 in Humboldt, Nebraska. When
two men, John Lotter and Marvin Nissen, discovered Brandon's secret,
they raped and killed him, as well as murdering two others who were
present in the house at the time.[54] While it was based on true events, the
movie borrowed heavily (consciously or not) from the traditional rebel
formula in order to mythologize Brandon Teena.

Brandon's courageous insistence on being himself in a small
Midwestern town made the film similar to, yet somewhat more
powerful than, classic rebel films. In the tradition of *The Wild One* and
Easy Rider, Brandon's unknown and anonymous character (played by
Hilary Swank) arrived in a new town. He was a mysterious male loner
with a police record and a closely kept secret, bereft of family and
adrift. From the outset of the film, when Brandon left his hometown of
Lincoln, Nebraska, and met his new friends, he was obviously thrilled
with risk. In one of the film's opening scenes, Brandon was chased
home by a crowd of young men, running from epithets like "Faggot!"
lobbed through the Midwestern night. Brandon entered his friend's
house, laughing and winded, after running from potential violence—
and continued the same daring behavior once he reached Falls City.

The story of Brandon Teena represents the most dramatic risk
minority rebels face when they climb into the dominant rebel's shoes
and fall in line with traditional male rebellion. As a transgendered
drifter seducing young women in the Midwest, Brandon's quest itself
was more transgressive than any heterosexual white male rebel. Brando
could wander in and out of town safely, no matter what happened in
between. But not Brandon. The director, Kimberly Peirce, portrayed him
as trusting and optimistic—as someone so desperate to escape the utter

isolation of his experience that he was willing to believe in nonexistent safety, even when his friend in Lincoln warned him repeatedly about the perils of hiding his identity and staying in Falls City.

But Peirce also disregarded some larger details contributing to Brandon's death, which would have added to the depth of his alienation and highlighted the larger forces that conspired against him in real life. After being brutally raped, he did report it to police, but the film omitted the fact that the Richardson County sheriff refused to arrest John Lotter and Marvin Nissen for the act. Sheriff Charles Laux only brought them in for questioning on December 28, 1993, three days after the rape—and three days prior to Brandon's murder.[55] According to numerous witnesses of the sheriff's investigation, he was more concerned with (or afraid of) Brandon's sexual identity than he was willing to arrest Lotter and Nissen on rape charges. Brandon is shown reporting the rape to the police, but the sheriff let Lotter and Nissen walk away after their questioning. Without this detail in the film, Brandon seemed ultimately responsible for the risk he took, and his gamble appeared to turn out tragically only because of Lotter and Nissen's ignorance. While the film was highly compassionate, it stripped away some crucial facts—the lack of protection and the societal forces that contributed heavily to Brandon's murder—and thus sent the message that such courage alone is deadly.

Considering the subject matter and Brandon Teena's nonfiction bravery, coupled with the film's radical content and Swank's nontraditional performance, *Boys Don't Cry* was a rebellious act in itself. And mainstream culture responded to it. As Janet Maslin wrote in *The New York Times*, " . . . [T]he character of Brandon Teena became a touching emblem of freedom: the chance to reach beyond the limitations of circumstance and bravely shape a different destiny."[56] Brandon's harsh reality became a landmark moment for the discourse, visibility, and advocacy of transgender rights.[57] Tellingly, in *The Stranger*'s 2007 queer issue, writer Kaley Davis referred to Brandon as "the great transgendered martyr of our time."[58]

Boys Don't Cry did bring more to the table than a dark, unrelenting story; it venerated both Brandon's strength in unwelcome territory and his faith in the people around him. However, Peirce also recast in more optimistic terms the degree to which Brandon's girlfriend, Lana Tisdale, accepted him; put Lana at the crime scene; and decided she would wake the next morning with Brandon's body underneath her. Brandon's heroic status is certainly deserved, and it was significant that the rebel myth was retold, but oversimplification—and thereby romanticization—of the story unfairly attributed Brandon's risk-taking and ensuing rejection to his own trust and need for love. As a result, *Boys Don't Cry* simultaneously cheapened true courage and illuminated the dangers of being oneself.

More problematic is how the images in *Boys Don't Cry* began steering the images associated with the case. Hilary Swank's picture has replaced Brandon Teena's as the go-to reference point for news about the actual case. When Marvin Nissen confessed to his sole responsibility for the killings in 2007, CNN's website ran a photo of Swank, rather than Brandon, with the story. It also referred to the case as "the 'Boys Don't Cry' case."[59] In 2003, on the ten-year anniversary of Brandon's death, *USA Today*'s website also featured a still from the movie.[60] No additional photo of Brandon Teena was included in either report. Swank is forever intermingled with the story's actual martyr—the simplified, fictional account diluted Brandon's story and pinned a new, recognizable, heterosexual, and wealthy image over the face of the actual, truly brave rebel.

Boys Don't Cry bore some surface similarities to the 2003 film Monster, the story of Aileen Wuornos, a Florida prostitute who was convicted of seven killings that occurred between 1989 and 1990.[61] Both Boys Don't Cry and Monster featured outlaw women, drifting and poor, who were deceptive but were represented compassionately. Although Teena and Wuornos were newsworthy for much more than transgressive behavior, Monster and Boys Don't Cry showcased each character's transformative love relationship as a major plot point— ostensibly to highlight their individual humanity for audiences who might have otherwise lacked sympathy for two such outcasts, particularly Wuornos.

Aileen Wuornos also embodied the rootlessness of the classic rebel, but she and Brandon both distanced themselves from that persona: Rather than being typically emotionally detached, they expressed their hunger to be loved and to experience human connection. Neither film, however, explored the complexities of such abject alienation. Brandon Teena's story focused so intently on the transcendental love between Brandon and Lana Tisdale, it was difficult to remember that their relationship lasted only about a week.[62] Conversely, Monster condensed the time Wuornos and her lover, Tyria Moore, knew each other—they were actually together for approximately four years.[63] The heavy dose of love in both films elicited empathy and lightened the mood of the stories, to some degree, but also detracted from the larger struggles, such as Wuornos's and Brandon's utter financial and social powerlessness. Wuornos made her living as a roadside prostitute, and Brandon indulged in check forgery. Although Brandon's risk taking was much less intertwined with the danger of living as a male in a small American town, money would have made it possible for him to wander beyond another bleak Midwestern landscape. Wuornos and Brandon both sought to escape from the personal danger that poverty created for them, but it was unattainable.

Society's role in deciding the fate of these outsiders, punishing them for being at odds with social norms, certainly could have been played up much more. Both movies lessened the impact of the deeper destructive forces at work while reinforcing the danger of personal violence to drifters who are female or transgendered. The retelling and simplification of true events like these can perpetuate the belief that female road warriors can never ride to safety.

*T*he iconic road maven Bonnie Parker was portrayed in the artful 1967 biopic *Bonnie and Clyde*. Again, the film itself was a revelation by Hollywood's staid standards of the day, personalizing the story of Bonnie Parker and Clyde Barrow, legendary wandering bank robbers in the 1930s. This intimate, roiling tale of two disaffected criminals was a grand departure from the other critical successes of 1967, which included banal Hollywood fare such as *Camelot, Doctor Dolittle,* and *Thoroughly Modern Millie,* but also *Cool Hand Luke, The Graduate,* and *Guess Who's Coming to Dinner.* Caught in the fold between forcefully happy old Hollywood and the years of the complicated American auteur that followed, *Bonnie and Clyde* was noted more often for its stark and lengthy hail-of-bullets ending[64] than for Bonnie Parker's emotional complexity. Faye Dunaway's performance revealed a very different leading lady—beautiful and temperamental, assertive and tough. Bonnie Parker wasn't the first female protagonist prone to brooding, shooting guns, or sinning, but she was certainly the first truly violent and simultaneously seductive lead woman in a Hollywood-endorsed and critically acclaimed film in decades, since gangster molls and denizens had been allowed to run amok in the 1920s and '30s.

We have Hollywood's Production Code, established in 1934, to thank for the long dry spell.[65] In fact, the Code helped to sustain predictable story arcs involving leading ladies who turned good in the end, or bitterly swallowed a dose of their own medicine. After pressure from the Catholic Church, which objected to story lines disagreeing with the religion's mores in the 1930s, the Studio Relations Committee enforced the code to assuage the threat of a movie boycott, resulting in a tight grip on the "decency" of film content.[66] Given the narrow moral values the Production Code Administration deemed acceptable, there was no way for Hollywood's leading women to rebel—or to do anything else worth watching. Mick LaSalle wrote of the code's effect on the fates of femmes fatales in *Complicated Women: Sex and Power in Pre-Code Hollywood:*

> *Women got the worst of it. Under the Code, it wasn't only crime that didn't pay. Sex outside of marriage didn't pay. Adultery didn't pay. Divorce didn't pay. Leaving your husband didn't pay. Getting pregnant outside of wedlock didn't pay. Even having a job often didn't pay. Nothing paid. The Production Code ensured a miserable fate—or at least a rueful, chastened one—for any woman who stepped out of line.[67]*

The Production Code had loosened its grip on Hollywood by the early 1960s, and was officially dropped when the Motion Picture Academy Association implemented the ratings system in 1968, but the leading ladies' legacy in postcode Hollywood was longer than their precode precedent. Precode cinematic content in the 1920s and '30s had allowed for the crimes of prostitutes, murderers, gamblers, thieves, and seductresses to go unpunished. But Hollywood—largely an assembly line of stock characters throughout the 1950s and through the late '60s—was still producing female leads (not to mention happy endings) that tended to fit the box-office ideal. This lack of variety explained in part why gritty '70s films like Scorsese's, not to mention *The Children's Hour,* were so subversive.

For all of Parker's transgressions—her eager delight in her new, forbidden lifestyle; the cool glance she gave the camera as she posed with guns; her forceful debasement of a police officer; her smoldering unhappiness; and her frequently expressed dissatisfaction with lover Clyde Barrow—she was also feminine putty in Barrow's hands, doing whatever he asked in order to seem more attractive to him. Despite her efforts, in the film and in reality, Parker ended life as a bullet-ridden gangster slumped over in an excessive pool of her own blood. At least the critical acclaim the film received, and its ten Academy Award nominations, including one for Faye Dunaway and another for Best Picture, vindicated her boisterous life and death. The movie's success—as well as that of Anne Bancroft's Mrs. Robinson in *The Graduate*—increased the demand for more visible leading roles for women who weren't slaving over a hot stove, sleeping in a cold bed, or smiling their way from beginning to ending credits.

In 2002, the film *Chicago* garnered major mainstream attention. A new take on the stage version from 1975, as well as a remake of a silent film produced in the 1920s *and* a remake of a 1942 film starring Ginger Rogers,[68] the twenty-first-century *Chicago* was not your average, chipper musical. It reflected the qualities of pre–Production Code Hollywood: Women were criminals and were rewarded for their crimes, instead of being sent directly to the gallows. Based on real-life murders that took place in the '20s, and on a play written in that same decade by Maurine Watkins, a female newspaper reporter in Chicago,[69] the plot revolved around a series of flappers who murdered their husbands. In the movie, Catherine Zeta-Jones's character, Velma Kelly, shimmied and shook like a burlesque star, but a mean streak ran through her bawdiness; Velma was powerful, scheming, and unapologetic. In the end, she and costar Renée Zellweger's Roxie Hart escaped death row, joined forces to seek fame and fortune, and tap-danced their way away from the previous cinematic reflex of guilt or longing for forgiveness. The film, though a complete fantasy (right down to Richard Gere's deftly edited tap-dancing solo), rewrote the script not only for criminal women, but also for the Hollywood musical, in which love is the ultimate ending and there's no blurring of the lines as far as comeuppances go: The "good" characters get rewarded, and the "bad" characters swallow their just desserts. *Chicago*'s happy ending sent two murdering women—women who'd killed their lovers, no less—off into the sunset, replete with sequins and sashays. Considering the way Billie Holiday was dragged through the legal system, the glory these women were rewarded with was wholly unrealistic for the time—or at least it would have been for high-profile black criminals.

Of the female-criminal tag-team films, the most crucial is *Thelma & Louise*. Here, the classic road story was appropriately deconstructed and illustrated the differing motives women and men in the open West have for shuttling off into the unknown. For Thelma, the trip was an escape from her abusive husband and miserable marriage. For Louise, the adventure changed from a weekend trip in the mountains to escaping the inevitable consequences of killing Harlan, a bar owner who attempted to rape Thelma in a parking lot. Acting on the impulsive rage of invaded women everywhere, Louise shot him. The killing sparked numerous incidents—usually involving acts of sexism any woman in America has encountered, such as a truck driver's delight in making obscene gestures—in which Thelma and Louise tapped into the criminal within them. The film also implicitly commented on how the U.S. criminal system treats survivors of both rape and violence (with overwhelming disbelief), and on its unforgiving stance toward female criminals themselves.

More than any other female-rebel film that has captured mainstream attention, *Thelma & Louise* was modeled after the traditional road and rebel genres, embracing women as viable lead characters, antiheroines, and serious criminal threats. For all its empowerment, comedy, and truth in between exaggerated moments of desperation (such as Thelma coolly robbing liquor stores), *Thelma & Louise* provided two hours of shoot-'em-up action made for women—with death, yet again, as the only escape option. The final moment was crafted to be uplifting: Accompanied by soaring music, Thelma and Louise expressed their love for each other, clasping each other's hands. But it's the aftereffect that stings: the belated, sinking realization that events set in motion by a rape and a murder have finally caught up with the initial sense of excitement and freedom in the women's adventure.

A different kind of rebellion, similar to that in *Norma Rae* and *Erin Brockovich*, appeared in the 1983 film *Silkwood*, a biopic about Karen Silkwood, who uncovered health hazards and safety risks in the 1970s at the nuclear power plant where she worked. The film effectively underscored the powerlessness of the plant workers, who were willing to ignore flagrant risks to their safety and the misgivings of plant management in order to retain their jobs, and dramatized Silkwood's bravery in the face of upper management's deception and manipulation. Karen, played by Meryl Streep, was portrayed as a devil-may-care, spirited, wisecracking woman, one so unfettered from behavior expected of women that she comically exposed her breast at work for shock value. Karen's charming personality was rebellious enough, but her willingness to dedicate herself to uncovering the truth, coupled with the damage it did to her live-in relationship with boyfriend and coworker Drew (played by Kurt Russell) made *Silkwood* and its female lead unique among other films about women released that year, including *Yentl*, a mostly comical musical about a woman dressing as a man to study Judaism; *Terms of Endearment*, which explored a mother-daughter relationship; and the steel worker-by-day, stripper-by-night story offered in the erotic *Flashdance*. *Silkwood* was the only film nominated for an Academy Award that year to offer a leading lady of depth and soul who was realistically sexual, unassuming, and intelligent, as well as poor. (Sure, *Flashdance* offered the poverty and the sexuality, as well as a sprinkling of soul, but director Adrian Lyne padded the film with enough objectification to distract from both the flimsy plotline and the positive points.) Even as Karen's work kept her from Drew, her coworkers, her roommate, Dolly (played brilliantly by Cher), and her children, she remained committed to exposing the plant's breaches of security and workers' rights.

Eventually, her entire house and body were contaminated with radiation, and her home's contents were removed. Soon after the contamination cleanup, in 1974, she died in a car accident on her way home from a union meeting. Tranquilizers were found in her bloodstream, but the sense of threat surrounding her throughout the film suggests that Silkwood died for a cause. The actual cause of her death remained a mystery for many years.

In almost all of these cases, the women martyred live on in our memory mainly because of their end. As a culture, we often ignore the ways minority rebels change the status quo while they are alive. The slices of life we embrace are the more acceptable, safe ones, and the darker sides become cautionary tales. In short, these women are no longer women; they're bits and pieces of the women they were—a saint, like Billie Holiday; or hopelessly ill-fated, like Thelma, Louise, Brandon, or Wuornos. Their appeal becomes whatever the culture chooses to remember. There is an upside to this scenario, however: While Plath, Woolf, Holiday, and Joplin may have suffered deeply in their lives, they were extraordinary artists who left behind work that remains vital regardless of their personal anguish (and at times, perhaps, because of it). These visionaries' true legacy has been to make generations of women feel alive and validated, and to give them permission to claim a wider, freer sense of self-expression.

chapter 3
Cherry Bombs

I pity weak women, good or bad, but I can't like them. A woman should be strong either in her goodness or badness.[1]

—Mae West

The most powerful, enduring female cultural icons in the United States have always been heralded for their beauty and sex appeal: Silent-film star Clara Bow was labeled the It Girl; Greta Garbo haunted audiences with a beauty that exuded both passion and anguish; Marlene Dietrich seduced with a deep, raspy voice, heavy-lidded, sometimes snide looks, and forays into cross-dressing. Mae West's bawdy strut was singular, tough, seductive, and always identifiable. Betty Grable's and Rita Hayworth's legs far outlasted their films in our memory. Sophia Loren and Brigitte Bardot brought a lush European sensuality to the United States in the 1960s, making even Marilyn Monroe look innocent on occasion. In the 1970s, sex symbols like Farrah Fawcett were better known as teenage-boy poster fare than for their acting talent or onscreen mystique. Madonna and her midriff became the popular definition of sex during the '80s—until supermodels took over in the early '90s. A stampede of laddie magazines followed later in the decade and allowed actresses known more for their sexuality than for their talent, such as Alyssa Milano, Yasmine Bleeth, Tara Reid, and Pamela Anderson, to moonlight as pinup girls. Also in the '90s, young women who were barely adults, like Britney Spears and Christina Aguilera, became mainstream sexual fantasies as the smoldering drama of '50s and '60s curvaceous seduction gave way to the allure of sexually suggestive schoolgirls. Like the restless iconic rebel, sex symbols generally enforce traditional gender roles, achieving titillation and not much else. The concept of what's considered arousing, too, has significantly narrowed since the middle of the twentieth century.

Erotic art and photographs have existed for as long as art itself, but the American sex symbol straddles a clearly marked fork in the road: the time before Marilyn Monroe, and the time following her death.

I think that sexuality is only attractive when it's natural and spontaneous. This is where a lot of [manufacturers of beauty] miss the boat. . . . We are all born sexual creatures, thank God, but it's a pity so many people despise and crush this natural gift. Art, real art, comes from it—everything. I never quite understood it—this sex symbol. . . . That's the trouble: A sex symbol becomes a thing. I just hate to be a thing. But if I'm going to be a symbol of something, I'd rather have it [be] sex than some other things they've got symbols of![2]

—Marilyn Monroe

Marilyn Monroe is instantly recognizable to most of us—her image, now most often of her wearing a white dress and standing over a subway grate during a promotion for *The Seven-Year Itch,* graces coffee mugs, purses, posters, plates, T-shirts, dolls, and statues, among other products. Monroe's official website alone also sells candles, a terrifyingly rendered Marilyn bust/cookie jar, salt and pepper shakers, magnets, makeup, and standing cardboard cutouts.[3] Since 2001, Monroe has consistently appeared on *Forbes's* morbid annual list of top-earning dead celebrities, with her image pulling in annual profits in the millions.[4] Her sex appeal is still as ubiquitous as her likeness: In 1999, *Playboy* named Monroe the "Number-One Sex Star of the 20th Century," and *People* magazine declared her the "Sexiest Woman of the Century."[5] She remains a prominent part of our cultural consciousness—even if her movies have taken a back seat to Marilyn memorabilia.

Whether Monroe would have liked to or not, she has remained eternally available, inviting, and sexy. She may not seem the rebel, but she is the ultimate example of the difference between male and female iconography—the embodiment of male fantasy, the eternally waiting woman, is the polar opposite of 1950s classic male-rebel cool. By 1957, when *On the Road* was published, Monroe's celebrity had exploded. She had already appeared in several films now considered highlights of her career, such as *All About Eve, How to Marry a Millionaire, The Seven-Year Itch,* and *Gentlemen Prefer Blondes.*

Long after the height of her fame in the 1950s, and long after her death in 1962, the male public considered Monroe the ideal celebrity, the dream date, and, generally, the ultimate sexual fantasy, or at least the recipe for the fantasy ideal she left in her wake. For women, Monroe is a different experience entirely. Monroe herself suggested in *Life* magazine that male journalists were kinder to her than female journalists[6]—an understandable comment, considering that for women, digesting Monroe's conflicted image as both powerful and submissive can feel like downing a tablespoon of sugar with a large dose of rock salt. In moving beyond her voiceless, near perfect product image, though, Marilyn Monroe can be more than merely the sexiest woman of the twentieth century. In the overstuffed library of Monroe biographies (including one embarrassingly hyperbolic, sexually frustrated Norman Mailer tome), she's alternately presented as an innocent or unknowing victim, a child, and the sexiest woman who ever lived.[7] But as Sarah Churchwell documented in *The Many Lives of Marilyn Monroe,* even a flood of words doesn't move Monroe beyond the strictures she suffered under as an actress, when she was repeatedly forced to play the dumb blond. Truman Capote once recalled her confiding to him, "I'll never get the right part, anything I really want. My looks are against me. They're too specific."[8]

It wasn't only her looks that were specific—the roles she played rarely fluctuated either, particularly in the romantic comedies noted as the pinnacles of her career. From *Gentlemen Prefer Blondes* onward, Monroe mostly affected a saccharine-sweet, soft voice in an impossibly high register, with her eyebrows yanked up in perpetual surprise as if she were a toddler seeing everything for the first time. Her character's relentless gold-digging was juxtaposed with her uncanny ability to be seduced by the mundane men surrounding her. In *How to Marry a Millionaire,* Betty Grable, Lauren Bacall, and Monroe play three single women on the hunt for rich men to marry. *Gentlemen Prefer Blondes* offered Monroe's rendition of "Diamonds Are a Girl's Best Friend," later mimicked by Madonna, the twentieth century's other most influential sex symbol, in 1985. In *Some Like It Hot,* Monroe's character, Kandy Kane, lamented that she always fell for musicians who left her, and vowed to find a rich, supposedly more stable man. The mess that was Monroe's most famous character—a soft-spoken, hopelessly naive, endlessly nice, perpetually dim woman hunting for a sugar daddy—superseded her public persona and caused her to be remembered as a dopey and doped-up sexpot, more than as a comedienne. Interestingly, too, the one thing she already had in reality—money (though she was reportedly given short shrift in her salary throughout her career)—was something her characters were starved for and chased doggedly.

Even with a trail of questionable, one-note roles behind Monroe, acting teacher Lee Strasberg (who also coached James Dean, Dennis Hopper, and Marlon Brando, among many others) once said "he encountered two film personalities of really great potential in his work at the Studio, Marlon Brando, and quite as good as Brando is Marilyn," Mailer noted in *Marilyn, a Biography.*[9] "However confused or difficult she is in real life," makeup artist Whitey Snyder once confessed to a production assistant on the set, "for the camera she can do no wrong. . . . And sometimes, I feel like telling her directors—don't fuss her, don't tell her what to do, just let her rip."[10]

There are ways in which Monroe shifted from being a simple sex icon to being a more complex figure, beginning with the raciness of her films and her raunchy quips to the press, which brought sex back to the fore in a puritanical Hollywood. In some ways, her hypersexuality made up for the sex Hollywood was constantly trying to shut out of its films. The dumb-bunny innocence blanketed with double entendres that never failed to make her leading men sweat also revealed the male sex drive's foolishly undiscriminating tendencies. *Time* magazine's May 14, 1956, cover story on Monroe quite dramatically drove home the extreme to which men reacted idiotically to her sensuality:

In Turkey a young man went so daft while watching Marilyn wiggle through How to Marry a Millionaire *that he slashed his wrists. The Communists have angrily denounced her as a capitalist trick to make the U.S. masses forget how miserable they really are. In Moji, Japan, her notorious nude photograph was hung in the municipal assembly building in an effort "to rejuvenate the assemblymen." In the radiation control laboratory of the world's first atomic submarine a picture of Marilyn occupies a prominent place in the Table of Elements. She is the subject of more unprintable stories than anybody since the farmer's daughter.[11]*

Such dramatic reporting mirrored the reactions of male characters in her films. In *Gentlemen Prefer Blondes,* Monroe's Lorelei Lee sat at dinner, surrounded by men, and shot off a series of rapid-fire questions (without giving the men any time to answer) as they gawked. She ended her falsely passionate, completely inane staccato reverie with "I just *adore* conversation, don't you?" while the men around her continued grasping for words.[12] By remaining fully oblivious to the cinematic messes she made of the men around her, Monroe revealed in an accessible way what ridiculous lengths men would go to for attention. And she almost mockingly exhibited what sells—and for millions. In perfecting the blond-bombshell role, she demonstrated, however inadvertently, *Orlando*'s revelation regarding men's fumbling reactions to glimpses of women's bodies: "What fools they are!"

For all the ways in which she can be read as a foil to the cool exterior of the quintessential American male, Monroe still sank back into a pile of mink myth, with any hint of rebellion or cynicism peroxided, airbrushed, or washed away. And her alleged perfection unveiled the other ultimate truth about men when it comes to beauty: The ideal will never be enough. While there are countless excited accounts of Monroe's public appearances, a few express disappointment at seeing her in public. In Colin Clark's *The Prince, the Showgirl and Me: Six Months on the Set with Marilyn and Olivier*, the author recorded his experiences working on the set of *The Prince and the Showgirl*, a film directed by Sir Laurence Olivier, starring him and Monroe, and produced in part by Marilyn Monroe Productions. (It was the only film the company produced.) Clark revealed his own expectations of Monroe when he described her first arrival on the set: "She looked absolutely frightful. No makeup, just a skirt, a tight blouse, head scarf, and dark glasses. Nasty complexion, a lot of facial hair, shapeless figure, and, when the glasses came off, a very vague look in her eye. No wonder she is so insecure."[13] The presumption that she awoke looking as naturally beautiful as a two-hour preshoot grooming session would make her appear is absurd, and it evidenced a male naiveté about female beauty that surpassed even Marilyn's characters' oblivion. Yet part of her cultural appeal was that her wholly unnatural physical perfection and her exaggerated, constructed sweetness seemed so effortless as to convince women that they could look like her, and men that they could have her.

Monroe also illustrated how charmed men were by a supposed lack of intelligence. The image of her as a willing, dumb blond perpetuated not only the blond stereotype, but also men's need to confirm their own power by being smarter than their lovers. As a powerful sex symbol, Monroe was tremendously appealing precisely because she wasn't an assertive, powerful, sexy, *and* intelligent woman—that would have been as emasculating to men as a rebel male's settling down with one of his swooning women on the road. If Monroe is still considered the sexiest twentieth-century woman, then the mainstream male version of women's perfection still includes female helplessness, and a need of being rescued and schooled. A woman who won't make a fuss, and a woman who won't mind taking a back seat to her partner, allows male audiences to achieve, or retain, unshakable macho cool.

But the mere idea that Monroe's intelligence was slightly below average isn't what's so offensive. Assumptions about it border on the ridiculous—for some, it seems, she was in a virtual coma throughout her professional life. "The question is whether Marilyn is a person at all, or one of the greatest DuPont products ever invented," director Billy Wilder (*The Seven-Year Itch; Some Like It Hot*) once noted. "She has breasts like granite, and a brain like Swiss cheese, full of holes. . . . The charm of her is her two left feet."[14] Clark's and the crew's impressions of Monroe (who was beyond difficult to work with, according to Clark's account) were also flippantly judgmental. Prior to Monroe's arrival in England, where *The Prince and the Showgirl* was shot, Clark speculated that the honor of playing opposite acting legend Olivier would have had to be explained to her.[15] Would an actress who had studied under Lee Strasberg need a talking-to about who Sir Laurence Olivier was, when he was highly regarded as one of the greatest actors of the day in the United States and abroad?

Unlike Hollywood's preferred, polished public images of the 1950s, the sexiest woman of the century was messy. She divorced three times, her weight fluctuated, she spoke openly about a difficult childhood, and she made witty sexual innuendoes to the press. On numerous occasions, it was reported that Monroe was "often bedraggled and stained" in public.[16] She was hardly the classic prim, glamorous, and PR-ready celebrity of the 1950s. She was a porcelain beauty who took advantage of a stereotype and blew it out of the water, and a celebrity who contradicted the "appropriate" dream-girl personality of the era by displaying her humanity publicly.

After her death in 1962, reflections on Monroe discussed an unending need to save her—again reinforcing traditional masculinity. "Marilyn has gone from sex symbol to a symbol of mourning, from a promise of the liberation of sex to a cautionary tale about the dangers of loneliness and spinsterhood," Sarah Churchwell noted in *The Many Lives of Marilyn Monroe*.[17] Scores of accounts display the cultural self-flagellation and dramatic, mournful writing that arose in the wake of Marilyn's death, notably Clare Booth Luce's 1964 *Life* magazine article explaining Monroe as a casualty of sheer loneliness and desperation. Luce theorizes about age as a possible motive for Monroe's suicide: "Her daily, often hourly encounters with her 'mirror, mirror, on the wall,' however satisfying and reassuring in the beginning, [became] summit meetings with her archenemy—time."[18] But for all the hand wringing, curiosity, and guilt that plagued the media in the days, months, and years after her death, her status as the biggest sexual fantasy of the century held on, and continues today.

In *Marilyn: A Biography,* Norman Mailer painted Monroe as completely lost, in desperate need of guidance, and having no balancing traits—most likely to assert Mailer's obvious fantasy of being able to rescue her himself. He constantly referred to her as having "little identity,"[19] which allowed her to remain lost and malleable, and incapable of assertiveness or autonomy without a guide (in this case, the obviously frustrated Mailer himself). Colin Clark called her "self-centered and sensitive"[20] and as "naive and well-intentioned as a puppy."[21] *Playboy* never let her sexiness go, as evidenced by its description of her dead body in 2005: "We are left with a haunting photograph of her—lying naked on her stomach in bed, partially wrapped in white sheets, with a phone receiver dangling from her hand, her face in a pillow, her hair a gorgeous mess of platinum blonde—taken on the morning of August 5, 1962."[22]

To remember Monroe for the fact that the men in her life used or abused her allows her no independent authority—which, at its root, leaves us with that mouthful of rock salt. But it also reminds us that one-dimensionality and exploitation can batter even the woman held as the ultimate male fantasy.

I want to be remembered as a woman who changed people's perspectives concerning nudity in its natural form.[23]

—Bettie Page

or all of Marilyn's mixed messages about female sexuality, she still had more autonomy than pinup Bettie Page. Monroe might have appeared sweeter and more directly seductive and submissive, but Page is virtually voiceless, with significantly fewer opinions, analysis, and criticism to stand for her life and work than Monroe had. Barring the 2005 biopic *The Notorious Bettie Page* and a handful of published interviews, Page's face and body have usurped her entire public persona. Monroe's history is littered with stacks of magazine features and interviews in which she was picked apart, studied, broken down, and defended, as well as with films that have since become classics. Onscreen, Monroe walked and talked, while Bettie Page was frozen in still photographs, permanently posed, ever coiffed, and gawked at. Due to her relatively short career and her subsequent retreat from the public eye, she has retained her youthful image for much of the last fifty years. We can project anything we want onto her, because the large majority of the population doesn't even know what her voice sounds like. Former photo editor Harlan Ellison's confession about Page says it all:

> *I'll tell you the simple truth.*
>
> *I never met her; I have no idea if she was a bright and cheery person or an emptyheaded tart; was she inordinately intelligent or a dumb bunny; was she a virgin till the day she vanished from our ken or did she make her living in shadier ways than merely posing for those naive cheesecake shots? . . .*

> . . . But like every male I've ever met who has seen a picture
> of her, I cannot to this day see a photo of Bettie Page without
> getting an erection. And that is the simple truth; and that is what
> it's all about.[24]

Like Monroe's, Page's image is plastered on cigarette lighters, candles, T-shirts, wallets, posters, shot glasses, and more. She remains a picture, a brand, a decoration, and almost her own fetish category. In the scores of photos of her, a curvy, fit Page stared the camera down defiantly or brightly smiled as she arched·her back, stretched, or danced in burlesque costumes or bondage gear. She wore bright red lipstick and had black hair with severely cut, trademark bangs and a wide, welcoming smile, as if the pinup trade were celebrating her sexuality alone. "She was *Playboy*'s Playmate for January 1955," Kevin Cook wrote in *Playboy* in 1998. "Indeed, Bettie was the perfect Playmate, for she was both naughty and nice. That smile suggested forbidden fruit as well as apple pie."[25] Where Monroe's photos often portrayed her shrinking back into bed or collapsing in a fit of prone lust, Page's photos boasted a healthy body in control. She stood with strong legs spread apart and arms in motion. Her eyes weren't glazed over with Monroe's come-hither longing. Instead, the camera captured her in the midst of doing something other than trying to captivate the viewer—a technique that made the viewer's seduction seem a footnote to Page's enjoyment.

Many of her photos depicted bondage scenarios—which were impossible finds in the sexually repressed 1950s. Cook wrote of the photos, "These Dark Angel photos led countless American men and boys to ponder a new sexual geography, a wet-dream-like land where

Miss America meets the Marquis de Sade."[26] But the bondage photos exude a sense of fun; Page looks slightly amused, as she is inflicting or receiving quite campy versions of pleasure and pain. In an era when any sex outside of heterosexual, married sex or *Playboy*'s cleaner, cheesecake variety was considered perverse, Page and the models she posed with created sexual normalcy out of supposed deviance. Beyond expressing a healthier vision of sex than what the zeitgeist was pushing, she handmade many of her own costumes for her photo shoots, claiming for herself a level of control and self-expression not granted to many models.

Bettie Page began her modeling career by posing for an amateur photographer in New York City in 1950.[27] At the time, models were hired for the day to be shot by groups of amateur photographers, who used the club's lighting and staging to practice portraiture. "I did it mainly because I could make more money in two hours as a model than in 40 hours as a secretary," she explained to Cook in *Playboy*.[28] She became legendary in the underground trade of girlie magazines when Irving Klaw, owner of a downtown newsstand in New York City, began staging scenarios for clients who were quietly requesting bondage photos on a regular basis.[29]

Page's pinup career took off soon after she began appearing in Klaw's photographs, and by the end of it, Bettie Page was the pinup version of a household name—if you lived in that sort of household. Page existed in the midst of a popular culture that relied on cinematic double entendres, like Monroe's, for sexual expression, and on thinly veiled euphemisms to make similar suggestions in rock 'n' roll. Page and other pinup girls provided sexuality that wasn't as "dirty" as the era insisted it was. The pinup queen was reportedly an agreeable and affable model while she posed for camera clubs, and as comfortable with her sexuality as her photos suggested. One shoot ended when the participants were arrested for indecency. According to one photographer's account, Bettie, offended by the charges and defending her own honor, refused to cooperate. "I am not indecent!' She yelled at the officers. 'I will not plead guilty to it! You'll have to charge me with disturbing the peace, too!'"[30] She fled New York in 1957 when Klaw became a repeated FBI target for obscenity charges,[31] and she was spiritually "born again" in 1959.[32]

"I put my other life behind me," Page told *Playboy* in 1998. "I threw all my bikinis in the garbage can. I threw out all my stockings and lingerie and panties, and lace bras. And I went to Bible school. First the Bible Institute of Los Angeles, then the Bible Institute in Chicago and the Multnomah School of the Moody Bible in Oregon. Did street witnessing and . . . helped with church services at a home for teenage mothers. . . . "[33] Page has spent the second half of her life recovering from mental illness that allegedly led to a handful of violent assaults. She has withdrawn from media exposure because she would rather remain the ageless pinup queen she once was.[34]

During the 1950s, Page exuded a friendly sexuality, one that celebrated the human body and looked comfortable with sex and its deviances without being submissive. She also represented a tougher beauty than the soft blond bombshell, proving that gentlemen preferred the darker side of blond, too. But her fantasy appeal hinged on the pleasure she radiated. Female photographer Bunny Yeager once said, "She was like a drawing—a perfect woman, fun, unreal, fantasy. Bettie always portrayed a woman that hinted she would be lots of fun to be with, someone who would never have a headache or a bad mood."[35] The

2005 film *The Notorious Bettie Page,* directed by Mary Harron, brightly showcased this side of Page, but did not document the pain her later life entailed, including the violent episodes and emotional instability that would have added texture to her frozen image. The movie also depicted Page as the living version of her famous photographs—as willing and cheerful in life as she appeared on film. As a result, it's easy to like Bettie Page, a woman for whom there was no fate, who was readily available, seemingly kind, and free from criticism for participating in the underground fetish world that was condemned by society at large.

Both Monroe and Page had troubled childhoods and sporadic relationships with their families. They both spent time in orphanages. They both admitted to being sexually abused—Bettie by her father and Monroe by a boarder of a foster family she lived with for a while.[36] The childhood suffering they experienced is believed to have greatly contributed to their intense need for approval, which many models and actresses seemingly experience during their careers. Monroe and Page also both had early marriages that ended fairly quickly; each explained that she wanted more out of life than an unsatisfying marriage—a desire that women rarely acted upon during the 1940s and '50s.

Page's first husband, Billy Neal, didn't want her to go to college,[37] and she left him after he returned from duty overseas during World War II.[38] Monroe's first marriage, to James Dougherty in 1942, ended in divorce when he returned from the war.[39] According to *Life* magazine, Dougherty attributed the failure of their marriage to Monroe's inability to "give him the feeling of self-esteem and self-confidence a man needs to keep even a sexual liaison going, no less a marriage.[40] In discussing her career, Monroe told *Life* in 1962, " . . . I guess I've always had too much fantasy to be only a housewife. Well, also, I had to eat. I was never kept, to be blunt about it. I always kept myself. I have always had a pride in the fact that I was on my own."[41] She and baseball player Joe DiMaggio, whom she married later on in her career, also parted ways over differences in what role Monroe should play in the marriage (DiMaggio would have opted for a housewife). Early on in both Monroe's and Page's lives, they wanted more than marriage, and they pursued it. Their efforts might not make them rebels, but it wasn't the usual tack for women of their era. In both cases, though, their husbands' tours of duty during World War II allowed the women solitary time in which to reflect on their own life goals, and to support themselves while their husbands were serving. They are both sometimes seen as the lucky inheritors of happenstance: Page began her career posing on a beach for an amateur photographer, and Monroe's factory work led to her early days as a model. Both women demanded more for themselves than the fates befalling other women of their decade.

"I guess I was soured on marriage because all I knew was men who swore at their wives," Monroe once said, "and fathers who never played with their kids. The husbands I remember from my childhood got drunk regularly, and the wives were always drab women who never had a chance to dress or make up or be taken anywhere to have fun. I grew up thinking, 'If this is marriage, who needs it?'"[42]

Rather than discussing women's sexual value to men, or how someone's undoing might stem not from childhood but from the singular way in which the public and the media perceived Monroe and Page as adults, writers profiling both women zeroed in on their difficult childhoods (which also makes for better copy). Their psychological speculation may certainly have some merit, but they seemed to have a compulsion, particularly with Monroe, to understand something deeper than the simple fact that modeling successfully was a solid way for women to create their own worth and wealth when they were unsatisfied by factory work (which Monroe did for a short period of time) or secretarial jobs (which Page longed to escape). The men producing the profiles—mostly journalists—were also the same men who limited these women's public personae. If women express the desire to expand beyond the role they've been pigeonholed in, men and society at large may be forced to reexamine the roles they themselves play in prolonging an ultimately damaging level of exposure. And that reexamination would certainly be less lucrative than continuing the girl next door–cum–dream girl charade. Consider this 1998 exchange that occurred between Page and Cook:

Cook: Men have always wanted things from you.
Page: That's part of why I had a nervous breakdown.[43]

This kind of brutal honesty about how even sex symbols might not appreciate, welcome, or want the drooling male attention they receive shatters the freshly scrubbed and coiffed fantasy of sexually willing women present only to please potential, distant, or imaginary lovers. The candid nature of both women is still shrouded in fantasies about their sexual submission.

After Monroe swooned for American men, few sex symbols proved to have her cultural endurance until Madonna came along thirty years later. Unlike Monroe's, Madonna's sexuality was never seen as completely subservient; instead, she used elements of earlier sex-symbol submission to soften her stronger side and harder edges. Clad in leggings, bracelets, hats, and biker jackets, she also bore her midriff and trimmed herself with lace. In keeping with her softer, more classically feminine fashion touches, Madonna could stare down the camera like a hardened, street-smart tomboy and *still* muster longing from her overly charcoaled eyes.

In the early 1980s, at the beginning of her career, Madonna had a good sense of how to push the culture's buttons (which were renewed by that decade's puritanical thrust), and used shock to garner heaps of press attention. In the early days of video, Madonna was a pinup version of a pop star: She appeared in video after video in different scenarios and costumes, often performing updated burlesque moves. It was in the video for "Open Your Heart" that she mimicked the 1950s pinup most directly, wearing long gloves, a black bodice adorned with fringe pasties, fishnets, and bright red lipstick, and dancing on a prop chair in a peep show. In her first major public transgression, she performed the 1985 single "Like a Virgin" in a wedding dress, rolling around suggestively onstage.

For the next ten years of her career, it was open season on shock value. The album *Like a Prayer,* released in 1989, inspired the video for the eponymous single in which she portrayed an interracial relationship, sang in front of burning crosses, and used Catholic imagery as a backdrop. Her ever-changing image continued to evolve in the '90s with the more commanding video for "Express Yourself," which featured a crotch-grabbing, bullet bra–wearing, shorn-haired Madonna. Her ultimate pinup moment occurred when she released a book entitled *Sex* in the 1990s, composed of sexually suggestive photos and a mock version of a journal. Unfortunately, while it was highly anticipated by the public and the press, the book was nowhere near as interesting or challenging to sexual mores as it could have been, and it came off as Madonna's effort to cash in on her earlier, more transgressive reputation. After weeks of media hype, the press panned it—even staid *Newsweek* sighed with disappointment. "Madonna, who throughout her career has been able to turn an exposed belly button into a major-league scandal, here couldn't parlay a legitimate publishing event into a hubbub worthy of [controversial singer] Sinead O'Connor's clipping file," the magazine declared, also deeming the book "neither groundbreaking . . . nor particularly sexy."[44]

Madonna's earlier image borrowed from everyone: from the confrontational punk women lining the bohemian streets of American cities to Dickensian orphans to, eventually, Monroe herself. While Madonna appeared to be simply co-opting a world of sexual and cultural imagery, she infused it all with her own sense of style and her own sexuality—at times looking like a cross between the bad girl next door and old Hollywood's softly lit glamour girls. She offered artistic interpretations of the sex culture that created her, alternating between the seductive nature of Monroe and the more commanding yet approachable image of Page.

In her 1990 video for "Vogue," Madonna recalled, in her lyrics, lighting, staging, and costume, the twentieth century's female sex and beauty icons, appearing in white satin robes, suits, and evening gowns against the backdrop of sets that recalled the drawing and dressing rooms often used in 1930s and '40s film. She also name-checked Harlow, Monroe, Dietrich, Lana Turner, and Rita Hayworth (not to mention Marlon Brando and James Dean). While Madonna's songs were gargantuan hits throughout the late '80s and early '90s, and while more cultural speculation has been lavished on her than on any other female musical performer of the period, she certainly used sexuality to her advantage without concretely changing all that much for women.

Madonna's brand of sexuality, while more overtly aggressive than Monroe's, still capitalized on the same ideas of eye candy and camera fodder. She found a balance between a powerful female character, a sexual persona, and just enough difference to shock—without breaking so many boundaries that she'd be knocked off the pop charts. She also retained a typically feminine look until she adopted a drag style (an updated version of Dietrich's aesthetic) for her "Express Yourself" video. She was often painted into the role of the rebel, but the culture sat up and took notice of her sexuality—which was certainly no different from how women have gotten attention in the past. Madonna managed, though, to retain a certain "street" quality that rejected the perfection demanded of Monroe. Although the pop star was physically attractive, she did have an everyday humanity about her—especially in earlier videos, before her later long and lean days. Madonna also never shied away from the strength in her sexuality—a feat that she could accomplish more easily than sex symbols of the past, given the era and the vast changes in sex culture since Monroe's ascendancy, including the mainstream proliferation of pornography in the 1970s. But the press addressed Madonna's conflicted image and ignored her more powerful transgressions. In the '90s, for example, *Entertainment Weekly* wrote:

> *Madonna's obsession with sex and the way she exploits her own body seem to be at odds with the artistic ambitions that permeate*

her more recent videos and the current tour. She clearly has a mind-body problem: No matter what serious message she wants to convey, she can't stop flashing her physical gifts. Love me for my brain, she seems to say, but don't stop there. Madonna is a sex object—by her own choice. She is also, however, a strong, independent woman with a multimillion-dollar business. "I think the public is tired of trying to figure out whether I'm a feminist or not," Madonna has said. "I don't think of what I'm doing as gender specific. I am what I am, and I do what I do."[45]

Then there are the beauties deemed too quirky-looking to be overtly sexual, such as Andy Warhol's mod muse, Edie Sedgwick, and 1960s cover girl Twiggy. The roles available to Hollywood actresses either accentuated their sexuality to no end, as in Monroe's case, or played up their innocence or refined their image so much that it was hard to think of them as sexual. Audrey Hepburn, the most notable example of the latter tactic, was recognized for being bright, fun, fashionable, and impulsive, though she was also an extraordinary actress and a dedicated humanitarian. Her thin, boyish figure made her more of a charming girl next door than a seductive being. *New York Times* critic Bosley Crowther described her as "a slender, elfin, and wistful beauty, alternately regal and childlike."[46] *Sabrina* director Billy Wilder remembered, "You looked around and suddenly there was this dazzling creature looking like a wild-eyed doe prancing in the forest. Everybody on the set was in love within five minutes."[47] While Page and Monroe were lurking animals in an exotic jungle, an equally gorgeous Hepburn, who lacked the curves and the overt sensuality attributed to Monroe and Page, frolicked girlishly, like Little Red Riding Hood.

Hepburn's most recognizable and widely celebrated character was Holly Golightly, in the 1961 film *Breakfast at Tiffany's*. Hepburn's career was full of signature roles, such as in *Funny Face* and *My Fair Lady*, but Golightly has captivated new, youthful audiences for decades. Her signature look—large sunglasses and a little black dress—has long been imitated, and images of Holly posed outside of Tiffany's abound. "Women can look like Audrey Hepburn," she once advised, "by flipping out their hair, buying the large sunglasses and the little sleeveless dresses."[48] The renowned black dress she wore in the movie even sold for £410,000 in 2006.[49]

Based on a story by Truman Capote, *Breakfast at Tiffany's* was about a lighthearted, flippant, restless, and roaming young woman. Her clothes were glamorous; she threw wild parties in her barely furnished apartment, forever smoking from a long cigarette holder. Golightly seemed ahead of her time: She was a single girl in 1961 who had no interest in domestic pursuits, didn't decorate her apartment, kept all of her possessions in a suitcase, named her cat "Cat," and was an incorrigible flirt. Even the leading male, Paul, Holly's neighbor and eventual suitor, had an untraditional role, kept as he was by a wealthy older woman (who was a foil à la *The Graduate*'s predatory vamp, Mrs. Robinson). As more of Golightly's life unfolded, it was revealed that she had once been a rural housewife—a life she had abandoned, not unlike Monroe and Page, to move to New York. She had since buried her past, and appeared to have come from the male rebel's "nowhere." When her husband tracked her down in New York to encourage her to move back home, Golightly told him, "You mustn't give your heart to a wild thing. The more you do, the stronger they get, until they're strong enough to run into the woods or fly into a tree. And then to a higher tree and then to the sky."[50]

The aesthetic of the film was entertaining and appealing (aside from the Asian equivalent of blackface found in Mickey Rooney's painfully stereotypical landlord role). Golightly was likable, wearing her quirks proudly. While her sex life was never openly discussed, as Paul's situation was, it was clearly suggested in her flirtations with suitors from whom she gleefully took money, and in her inability to contain her excitement at meeting rich single men who were obviously a dull match for her. Like Monroe's characters, all of the men Golightly actively pursued in the film appeared even more average than they already were when they were juxtaposed with Golightly's ebullience and style—average, that is, except for the size of their wallets.

Holly's insubordinate edges blurred further when the story revealed that she had a sponsor in prison, who paid her a bundle of cash to regularly pass him messages from a source on the outside—but she was somehow completely oblivious to this act's criminal nature, and when scandal broke, she passed through it completely unscathed. It was a nice touch, in light of women's history of being punished much more harshly for lesser crimes, but it cast Holly as truly clueless about the underbelly of the city she inhabited.

The rebelliousness that Golightly happily, unabashedly demonstrated collapsed when she received news that her brother Fred was dead, and she began to unravel. Paul finally confessed his love for her, and the film ended with the two of them in love and committed to each other. Initially, Golightly relied on rich men for financial stability openly, unapologetically, and almost joyfully, without the same comic desperation of other cinematic gold-diggers—and then she chucked it all away for predictable marriage, thereby disempowering her "wild thing" speech. Unfortunately, Hepburn is not as widely acclaimed by younger audiences for her witty, assertive, and vibrant roles in other films, such as *Charade,* in which her advances toward Cary Grant's character were met with strong discomfort and awkwardness on his part, while she remained relaxed, vital, and light.

Throughout the twentieth century, in all forms of art, women's sexuality was the most effective tool to mark a woman with power— or to rip the rug out from under her. Rarely, if ever, has Hollywood succeeded in balancing female sexuality with a likable, complicated character who *hasn't* capitulated to the saccharine Hollywood ending, or ended up suffering fates worse than those of Salem witches. From Monroe's cotton-candy siren to Hepburn's coquette to the unbridled sexuality of the late 1960s, sex remains the most accessible signifier of a woman's difference, or means of making an uninteresting character more engaging—for men, at least. All of Monroe's wistful, lasting desire couldn't hold a candle to the 1987 film *Fatal Attraction*—possibly a more harmful influence on sexually liberated women than a century of sugary-sweet pinup girls.

Like director Adrian Lyne's cinematic treatment of leading women as virgins, whores, or as simultaneously bewitching and evil, *Fatal Attraction*'s plotline is simplistic: Married man (whose wife is beautiful and kind) meets single woman. Single woman is attractive and fairly mysterious. Married man's gorgeous wife is out of town. Man sleeps with woman. Woman cannot stand being rejected, and creepily, violently, stalks married man to the point of insanity, from cutting her wrists to boiling his daughter's pet rabbit, until his wife eventually shoots and kills scary single woman. Cheating married man becomes heroic and remains with his wife. Single female threat is killed, and happy ending prevails.

Fatal Attraction was a tremendous box-office success, due to its extremity from beginning to end. Its high level of suspense, Glenn Close's completely unhinged single female, Alex, and her now classic blow-job scene with Dan (Michael Douglas) in an elevator all conspired to make it one of the most successful movies of 1987 and landed it six Oscar nominations, including one for Close. What made *Fatal Attraction* box-office gold was also the most damaging aspect of the film: A woman with a career—who was also clearly sexual and seductive—became absolutely psychotic without a man, or from rejection. Instead of remaining happily single, or, at the very least, wistfully dejected, Alex's only aim is to force Dan to fall madly in love with her. The film promotes the idea of an otherwise smart woman instantly, violently, and unequivocally equating a sexual encounter with falling deeply in love.

For much of America, seeing *Fatal Attraction* was like being riveted by a freak show. Alex differed from the mostly sedate characters leading women played in the '80s. She was urbane. She had a successful publishing career. She was stylish, smart, and sexually aggressive. She was also pathetically, frighteningly alone. She did things other women in films, who appeared mostly in romantic comedies and as horror-film victims during that decade, wouldn't do . . . but those things included boiling live rabbits and terrorizing suburban families. As Pauline Kael noted in her review of the film, and as Susan Faludi discussed at length in her book *Backlash, Fatal Attraction* pounded home the message of the religious Right, which spent the '80s padding its ranks with antiwomanists like Pat Robertson. According to Kael and Faludi, the movie underscored the demise of the American family at the hands of independent, self-sufficient women who secretly didn't want to be independent or self-sufficient.

Even more torturous was the long parade of insane vamps trampling single womanhood in Alex's wake, from Jennifer Jason Leigh in *Single White Female* (1992) to Alicia Silverstone in *The Crush* (1993), Rebecca De Mornay in *The Hand that Rocks the Cradle* (1992), and, of course, Sharon Stone in *Basic Instinct* (1992). Hollywood tossed one seductive, crazed woman after another onto a witch-burning pyre. Most of these films weren't as successful as *Fatal Attraction,* but for five years after that movie was released, celluloid's single women spent much of their time marring otherwise happy families—without other complex female roles to balance out the image. As Kael wrote of *Fatal Attraction,* "This shrewd film touches on something deeper than men's fear of feminism: their fear of women, their fear of women's emotions, of women's hanging on to them."[51] She also commented, "This is a horror film based on the sanctity of the family—the dream family. It enforces conventional morality (in the era of AIDS) by piling on paranoiac fear. The family that kills together stays together, and the audience is hyped up to cheer the killing."[52]

While the more recent *Notes on a Scandal* (2006) may seem a world away from *Fatal Attraction,* the film also generated Oscar hype and media attention. Cate Blanchett played Sheba Hart, a bohemian mother and teacher whose spirit was squelched by her seemingly suffocating home life. She began having a sexual affair with one of her high school students; it became the scandal of her town when a colleague (Judi Dench) reported her. While Sheba could have rebelled in other ways, her escape from the life she found so unsatisfying was through sex.

Dench's Barbara, a lonely colleague and friend of Sheba's, enhanced the sexual rebellion by being a lesbian who was in such desperate, obsessive love with her friend that she ruined Sheba's life. The madness and sexual deviance both characters displayed didn't leave any room for female normalcy, or for any positive images of sexual rebellion. It's hard to say which transgression was worse: Sheba's, for having an affair with a student, or Barbara's, for betraying the woman she loved. By the time Sheba's scandal hit the papers, she had descended into pure mania and neuroses. For Sheba and Barbara, sexually unorthodox behavior was equated with madness, and sex appeared to be the only means of revolt for a lonely or dissatisfied woman.

*B*ecause the movies so often present female characters who are in touch with their sexuality as crazed or abnormal, Mae West—who was rebellious, funny, and sexual, all at the same time—has emerged as one of the most refreshing and undervalued pop-culture sex icons. West began her career in vaudeville in 1911 (when she, too, embarked upon a short-lived marriage), moved on to Broadway and playwriting in the 1920s and into film in the 1930s. She was a buxom blond who dressed for performances to exaggerate every curve and accentuate her cleavage. To her, the female ideal and the men who surrendered blindly to it were comic fodder ripe for mockery. Her walk hovered somewhere between a shuffle and a strut, her shifting shoulders moved more than her heeled feet did, and clever one-liners for which she became infamous leaked from her lips so slowly as to intimate that she'd just been dragged out of bed and away from a lover to deliver them. Her best-known quip was "Come up and see me sometime," but others, such as "A hard man is good to find," also remain in the cultural consciousness—even if West's more Rubenesque body type does not. The sexual suggestion she built into her work positioned her as the sexual aggressor—and she would make it clear that she preferred to take the lead. She might have been ever available, but she presented herself as sexually indulgent in her own desires, rather than sitting pretty to make men comfortable. She also staged plays such as 1927's *The Drag*, the story of a gay man married to an unassuming wife, and wrote the controversial *Sex*, about a prostitute choosing between a man who understood her profession and loved her anyway, and one who was oblivious to it. (The prostitute, a strong, independent woman, eventually chose to be with the man who accepted and understood her past.)

As a sex icon, West may not have met the beauty standards upheld throughout the second half of the twentieth century, but she pushed the envelope insofar as she spoke publicly about sex, battled obscenity charges, and presented openly gay characters and themes in her plays. Her extravagance and exaggerated hedonism were truly at the heart of her charm, as though the more the public was offended by her bawdiness, the more she liked to flaunt it and smile. After being sentenced to ten days in jail for staging *Sex* in 1927, for example, she allegedly arrived at the prison carrying dozens of white roses.[53]

Along with *Sex, The Pleasure Man* was raided, and the cast arrested, directly following its Broadway premiere in 1928,[54] but charges were eventually dismissed.[55] *Diamond Lil,* the play on which her 1933 film *I'm No Angel* was based, was closed by police in Chicago.[56] Such frank productions posed a threat to moral crusaders, who firmly believed that sex and sexuality should be neither seen nor heard. By continuing to write, produce, and act in plays targeted by the police and the district attorney for their content, West defiantly resisted the censorship that was alive and well in 1920s New York City.

Although Broadway was loaded with sexual themes when West performed and wrote her own plays, other productions were "obedient to the unwritten rule that prescribed ruin for fallen women."[57] West's stage characters reflected the same unconventional dominant female stance she would later bring to the screen. In *Sex,* for instance, Margy, a prostitute, confessed, "All I've been is a physical attraction to men. I'm sick and tired of being that sort of thing. Now I want a man whose love goes beyond that."[58]

West's stage reputation preceded her by the time she hit Hollywood in the early '30s. As a playwright, she had already presented her most tangible and overt social subversions. Hollywood, though, made her work more accessible than her theatrical celebrity, opening her up to a much wider audience. She became more than stage spectacle, censorship target, and vice-squad martyr. Onscreen, the wisecracking West reveled in the glories of deviance. Her obvious and exaggerated delight in sexual indulgences created a magnified version of womanhood, from her crown of gleaming blond hair and her ever-present mask of makeup right down to her perfectly curved, highly accentuated hourglass shape.

West's insubordination went deeper than onscreen seduction. She arrived in Hollywood on the heels of the 1920s flapper—whose smoking, drinking, heavy lipstick, and socializing with the boys also made the moral police shudder. Flappers boasted femininity (hidden beneath loose, boxier dresses) and frivolity. West flew in the face of fashion and flaunted curves and cleavage that the twentieth century hadn't yet encountered on the silver screen. The most famous film stars of the

1920s were petite (or appeared so) and, whether playful or intense, they were overwhelmingly delicate-looking: Louise Brooks, Clara Bow, Greta Garbo, Jean Harlow, and Marlene Dietrich were all known for their dynamic individualism and power onscreen, but they were all soft and slight. Among their artfully arched eyebrows, soft lighting, often ultrafeminine clothing (except for Dietrich's), and slender limbs and torsos, West almost represented another gender entirely.

In the midst of the economic drought of the 1930s, West was also haughtily draped in diamonds and sequins—a completely escapist, indulgent image in a dire economic era. Furthermore, she arrived in Hollywood in 1932[59] when she was approximately thirty-nine years old.[60] Hollywood's age standards haven't changed much since the '30s: Jean Harlow and Greta Garbo were in their early to mid-twenties in that same year.[61] With a dash of sauciness, West eschewed the eye-candy submissiveness of later sex symbols, cast off Dietrich's and Garbo's otherworldly qualities and other peers' feminine severity, and became a lasting, comedic Hollywood legend. She managed to encompass sex *and* smarts, rather than being known for one or the other.

She was also able to seduce men with her tongue planted firmly in her cheek. While *The Pleasure Man* berated men for seducing women and leaving them behind, West made a joke of her ability to do the same. In 1933's *I'm No Angel,* she played a burlesque dancer and lion tamer who invited a male target to her room and played music for him (a longtime lothario strategy). When she found out he was from Dallas, she shuffled through a stack of recordings, passing "No One Loves Me Like That Frisco Man" and "No One Loves Me Like That Memphis Man," until she came across "No One

Loves Me Like That Dallas Man." All West had to do after placing
the needle on the record was shuffle around the room, halfheartedly
spraying herself with perfume, and her suitor from Dallas fell for it.
West's seductiveness was always seemingly effortless, derived from
a bag of surefire tricks that, like male aficionados of seduction, she
relied on. Those tactics might have become predictable in a man's
bedroom, but in a woman's boudoir, they represented critiques of a
tired formula.

West experienced near instant popularity with film audiences.
Even Monroe decorated the corners of a handful of films before she
had a hit. But the first films in which West had a leading role, *She
Done Him Wrong* and *I'm No Angel,* made more than $2 million each,[62]
and she became the highest-paid entertainer in the country by 1934.[63]
Judging from the millions she made for Paramount in the '30s, her
massive financial success, and the gleeful way she was covered in the
press, West's comic sexuality was welcome and wildly popular.

Morality, as always, had poor timing: The Production Code began
being actively enforced soon after West's first two leading roles. Her
films following *I'm No Angel* were received less warmly, with critics
pointing to a lack of sassiness in her dialogue. Altogether, she made
ten films between 1932 and 1944, and two comeback films in the
1970s,[64] as well as making numerous television appearances until her
death in 1980. West was smart, sassy, over the top, and in control
of story lines, plot, and her dialogue. The author of six produced
plays and two books, she was a prolific writer and became a fixture in
Hollywood history.

Like other cultural icons who have relished their shock value—
Madonna, Elvis, and Kerouac, to name a few—West borrowed

phrasing and her singing style from blues music and shimmied juke joint–style, invoking black culture and causing conflict when her work was praised.[65] Her character was also somewhat of a one-trick pony—a strong, flirtatious, funny, self-satisfied one-trick pony that prohibited anyone else from holding the reins—but her singularly sexual focus also drove her career. However repetitive the joke, a woman armed with a casual attitude about sex who doesn't capitulate to men has traditionally been a Hollywood rarity. West was an anomaly who upended female sexuality by infusing it with joy, rather than conflict. Beyond her strut and drawl, her lasting legacy is that she used her controversial reputation to force public dialogues about deviant sexuality, illegal, salacious behavior, and the parameters of what's culturally acceptable.

Not only have our lasting sex symbols been predominantly white over the last hundred years, but they've almost always been blond as well. That's not to say the culture doesn't eroticize minority women—male culture has long objectified the Asian cliché of kinkiness or submission, and the sexual stereotypes of the black hip-hop vixen and the Latina lover. In recent years, singer-actresses Beyoncé Knowles and Jennifer Lopez have risen to high-profile fame for being perceived as both beautiful and talented. In 2007, Knowles sang "Diamonds Are a Girl's Best Friend" to promote Armani's Diamonds fragrance line. She stood solo at the microphone, though, leaving behind the tuxedoed men that have been hired in the past to cart Monroe and Madonna around. Beyoncé also recast the notion of the blond bombshell, not only because she was a black performer, but also by showcasing her own vocal style rather than imitating Monroe's. Yet both Knowles and Lopez, however prestigious, have slipped into mainstream pop culture, producing and performing sweet songs about love, embracing even-keeled pop-star images and neatly avoiding subversiveness.

Today's mainstream rebellion resides in hip-hop, rather than in pop music. Its biggest, most popular and successful artists are men: 50 Cent, Kanye West, Jay-Z, and Ludacris have led the hit parade for years, enjoying profits in the millions and heavy rotation on mainstream radio and MTV. Hip-hop's women only sporadically gain the success and accolades showered on male hip-hop stars, and the attention is usually short-lived. "Women in hip-hop performance and culture," wrote journalist Karen R. Good in 1999, "are so often reduced to machismo fodder and background performance; a bit of rhyming, definitely singing and dancing, or, primarily, watching backs."[66] As rebellious as hip-hop can be, the most visible women in recent years have been more sexual than anything else. While male hip-hop stars vocalize their status and success, the women surrounding them— mostly in the genre's videos—voicelessly adorn men as much as the material goods the genre's stars brag about. Typically, women appear draped on the arms of male stars, as dancing backdrops, partygoers, and often, as the foil for men's fun, as in Kanye West's smash single "Gold Digger," for example. Women rarely hold the mike. Raunchy rapper Lil' Kim has spent years trading sexual rhymes for shock value, and has been subjected to much criticism. Kim, like Madonna, is constantly reinventing her image, but her overblown sexuality, most often illustrated through blunt, aggressive lyrics describing sex acts performed on her, gives voice to the video-vixen image, rather than to a streetwise, political tough girl.

With all her sex talk, Lil' Kim's empowerment is ambiguous. On the one hand, her lyrics have added another female voice to a subculture dominated by male artists, and—dressed in skimpy, seductive clothing—she occasionally succeeds in tapping into mainstream men's sexual fantasies while appearing to be in control. On the other hand, much of the attention she receives comes from a self-deprecating place: She relies on a submissive sexual quality that many women in pop music use to make men take notice, and her lyrics are often more shocking than self-aggrandizing. In addition, Lil' Kim's look undermines the strength she may gain through her rhymes. She emulates white beauty standards, as well as the usual markers of the sex symbol: She often dons blue contacts and long blond hair, suggesting that even when women of color make space for themselves among their lily-white sex-symbol peers, the traditional blond-icon look has retained its hold over our culture's measure of what is considered erotic.

The female hip-hop star who's had the greatest impact recently is Missy Elliott. Elliott has been producing inventive, surprising, fun music since her 1997 debut, *Supa Dupa Fly.*[67] She has been able to express her enjoyment of sex with her integrity intact, most notably in her hit "Work It," and manages to do it with humorous, blunt, sexually aggressive rhymes. Her lyrics celebrate her erotic passion, submissive to no one, and sexualize her larger body type. Sex is fun for *her;* she's not available merely for others' entertainment. Physically, Elliott affirms the idea that neither women in hip-hop nor women in mainstream pop music have to invoke the traditional sex symbol to be successful and engaging. Instead, she adds a sexy slant to the undervalued tomboy. In the hypermasculine, decorative, and erotically one-dimensional realm of hip-hop, though, Lil' Kim is seen as a sexpot, while Elliott's sex appeal is muted. Still, however dissimilar they are, Lil' Kim and Missy Elliott both propagate the beauty of frank, strong black women forging ahead in an industry that often makes the battle an uphill one for them.

*I*n the wake of lasting American sex symbols, other subversive women in recent years have moved beyond the shallow sexuality presented in pinups, onscreen, and in mainstream music. Underground artists like Lydia Lunch, Annie Sprinkle, and Karen Finley have all delved deeper into the realm of female sexuality through their theatrical and experimental-film explorations. Of course, while their work is complex, blunt, empowering, and intricate, and often renders them simultaneously powerful and vulnerable, none of these artists have been lauded by mainstream audiences or critics.

Today's stars and the press continue to rehash iconic females' trademarks—and women who are often less intriguing than their pop ancestors appropriate them. Lindsay Lohan graced the cover of *New York* magazine and re-created Marilyn Monroe's last photo shoot in its February 2008 issue. The photos did nothing new, besides elevating Lohan to a level of fame that her career does not warrant, and drawing a parallel between Lohan's well-publicized addictions and Monroe's troubled side. In addition, a photo of Paris Hilton that has made its way around the celebrity-gossip blogs features the wayward heiress posing as a cheap Holly Golightly knockoff. Never mind that the generous and often selfless Hepburn is probably rolling over in her grave at the comparison—Hilton, Lohan, and their rabid press opt to bank on the attraction of older icons to boost their reputations and get more publicity.

Photo shoots connoting past celebrities are fairly common in consumer publishing. *Vibe,* for example, recreated Michael Jackson's *Off the Wall* cover for a Janet Jackson cover shoot, also in 2008. Re-creations like these can sometimes be interesting and fun for viewers, models, and photographers alike, but it would be infinitely more interesting to let go of the parallels, open up space in which newer public figures could express themselves, and let the consumers' imaginations make their own associations. The longer we rely on our older icons to "own" particular images, as Marilyn does sex and femininity, the less likely it is that we'll ever add dimension to our predictable definitions of sexiness, or move on from the three or four women we keep recycling as paragons of style, beauty, and sex.

Pop culture continues to hold up images of female sexuality disguised as rebellion. But even icons who have long reveled in their seductiveness can be remembered for something deeper. Rather than simply decorating the beds, kitchens, corners, and locker rooms of male culture, Madonna and Mae West insisted on becoming women who were intriguing beyond their decorative qualities. As for Bettie Page and Marilyn Monroe, their careers resulted from their wanting something more from life than what was expected of them, from their need to support themselves, and from their healthy attitude about sex in a culture unwilling to recognize any sexual activity that wasn't preceded by a minister and a ring. When we investigate sex symbols' histories, we realize that they acted more like flawed human beings than like the untouchable yet available women—ready to indiscriminately indulge male fantasies—they were branded as.

While it might have benefited men for Marilyn to remain untainted, reports of her appearing in public as a "bedraggled" sex star can be a good thing for women. In becoming aware of sexpots' fully human characteristics, and the ways in which they subverted what they could in their time, women might eventually be relieved of the pressure to achieve the same silent, smiling, and perpetually naive perfection. If *Marilyn* couldn't appear perfect all the time, then why should we feel obligated to try to? And if men's constant desire did, in fact, partially cause Bettie Page's mental illness, as she sought something more satisfying and meaningful than male attention, then knowledge like this might encourage other women to refuse to be eternally game for pandering to traditional sexual fantasies.

A shift in the way we view sex symbols—as real women, not goddesses—might make room for louder, more aggressive, more socially conscious women to thrive in mainstream culture, and to simultaneously appear as sexy as Monroe did. And maybe then we can even start celebrating Marilyn for her irreverence, too.

139813
CLEVELAND
32 5' 8 126
NOV 3 1970

chapter 4
The Political
Gets Personal

Miss Susan B. Anthony considers it her mission to keep the world,
or at least her part of it, in hot water. Gentlemen, take notice.[1]
—The Revolution, 1869

Sex symbols preen and pose, but other women have shaped our real female sexual liberation. No matter how consistent their activist history has been, politically outspoken and active women are considered few and far between—more as oddities than as a steady part of political and cultural history. Even the perceived chronology of the women's movement itself—first, second, and third waves—minimizes feminism's continuous history of political endeavors by intimating peaks of activity, and inaction in the valleys between them.

Mainstream notions of sexual rebellion, and particularly of female rebels who concretely criticize the overall power structure, are often reduced to caricatures or stripped of any depth, either to diminish the power of the women's message or to maintain pop culture's economic viability. Television network sponsors held out on committing to advertising during the sitcom *Ellen,* for example, when rumors about her character coming out surfaced. The music industry's brief foray in the 1990s into endorsing a string of female singer-songwriters, such as Jewel, Gwen Stefani, and Alanis Morissette, added up to temporary success, while it ignored indie and punk female artists with something more meaningful (and possibly more alienating) to say. Instead of getting behind spirited, gung-ho women staring down the power structure like the cowgirls they are, pop culture upholds images of politically and socially powerful women, only to rip them down again or recast them when popular trends change.

Rather than being memorable for individual defiance, feminism has been an iconic rebellious movement. It's been populated with a multitude of voices, images, attitudes, personalities, and priorities, and seen its share of academic and grassroots uprisings. Feminists have endured internal battles and fights against the general public perception. They have also significantly impacted female rebellion, and notions of what rebellion means, throughout modern history.

Feminism has been kept on a short leash in mainstream culture, too, through repetitive representations of raging, physically undesirable women. In ensuring that politically articulate, challenging women seem unattractive to the mainstream, popular culture can remain comfortable by acknowledging the existence of differing viewpoints, while its mostly negative images avoid alienating conservative or critical audiences. Clearly, pop culture and, more specifically, the media aren't going to represent rebellion that directly threatens their own livelihood by criticizing and rejecting their messages. Advertising does its part, too, in tempering more powerful and controversial messages by sidling up next to them with consumerism. On commercial television, for instance, it's a game of bait and switch: Any inspiring, radical transgression or image of a strong woman can be countered immediately by commercial breaks that target consumer insecurities. But sometimes there are happier reversals: Figures like Rosie the Riveter and Wonder Woman who supported mainstream political agendas were later embraced as symbols of feminism. Whether at the hands of revisionist history or television marketing, the more threatening the female, the more maligned, misunderstood, or misrepresented she becomes.

> *You have to make more noise than anybody else, you have to make yourself more obtrusive than anybody else, you have to fill all the papers more than anybody else, in fact you have to be there all the time and see that they do not snow you under, if you are really going to get your reform realized. That is what we women have been doing, and in the course of our desperate struggle we have had to make a great many people very uncomfortable.[2]*
>
> —Emmeline Pankhurst, 1913

Women's history of modern, mainstream activism, its misrepresentation, and its sporadic exposure in the media began with the late-nineteenth-century movement to gain the (white) women's vote. Suffragists were guilty of their own exclusions, too: Sojourner

Truth, a nineteenth-century speaker and former slave, challenged the suffragists to fight for the black vote in her famous "Ain't I a Woman?" speech, which has been shunted from our usually brief educational references to suffrage, leaving black women's voting rights out of the cultural conversation altogether.

While sexuality never goes out of style for pop-cultural women, typical historical accounts have also lost sight of sexual-liberation pioneers like Margaret Sanger, a staunch and dedicated birth-control advocate; the renegade network of abortion providers known as Jane, which operated prior to the passage of *Roe v. Wade;* Shirley Chisholm, the first black congresswoman; newspaper publisher, stock broker, and female presidential candidate Victoria Woodhull; and the early-twentieth-century labor activists Mother Jones and Elizabeth Gurley Flynn. These heroines have all become cultural footnotes, relegated to lefty literature if they are included at all, and the minimization of their victories downplays the long-term impact of their extraordinary revolution. Then real rebellion—that which upsets the power structure, rather than reinforcing it—is often stifled, eradicated, or, in terms of pop culture, construed as "uncool" or embarrassingly sentimental. And women who aren't already committed rebels therefore hesitate to get on board, because doing so is a socially dreadful prospect.

If our culture gave feminists' hard-won victories and radical actions their due, the fictional images of rebellion that society privileges would fall flat—but the current exclusion of the former makes the latter seem more glorious, potent, and desirable. Compared with the accomplishments of real-life radicals—the risks they took and the criticism they faced—the fictional, iconic rebel weakens. Women's political movements make the archetypal loner male seem hardly a rebel at all.

Women's reclamation of social and political resistance affirms our long-standing commitment to rebellion, whether or not history remembers our revolution. Although conventional U.S. history positions the suffragist movement as the beginning of women's fight for equality, Mary Wollstonecraft wrote *A Vindication of the Rights of Woman* as early as 1792. Women who gathered in 1848 in Seneca Falls, New York, at the behest of suffragist leader Elizabeth Cady Stanton collaborated on "A Declaration of Sentiments and Resolutions," which revised the wording of the Declaration of Independence to include women in the document's classic proclamation that "all men are created equal."[3] In 1872, Susan B. Anthony, the nation's most famous nineteenth-century feminist, was quickly arrested for illegal voting when she insisted on being registered to vote in the presidential election, regardless of the fact that the word "woman" did not appear in the Constitution.[4] Emma Goldman and Victoria Woodhull were proponents of "free love" for women, and Margaret Sanger advocated for birth control in 1920, long before the "free love" catchphrase (not to mention the Pill) was permanently linked to 1960s counterculture.

However short on detail, even educational nods to suffrage include the fact that nineteenth-century proponents of it fought long and hard for the right to vote. The suffragists—aside from Anthony and Stanton, women such as Lucy Stone, Lucretia Mott, Paulina Wright Davis, Amelia Bloomer, and Antoinette Brown Blackwell[5]— also raised a host of other feminist issues that majority accounts of suffragist history have omitted, such as domestic violence, freedom from unwanted childbirth, socially acceptable single womanhood, and working and making a living wage.[6] A critical and often oppositional press, as well as an all-male government, hammered at the suffragists with insults and poorly constructed "logical," "moral," and "rational" arguments, and rejected state measures requesting women's right to vote. These historical oversights limit the general cultural perception of just how forward-thinking suffragists were— and reduce their rebellion to the singular goal of gaining the right to vote with the passage of the 19th Amendment.

Women's political visions were belittled, and so were the individuals who espoused them. As Susan B. Anthony published her own newspaper and lectured tirelessly throughout her life, demanding almost all of the rights the second wave of feminism managed to implement almost a century later, she was infamous, admired, and yet endlessly ridiculed in the press and by the public at large. In 1905, for example, Grover Cleveland published his opinion on suffrage in *Ladies' Home Journal*—a publication that would also play an integral role as the site of a much-publicized sit-in during the 1970s movement. Cleveland called women's dissatisfaction with domestically bound life "perversions." He called suffragists "dangerous," "aggressive," and "extreme."[7] The *Philadelphia Public Ledger and Daily Transcript* weighed in by saying the city collectively viewed women as nobodies.[8] Other editorials found the public to be "disgusted" by Anthony's lectures, while Anthony was "personally repulsive."[9] Demonstrating suffragists were viewed as "unsexed"[10] and "ugly as a mud fence."[11] The reasons for these reactions are obvious now, yet they still reflect the reality of what was expected of women, which was to lie back and take it, in every sense of the word. It's an idea that never fully disappeared, and that resurfaced with vigor during the 1960s and '70s.

In attempts to cripple the power of revolution for women failing to satisfy societal expectations, the unwed Anthony was also accused of being bitter about being single and childless, and was prodded in the press about her "spinsterhood" throughout her life (she always handled it gracefully).[12] Consciously or not, the media's decision to deflect the argument away from the issue of letting women vote, and to move toward criticizing how a woman looked in public and concentrating on her ability to physically attract men, was altogether easier than reenvisioning women as citizens, or taking their demands seriously. The suffragist rebellion could then be presented as outrageous rather than rational, populated as it was with social anomalies and spectacles. In reality, other suffragists leading the movement were wed mothers: Antoinette Brown Blackwell and Elizabeth Cady Stanton, for instance, each had seven children.[13] (Clearly, the excessive-childbirth issue hit close to home.) Individually based ridicule turned public attention away from the real issue, women's rights, and toward women's private lives. It was a reaction used against rights movements throughout the twentieth century—except when the participation of women and other minorities was necessary for mainstream political causes.

Heroic females—and, for once, their victorious fists—appeared in 1940s World War II campaigns for women's participation in the war on the domestic front. *Wonder Woman* also debuted (as an uncomfortable, simultaneously pro-war and pro-woman cartoon) during that decade. The comic story line began with Wonder Woman visiting the United States from the all-female island of Amazon, sent to return a soldier who had crashed on the island. She stayed to protect him and rescue him from various and nefarious dangers. While Wonder Woman has remained a strong figure for women since the 1940s, she reinforced the very female, very traditional notion of tending to the needs of men. And rather than heralding her as the subversive Amazonian force she could have been, covers of the comic repeatedly promoted her patriotism.

The original Wonder Woman wore a blue and white–starred skirt and her signature, strapless bustier emblazoned with a gold eagle. Over time, her political nature (not to mention her skirt, which was trimmed down to blue and white–starred panties that exaggerated her crotch) lessened in inverse proportion to her increasing bust size. Considering Wonder Woman's strangely exaggerated crotch line, it's none too surprising to learn that a man conceptualized her. Her creator, William Moulton Marston, was a psychologist and early proponent of the lie detector (truth-telling lasso, anyone?).[14] Marston once explained the goal of his Wonder Woman concept:

> Frankly, Wonder Woman is psychological propaganda for the new type of woman who should, I believe, rule the world. . . . Woman's body contains twice as many love-generating organs and endocrine mechanisms as the male. What woman lacks is the dominance or self-assertive power to put over and enforce her love desires. I have given Wonder Woman this dominant force but have kept her loving, tender, maternal, and feminine in every other way.[15]

As powerful as the idea appears, any sense of empowerment the quote provokes is deflated when Marston tumbles into the *reason* why this "new type of woman" should rule the world. Predicting behavioral characteristics based on biology has been well critiqued in gender theory as an extension of sexism. Being "too emotional" was also an argument that was leveled at suffragists, to imply that because of their gender, they would vote with their hearts instead of their minds. Furthermore, the alleged "love" Wonder Woman was supposed to promote was aligned with pro-war propaganda—hardly a shift from traditional male images of power.

By the time television took hold of her image in 1976, actress Lynda Carter's Wonder Woman still righteously wrangled the truth, repelled bullets, and leaped tall buildings—but she had none of the characteristic strength of her male supercolleagues and lacked the seriousness of Wonder Woman in print. She didn't convey the urgency of her comic alter ego, either. Her body was sculpted but distinctly feminine; she was gorgeous, flashing her blinding white teeth and sparkling eyes victoriously, and had a maddeningly perfect makeup job. Without an active political campaign to make her justifiably aggressive (after all, she was protecting the boys), Wonder Woman fizzled into a simpler glamazon. Still, she was a television hit, and her image has endured for decades.

Wonder Woman the comic book is still in print—although with her body type and shining, untamed locks she now resembles a porn star more than an Amazon. Wonder Woman's strong physical stature, though, continues to exude sensuality, power, and intelligence, and she has gained ground as a feminist icon—regardless of having been once steeped in overt patriotism and twisted biological theory.

Rosie the Riveter also emerged during World War II. An illustrated image of a female factory worker, Rosie represented the women who were working within the United States for the war effort. She had a pert, pretty face, wore a red and white bandanna and a generic blue factory uniform, and flexed her bicep for the viewer. Redd Evans and John Jacob Loeb wrote "Rosie the Riveter," a 1942 song praising female factory workers. Norman Rockwell also painted a portrait of a working, dirty, haughty Rosie, who appeared stepping on a copy of Hitler's Mein Kampf on a May 1943 cover of The Saturday Evening Post.[16] The government used the more widespread image of Rosie for female-factory-worker recruitment campaigns. The woman in this illustration, seen only from the waist up, was thinner than Rockwell's subject. She was also less insolent than Rockwell implied. Instead, she was closer to a pinup version of a factory-employed poster girl with a freshly scrubbed face, and her likeness was framed by the slogan "We Can Do It!" (A photo campaign documenting female factory workers— the "real" Rosies—featured a not yet discovered Marilyn Monroe, still using her birth name, Norma Jean Baker, working at a Los Angeles plant.) Rosie sported rosy cheeks and slightly sinewy forearms, with a daring look in her unblinking eye that seemed to challenge viewers to a fight. Apparently, when the glories of working women benefited the government, women with muscle were welcome.

As Betty Friedan recounted in The Feminine Mystique, women who weren't working prior to World War II were expected to revert to home life and babymaking after their husbands returned home from their tours of duty.[17] The strong, encouraging Rosie the Riveter shrunk into cultural obscurity with them—until women adapted her as an image for the feminist movement in the late twentieth century. Both Wonder

Woman's and Rosie's images were reclaimed by women's art and politics, and now decorate artwork and various apparel, household items, and printed products. Both figures were powerful visual statements about women's equality, and the empowerment they connote is still palpable today, somewhat negating their pro-government origins.

Just as suffragists excluded some women from their ranks, the women's movement of the late '60s had its own pariahs. More moderate 1970s feminists separated from rebellious allies, such as lesbian feminists, separatists, and women with far-left political ideologies. While these exclusions are difficult to accept, it's likely that the modern women's movement, in reaction to negative media portrayals, was fearful that its more extreme factions threatened to turn the tide of opinion away from the issues. Likewise, personal attacks on women such as Anthony might have been perceived as obstacles to the later movement's alignment with more marginalized women. Composed partly of members of the media, the women's movement knew to present itself as more palatable to media outlets that typically pounced only on shock value. The result? Self-censorship affected by a history of misrepresentation.

> *Honey, if men could get pregnant, abortion would be a sacrament.*[18]
>
> —Unknown

The turning point of post–World War II American sexuality is usually attributed to the Pill, but the single greatest, most beneficial, and most direct influence on sexual freedom and women's position in America is the 1970s feminist movement. Still, according to a 2001 Gallup poll, only 25 percent of women in the United States identified as feminists.[19] While viewpoints on working women and mothers, sexual behavior, sexual violence and harassment, and the behavior of single women and single mothers have evolved dramatically since feminism's third wave in the '90s, some women's hesitation to identify consistently as feminists, even as they enjoy the benefits of women's movements, derives directly from the backlash against feminism promoted through terms such as "feminazi"—a conservative-right-wing creation to imply a shrill, argumentative, humorless woman waving a burning bra and abstaining from sex and anything pleasurable. This idea is generally what the mainstream media's revision of the feminist legacy has maintained since the early 1970s, when consumer magazines such as *Esquire, Playboy, Mademoiselle, Newsweek,* and *Time* ran features on the women's movement.

Television used images of raging women to improve its ratings, too, and feminists gained exposure on talk shows heavy with volatility. *Time* noted, "Many of the new feminists are surprisingly violent in mood, and seem to be trying, in fact, to repel other women rather than attract them."[20] Hugh Hefner, often a target of 1970s feminist criticism, demanded an article for *Playboy* on feminism that was "a really expert, personal demolition job on the subject."[21] Possibly the most famously ignorant assertion of all was uttered by televangelist Pat Robertson at the 1992 Republican National Convention, when he deemed feminism a movement that "encourages women to leave their husbands, kill their children, practice witchcraft, destroy capitalism, and become lesbians."[22] The rhetoric of the religious Right is stuffed with venom for feminism, but the media's misunderstood, sweeping portrayals are more accessible and repetitive.

No matter how they were portrayed in the press, feminists approached much of their cultural disapproval with a sense of anger—and humor to match. The movement's most recognizable representative, Gloria Steinem, wrote a hilarious and mocking satire of what would happen if men got their periods. (They would announce their cycles to their friends on street corners, exchanging high-fives as they discussed tampon absorbency.[23]) When asked on television in 1970 how she defined women's liberation, Susan Brownmiller replied, "When Hugh Hefner comes here with a cottontail attached to his rear end, that's the day we'll have equality."[24] The 1980 film 9 to 5, inspired by an eponymous organization for women in the workplace,[25] playfully followed three women plotting to kill their sexist boss. Today, a parade of blogs, zines, films, music, and other cultural products indulge in the playful side of feminism. Among them, feminist comediennes such as Jennifer Saunders, Margaret Cho, Roseanne, Kathy Najimy, and Mo Gaffney continue to supplement their feminist wit with satire and politics; Hothead Paisan, a comic by Diane DiMassa billed as the story of a "homicidal lesbian terrorist," comically expresses militant-lesbian-feminist anger. And Bitch magazine has been publishing tongue-in-cheek, thoroughly smart feminist criticism since 1996.

Radical humor, however, hasn't been the movement's most marked rebellion. Both the maligned suffragists, and later, feminists, embodied unequivocally brash lifestyles that their opposition feared. For example, the common argument against the passage of the 19th Amendment, that women might not vote with their brains and would instead let their feelings sway their decision, implied female voters were biologically bursting with as much love as Wonder Woman's creator suggested. Suffragists and 1970s feminists not only were dueling with legal and social-rights restrictions, but also were expanding societal perceptions of what being a real rebel was, contrary to the definitions the media offered. As they envisioned the world with new, laughing—and often misunderstood—eyes, and implemented scores of passionate strategies for permanent social change, these women seemed entirely more revolutionary and intriguing than they would have been had they merely mimicked stereotypical, mostly unqualified rebel angst.

The media's attention to feminism did have a silver lining. Pop culture imitated the feminist example once public interest generated by the women's movement became apparent. Hollywood released poignant films about women of depth, such as *The Way We Were* (1973), which starred Barbra Streisand as Katie Morosky, a politically passionate, educated woman in love. Katie wasn't Hollywood's average leading lady, even in 1973. She was fiery and down to earth, articulate and honest, and her intellect fueled her love affair with Robert Redford's Hubbell Gardner. After she and Hubbell separated, Katie continued to derive joy from her political work, while Hubbell found love elsewhere. She didn't revel in heartbreak, though— the film ended on a hopeful note, as she graciously conversed with Hubbell, whom she had run into on the street, and turned back to work.

Sally Field starred as an unlikely resistant, righteous factory worker in 1979's *Norma Rae*. *Coming Home* (1978) investigated the personal effects of war on soldiers' lives, placing a conflicted army wife between her husband and a disabled vet with whom she fell in love.

Martin Scorsese's 1974 film *Alice Doesn't Live Here Anymore* followed the development and discoveries of a woman leaving her husband and starting over, learning to support herself and her son. It also offered Alice a new relationship with a sensitive, emotionally open, supportive leading man. All of these films presented challenging roles for actresses, and most explored characters facing deeper challenges than cheating husbands or men who couldn't commit. They planted women in roles that permitted their interaction with the larger world, rather than continuing the simpler, longer cinematic history of women's interacting mostly with men. These movies also finally allowed women to play intimate and heroic roles that were more grounded in reality than mysteries, thrillers, or musicals. They all cropped up on the silver screen before the end of the '70s, and they were all nominated for Oscars. Even some 1970s B-movies acted politically responsibly: Pam Grier avenged exploitation of urban communities, and women specifically, in *Coffy* (1973) and *Foxy Brown* (1974).

On television, *All in the Family* (1971) pitted Archie Bunker's old-school, stick-in-the-mud ignorance against his new black neighbors and the political passions of his daughter, Gloria, and her husband, Mike. Gloria's tirades against sexism and racism were regular features on the show, while Mike played the new, sensitive, politicized man. Bunker was often confused and angered by the changing world around him. His character's social stupidity was the butt of the show's jokes, but the opposing, new, and progressive world was vindicated by episode's end. Bunker's narrow-mindedness and blatant racism were squelched by characters and situations that failed to reinforce his outdated opinions.

Mary Tyler Moore, a single career woman supporting herself and working in television news, was the grounding professional force in a newsroom full of wacky on-the-job sidekicks on *The Mary Tyler Moore Show* (1970), and *One Day at a Time*'s Bonnie Franklin struggled as a single mother raising two teenage girls who offered audiences comic relief and were far from the toothy offspring of 1950s television's suburban dream. *Wonder Woman* made its prime-time debut a year after *One Day at a Time,* in 1976.

Relatively complicated women and their ideas began appearing consistently on the pop charts, too: Helen Reddy's "I Am Woman" hit the number-one Billboard chart position in 1972;[26] Joni Mitchell charted four times between 1972 and 1975;[27] Aretha Franklin hit the Top 40 fifteen times during the 1970s;[28] and Fleetwood Mac surfaced there nine times.[29] *Ms.* magazine made its debut in July 1972—with Wonder Woman gracing its cover—and feminist art, fiction, and journals were a vibrant part of a women's creative subculture.

After a respite from such programming in the less politicized mass culture of the '80s, Roseanne Barr's hit show *Roseanne* gave dry comic voice to the problems of the working class with some modern, progressive twists. She even wove a series of gay and bisexual recurring characters into a few seasons, and by the end was dropping the names of feminist punk bands like Bikini Kill. Roseanne's family fought and yelled, and her children repeatedly defied their parents by doing everything from emptying the liquor cabinet to getting married and pregnant as teens. The plotlines and lead characters did retain some sense of traditional stability, though. Roseanne and her husband, Dan, remained married through most of the series. The children always returned to their parents' house—the classic hub of sitcom activity since the 1950s—and even brought boyfriends and husbands home to live with the family.

The 1970s and early '80s were rich with new representations of women, a direct result of widespread changes in women's lives. The fact that producers of pop-culture material were willing to present progressive viewpoints highlights the fact that mainstream culture reacts to what will woo audiences; when a product with a broader point of view is successful, a number of similar ones are born in its wake. However, forward-thinking efforts on television were ditched later in the '80s once the cultural tide turned toward Reaganism's conservative reign. While feminism clearly affected pop culture in positive ways, presenting women with gradations of love, anger, and righteousness, or as people fumbling quite naturally with the changing world around them, it still broadly posited feminism as a negative political stance whose proponents were prone to knee-jerk reactions born of blind hypersensitivity—no matter how much feminism permanently influenced cultural content.

In the 1990s, third-wave feminism ushered in new feminist misrepresentations by antifeminists whose careers had, arguably, benefited from feminist cultural advances. The movement itself was swept up in the fervor of Anita Hill's sexual-harassment testimony against Clarence Thomas, and in the third wave's signature focus: combating widespread rape and sexual abuse. Campuses and culture were replete with feminist-activist voices, women's studies classes, and a new body of feminist literature and music. Everything from zines to punk rock made room for women's voices, including inflammatory work by writers such as Katie Roiphe, whose 1994 book *The Morn-*

ing After: Sex, Fear, and Feminism excoriated feminism's approach to sexual violence. Camille Paglia, who published Sexual Personae: Art and Decadence from Nefertiti to Emily Dickinson in 1990 and Sex, Art, and American Culture: Essays in 1992, spent the decade pushing buttons and loudly criticizing feminism while obsessively showering unabashed, slightly embarrassing praise on Madonna. And in 1995, Christina Hoff Sommers released Who Stole Feminism? How Women Have Betrayed Women. During the early '90s, one would have thought the culture's truly rebellious females were antifeminist—as if feminism were the nation's standard viewpoint.

Media coverage of feminism and products of pop culture wavered between acknowledging feminism's tremendous impact and anxiously wiping away anything that might threaten its own cultural power. In the late '90s, the term "girl power" was ubiquitous on T-shirts after becoming the motto of the Spice Girls, another uncomfortable incarnation of pop culture's forays into feminism in the form of five trendy, thin, beautiful women who sang heavily produced and sugary pop hits. They didn't exactly make a good case for "girl power," and they certainly weren't rebels.

Pop culture constantly removes rebellion from the equation to avoid veering into the territory of questionable content; instead, it constructs its own diluted, safe version of feminism—call it "feminism lite." Take, for instance, the twenty-year-old pattern of the glut of women's glossies. Articles on careers, motherhood, rape, accepting one's body type, overcoming the odds of being female, and increasing one's sex drive are sprinkled in between advertisements and articles on dieting and cosmetics, preying on the very fears discussed in the magazines' more conscious articles. The Lifetime and Oxygen television networks ostensibly offer "television for women," as Lifetime's catchphrase goes. The network packs its schedule with scads of programs about victims of violence, murder, and abuse, not to mention crafts and cooking, as well as advertising fare for cleaning solutions and traditional household and cosmetic products. Lifetime could remedy the problem by airing Hollywood hits featuring rebel women (or close facsimiles thereof), but instead opts for light and palatable twenty-year-old reruns of made-for-TV movies that have already been whitewashed to make women's behavior and programming contents more acceptable.

Oxygen isn't much different. It shows *The Bad Girls Club,* a reality program featuring women living together and behaving badly—and it never strays far from reality television's cat-fighting female characters. *The Janice Dickinson Modeling Agency* is another Oxygen staple, in which the charming, Botoxed, lifted, silicone-laden former supermodel rips her models' bodies to shreds when she's not wrangling assignments. Rare progressive programming, like *Talk Sex with Sue Johanson,* featuring a straight-talking older woman offering frank, nonjudgmental sex counseling to callers, is relegated to late-night time slots, while Janice psychologically tortures beautiful young women throughout the afternoon. "Television for women"—like other pop-culture products hoping to please both their advertising base and their female audience—invests in women who are vulnerable enough to buy its advertisers' products and yet still view themselves as rebellious.

Feminist rebellion as a concept isn't always what these networks co-opt, however. Individual outspoken women are also fodder for media feeding frenzies.

Peter Fonda is famous for the cool biker role he played in *The Wild Angels* and for his Captain America role in *Easy Rider*. But it was his sister Jane who was the subject of a ten-thousand-page FBI file compiled during the late 1960s, a target of a Nixon administration hate campaign, and one of the most controversial and polarizing figures of the '60s and '70s antiwar movement. Fonda forcefully rejected the Hollywood that had raised her—which had fostered its own "good" rebels possessing few of the messy complications of radicalism—and she was powerful enough that the media and the Right used her as a bull's-eye to target the peace movement.

Fonda is a fascinating and unique product of the '60s; she both inhabited the sex symbol for her part in the campy, sci-fi *Barbarella* and later was a tireless and outspoken antiwar and feminist activist. While the media sexualized the public faces of feminism, such as Gloria Steinem and author Germaine Greer, after their involvement with feminism began, Fonda had long lived with widespread, public objectification and chose to reject it, rather than riding it out. The public witnessed her transformation from its inception, while other activists became infamous only *after* political movements had absorbed them.

Fonda began her radical odyssey in 1968, when she became aware of the GI resistance movement.[30] Soon after, she became active within it, visiting army bases and covert gathering places for antiwar GIs. She toured with Dick Gregory, Peter Boyle, Barbara Dane, and Donald Sutherland, entertaining the troops with a comedy skit that playfully criticized the Nixon administration in an attempt to counter the "pro-war, testosterone-driven" attitudes so prevalent in Bob Hope's USO tours.[31] She spoke publicly for peace and an end to the war—efforts that culminated in a fateful trip to Hanoi in 1972. Her behavior during that trip shocked the nation back home. She broadcasted antiwar radio shows directed at U.S. soldiers and was captured on film—during a truly misguided moment—smiling, surrounded by Vietnamese men, and perched behind an anti-aircraft weapon.

After she met with several American POWs, comments Fonda made questioning the torture of POWs were construed as unclear, offensive, or misinterpreted, depending on who was listening. Her trip still generates anger among vets and the Right, and granted her the derisive nickname Hanoi Jane when the story of her trip hit the press. In 2005, the shadow of her Hanoi Jane moment surfaced again when she released her autobiography, *My Life So Far*. Hate campaigns against her are still splashed on the Internet, and a Vietnam veteran spit tobacco juice at her during a 2005 Kansas City book signing.[32] Among supporters of war, her widely publicized and divisive actions have also perpetuated the inaccurate equating of "antiwar" with "antisoldier," even today. Much like the reduction of feminists to shrieking harpies, the suggestion that antiwar activists are automatically antisoldier is a damaging tactic used to dilute the possibility of mobilizing for peace. Apparently, it works—the Bush administration has also frequently relied on such conflations throughout the Iraq war.

Fonda recognizes the controversy surrounding her image, the turmoil of opinion about Vietnam, and the reactions she continues to invoke, keenly aware of transgressing her insider's status with her activism:

I am Henry Fonda's privileged daughter who appears to be thumbing my nose at the country that has provided me these privileges. More than that, I am a woman, which makes my sitting [behind an anti-aircraft weapon] even more of a betrayal. A gender betrayal. And I am a woman who is seen as Barbarella, a character existing on some subliminal level as an embodiment of men's fantasies; Barbarella has become their enemy.[33]

While Fonda's antiwar comments and actions might have been misconstrued by and offensive to some, what hasn't been acknowledged, either by Fonda herself or by her widespread coverage, is the fact that until recently, representations of female support of the military—and, implicitly, of the only way women could be worthy of soldiers' appreciation—had transitioned from images of Rosie the Riveter toiling away in the factory for the boys, or Wonder Woman protecting soldiers from death and violence, to cheerful and leggy Marilyn Monroe greeting wolf-whistling soldiers. Fonda worked to end the war and challenge the government; she wasn't trying to demoralize the troops. But female support for war in the past has meant offering one's heart and body, not one's mind or politics.

Fonda's antiwar activities were an easy target for the government, and provided a convenient diversion from the issues plaguing U.S. involvement in Vietnam—an idea that was highlighted when she declared Richard Nixon a traitor upon her return from Hanoi in the summer of 1972.[34] Proving the threat she posed, or perhaps merely affirming Nixon's spite, Republican representative Fletcher Thompson attempted to subpoena Fonda for interrogation after her trip. (The House Internal Security Committee rejected the request.)[35] A number of smear campaigns, including a phony letter sent from J. Edgar Hoover's office to a gossip column regarding a yarn about

Fonda's behavior at a 1970 Black Panther rally,[36] as well as tapped phone conversations and records of her actions, worked to detract from her power as an activist and to discredit her as both a radical and a credible source of information.

Fonda's willingness to learn and the eagerness with which she jumped into the fight and risked her career were certainly rebellious acts. But it's important to note that she also gained entry to places such as GI bases and GI antiwar enclaves because of the privilege of her fame. Her status made her a more accessible object of criticism and a common reference point for pundits and opposition seeking public support. Her fame mostly worked against her, but it also aided her rebellion and, in some ways, made it a bit less risky. She had time to educate herself, and access to information and places that were off-limits to other countercultural individuals. Also noteworthy is that many people fell victim to FBI and CIA investigations during the 1960s, and to CIA sabotage and harassment within activist organizations such as the Black Panthers. Activists like Tom Hayden, Abbie Hoffman, and Angela Davis, who were not as financially privileged as Fonda, were scrutinized extensively. Fonda was certainly not the only martyr of underhanded government tactics attempting to suppress citizen subversion during the '60s. She is, however, the most famous living American woman who was a target of government and public derision, and who remains vilified for actively opposing the war.

In 1980, the press was still discrediting Fonda's '60s radicalism. Journalist Gail Sheehy snidely commented: "Eager as a teenager with a chemistry set, she suspends her own identity while testing the most colorful and incendiary elements to make herself a new compound."[37]

When female rebellion isn't being taunted for its unfeminine qualities or its humorlessness, restless, dissatisfied, or seething women who change their mind or change their political viewpoint are seen as weak or unknowing. Such shifting attitudes lead to constant speculation that these women lead a childlike life, rather than to an understanding that they are on a journey to uncover the truth about who they are. When women have opinions and express them publicly, plainly, or repeatedly, we're often treated to the equivalent of a pat on the head. But is it worse to be seen as a child or to be portrayed as an emotionally unstable, irrationally angry woman?

We get up every morning, and every morning we see this enormous mountain in front of us. We can't go through it, we can't go under it, so we have to go over it.[38]

—Cindy Sheehan

Just as Jane Fonda became a vessel for public opinion about Vietnam, the deceptions, public confusion, and polarization tied up with the Iraq war have found their own lightning rod. The Bush administration and the conservative Right have maligned the antiwar movement as a whole and have also aimed their venom squarely at outspoken activist Cindy Sheehan. A little more than a year after Sheehan's son Casey was killed in Sadr City, Baghdad, on April 4, 2004, Sheehan demanded to speak to Bush about the U.S. government's reasons for the war, and about the faulty evidence it used to make its case for invading Iraq, as a means of understanding her son's death. She became highly visible in 2005 when she set up camp in Crawford, Texas, the site of Bush's vacation ranch. Supporters from around the country quickly joined her, and Camp Casey, as her campsite was christened, became a landmark for the contemporary antiwar movement. Sheehan also founded Gold Star Families for Peace, an antiwar organization for the American families of military casualties. Whether Sheehan will outlast her generation is questionable, but she has been the Iraq war's most visible and consistent opponent thus far, and is the most recognizably rebellious American female in this context. Her anger and dogged pursuit of the truth are admirable and worthy of positive attention, yet it's important to remember that her great loss, her son's death, catalyzed her rage and action.

Once, when asked what motivated her to camp out, Sheehan said simply, "Being a mother."[39] She expounded upon this idea in a 2006 interview with *The Progressive:*

> *I was tired of the lies, I was tired of the media not asking George Bush the right questions, I was tired of Congress not holding him accountable. And I just thought, you know what, if these people who are in power won't do something, I'm going to try and go down and get the answers.*[40]

Similar to journalist Gail Sheehy's characterization of Jane Fonda as "experimenting" like a "teenager" with her behavior and beliefs, *Time* magazine began a mostly sympathetic 2005 article about Sheehan with a telling line: "Cindy Sheehan, 48, is not a natural-born revolutionary. She speaks in a high, almost childlike voice."[41] Sheehan's "childlike" voice is simply female. Reporter Amanda Ripley ended up shallowly equating revolt with a voice in a deeper register—quite possibly a male one. Eve Ensler reported in 2005, "I ask how she feels when columnists and TV pundits say she's being used by the 'left.' She notes that she was speaking out publicly for a year before the antiwar movement began rallying around her. 'It makes me feel insulted that they don't think I can speak for myself,' she says. 'Are they saying that just because I am a grieving mother I can't have my own ideas?'"[42] The same *Time* article that deemed Sheehan an unassuming revolutionary tumbled quickly into an account of her blind neglect of her other children and marriage, as if this loss were her rebellion's most unforgivable offense:

> *Back home in California, her family is imploding under its grief. . . . Husband Pat, 52, couldn't bear having Casey's things at home and put most of them in storage. "We grieved in totally different ways," Cindy says. "He wanted to grieve by distracting himself. I wanted to immerse myself." The couple separated in June.*
>
> *Surviving son Andy, 21, supports his mother in principle but recently sent her a long e-mail imploring her "to come home because you need to support us at home," he says.*[43]

When men are committed to a cause, no one mentions how their families get left behind, and rarely is there mention or wonder at their lack of attachment to their family lives. If trivia about men's personal lives is present at all, it's certainly not nestled in an article's first few paragraphs. Women's rebellion is perceived to occur at the expense of families and traditional domesticity, and it's also seen as our greater, more painful sacrifice than the home life of rebel men is. Sheehan's struggle presents an ongoing problem for the

Bush administration and public supporters of the Iraq war. If she is not interpreted as "crazy," "disturbed," or "misinformed," the Right is challenged to answer military families who question why their children are being sent to war. Making Sheehan's rebellion appear emotionally imbalanced is easier than addressing the questions she raises. After all, the media has already set a precedent for that sort of response: It has historically portrayed opinionated, demanding women as irrational.

Sheehan's independent decision to "do something" in the face of apathy—"I think I'll go sit outside Bush's ranch until he talks to me"—is a prime example of how women have always had to work toward viable change: by simply *beginning*. In fact, it's how we got the right to vote. And there's no doubt that Sheehan's acting, speaking, and campaigning against the war reenergized the peace movement.

*L*ooking back on a road littered with insults, smear campaigns, misinformation, and a sparse mainstream history of the feminist movement, it's little wonder that there aren't more women rebels out there upending things—the personal risks are more prominent than the accolades. With producers of pop culture eager to please audiences, and with advertising seeking profitability over quality content, the media's self-sustaining presentation of lighter versions of rebellion is inevitable. Renegades and questioning women get lost in the shuffle.

Over the last century, a flood of negative reactions has replaced radical legacies with images of humorless, difficult, crazy, lonely women. Women's extended lineage of real-life rebellion has also been hindered by our tremendously long history of being evaluated first for our looks; second, based on our marital status; and third, on how much our rebellion hinders our ability to behave well, and look and sound pleasing, for men. If a woman appears to be free from cultural criticism when she's worshipped for her exterior and her ability to sexually engage men, but is hated or ignored for having other kinds of passion, the majority of young women, not surprisingly, will prefer to imitate behavior that's received positively and to sidestep a potential onslaught of criticism for expressing other kinds of love. While such societal demands have lessened in the twenty-first century, women rebels haven't succeeded in overturning those criteria on a mass scale. Until we do, only rarely will girls be brave enough to dig up and follow the paths of the extraordinary women our culture still prefers to confine to obscurity.

Despite all the ways in which the press and the culture at large negatively viewed women's political and social change in the twentieth century, some of those developments did snake their way into popular culture and gain entertainment exposure—even if the ideas, like pop culture's tentative embrace of feminism, come in waves. Here's how the mainstream representation of rebellion can change: If we begin to identify public acts of social change, anger, and sharp wit as being as important to women's growth as intimate love is, then more prevalent, positive ideas about women's rebellion will remain in our pop consciousness, rather than appearing only when they're deemed profitable. Tactics used against politically outspoken females—such as when cultural pundits and media outlets declare opinionated women "crazy"—are perpetuated only because they've worked so well in the past. When they don't work, they won't be relied on anymore. The intriguing part of real-life rebellion is that its outcome is never guaranteed; there will always be unpredictable factors lying in wait. True rebellion doesn't end when the credits roll, nor is every story wrapped up neatly or resolved, with the leading lady socially accepted and victorious at the end. Even when media attacks get personal, political women's bravery is far more compelling and inspiring than the bravest fictional rebel heroes.

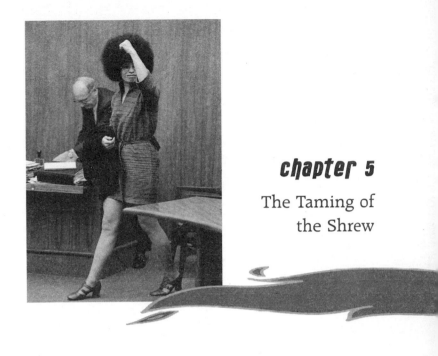

chapter 5
The Taming of
the Shrew

*. . . [W]hen I believe, after weighing the evidence, that what I am
doing is right I go ahead and try as hard as I can to dismiss from
my mind the attitude of those who are hostile. I don't see how else
one can live.*[1]

—Eleanor Roosevelt

The cultural taming of the shrew—out-and-out punishing women
for their behavior, and effectively silencing them or proving them
wrong through censorship or mockery—usually involves more than
creating a distorted or overblown image to dissolve their dissent. The
reaction of the media and politically opposed critics casts women
who act independently or politically, or who speak their minds

unapologetically in public, not only as "wrong," but also as forces to be stopped. And sometimes women quietly acquiesce in order to save themselves or their shaky careers.

Twentieth-century women could be tamed the traditional way, by having their work censored, taken out of context, or ignored (in the cases of Judy Blume, Sinéad O'Connor, and Alice Walker), or they could be fictionally monitored through television and film roles (as characters played by Lucille Ball, Joan Crawford, Bette Davis, and Katharine Hepburn were). Politics has had a tremendous impact on the denigration and disciplining of outspoken women, too—actresses such as Barbra Streisand, Janeane Garofalo, and Susan Sarandon and musicians like the Dixie Chicks are still harangued for their personal politics. The political arena itself attempts to use public opinion of women's misbehavior to temper the potential popularity of female candidate's opinions. Women working toward their own political goals—like Eleanor Roosevelt or Hillary Clinton—present such a threat to the status quo, they become tamed by public criticism that depicts them as emasculating or overly power hungry.

In other words, women leveling the same amount of criticism as men have throughout modern history tend to terrify, and subsequently outrage, the public much more dramatically than men do. It's the political equivalent of the saying "Everything Fred Astaire did, Ginger Rogers did backward and in high heels." Women have to work twice as hard to prove themselves politically and socially, only to find themselves twice as judged and their weaknesses, emotional or otherwise, picked apart. Or candid, on-the-run women like Angela Davis are used by traditional authority as an example of the negative result of radical activism, in order to instill fear in and silence other rebels.

Pop culture is, of course, rife with examples of how women and other cultural outlaws have been chastised. Madonna has been a favorite target of castigation over the years. She faced censorship and much flak in 1989 from the Catholic Church for her supposedly blasphemous album *Like a Prayer*, run-ins with police for live performances, and late-night video spots for racier videos like "Justify My Love." The fever-pitched opposition to Madonna and other artists at the time mirrored conservatives' hostile reactions to rock 'n' roll in the 1950s—the same old fear of "the other" nestled at their root.

One of the most damaging institutions to leftist political dissent was the House of Un-American Activities Committee (HUAC), which sought out "red" Hollywood in the late '40s and 1950s, investigating and blacklisting anyone with supposedly "communist" (read: liberal) tendencies working in the film industry. Along with the Production Code of 1934, the witch hunt caused studio heads to tiptoe around any potentially subversive themes found in films prior to the code's enforcement. Hollywood's Red Scare pitted conservative actors against liberal colleagues, heightened paranoia, and ruined more than a few entertainment careers. Women like Lillian Hellman, the screenwriter and playwright who wrote *The Children's Hour*, and writer Dorothy Parker, as well as numerous actresses and writers, targeted for their political opinions or their refusal to out other suspected communists, saw their careers halted for as long as the blacklist held, from 1947 to approximately 1960. Overall, the blacklist didn't target women specifically, but it put the brakes on the dissemination of anything but the most moderate and conservative cultural ideas. Any ideas that strayed from support for the Cold War and traditional American values undoubtedly hushed women who spoke up, and kept them nimbly skirting behavior that defied HUAC's demanding patriotism.

Women's political dissent has never had to be far leftist, marginal, or "communist" to inflame detractors—it has merely had to oppose the existing viewpoint to be defined as radical. Negative reactions toward antiestablishment women have reached all the way to the White House. Case in point was Eleanor Roosevelt, the First Lady in every sense of the word. During her husband's first presidential campaign, *The New York Times* compared her viewpoints and behavior with the expected role of the president's wife: "The President's wife must be a silent partner. The unwritten law is that the First Lady gives no interviews, makes no public utterance. . . . She must never show weariness or distress."[2] And in 1933, Mildred Adams wrote, "[T]he country at large has a much more set and stereotyped picture of what a President's wife should be, and the bewilderment which Mrs. Roosevelt's activity and widespread interests in many things evokes in small towns is a testimony to the novelty of her type in politics."[3]

Roosevelt's tirelessness and her flagrant disregard for her critics might appear to have been qualities as unattainable for some women as attaining Marilyn Monroe's lush body was for others. But Eleanor didn't spend her childhood kicking up dust; she found her voice only after her children were raised and her political life had begun. As a new wife, she began her public existence as a shy, unglamorous, and unassuming spouse and mother who was fearful of social situations and unsure of herself. In short, she was a wholly ordinary woman (regardless of being the niece of Theodore Roosevelt) who was thrown into extraordinary circumstances that challenged her own potential. She even admitted to becoming interested in politics because of her husband's career. In her autobiography, Roosevelt recalled the requirements of a dutiful wife, who was expected to blindly take up her husband's interests.[4] And while Franklin was an assemblyman, the later strident feminist remembered her youthful reflex to defer to her husband about politics. She even confessed to supporting the suffragist viewpoint due to his influence.[5] With the evolution of her political career, however, came the development of her own beliefs.

As for rebellion, well, she could easily have slipped into the dainty role of a First Lady focused only on teas and cucumber sandwiches, leaving her passionate political concerns at the White House door in order to please the public. But her fiery, restless nature would have seethed at the thought. And so Roosevelt chose to charge onward, to follow her conscience and let her unpopular political beliefs lead her to a louder, more active life, rather than bowing to a culture telling her to pipe down. "[F]or myself, I was deeply troubled," she recalled about the onset of her first term as First Lady. "As I saw it, this meant the end of any personal life of my own. I knew what traditionally should lie before me. . . . I cannot say that I was pleased at the prospect."[6] Instead of maintaining her own political views and identity, which was clearly her intent during her adventurous later life, she was sometimes painted as a mere nuisance to her husband.

As a First Lady, the only public criterion Eleanor met, according to journalist Adams, was having immense energy—otherwise, she was unlikely to be silent. The press highlighted her unique involvement in high levels of politics, and noted how engaged she became in political affairs. "Her prodigious publicity has had several effects," said *Time* magazine in 1933:

. . . to pain people who think the First Lady should be her husband's wife, not a front-page solo character; to gladden people who think it is fine that the country has a woman at its head as vitally interested in almost as many public movements as her husband. . . .

Her impulsive bobbings in and out of the President's office may seem incorrigibly undignified to her husband, but they make good copy.[7]

While a male might be seen as driven, focused, or passionate, the press characterized Eleanor's commitments as "impulsive bobbings," and her commitment as an undignified bother (not to mention revealed reporters' own undignified projections of what it might be like to work with *their* wives). *Time* speculated about FDR's reaction to Eleanor's political involvement in the White House, and Eleanor herself denied a heavy influence on her husband's policymaking and admitted her advice was occasionally unwanted.[8] FDR did assign her roles in the field, though, sending her to investigate mining towns, areas of poverty, and the educational system, as well as to evaluate support for various bills—proof that her "incorrigibility," if the term must be used, was matched by intellect, spirit, capability, and ideas.

For a formerly shy and retiring wife and mother, Roosevelt ended up carrying the burden of the shrew throughout her husband's terms in office. Constantly scrutinizing her for her own possible hypocrisy surrounding wealth and spending as she focused on the poor, her critics attempted to chip away at Roosevelt's beliefs by pitting her privileged lifestyle against her attentiveness to social issues, about which she was famously vocal. When her husband began hiring women for high political positions (an idea that she did admit to suggesting,[9]) it was presumed she was acting as an unofficial political adviser. Eleanor did bring feminism to the White House during a time when the idea of a large female workforce took a back seat to the Depression's dire unemployment problem. The majority opinion was that the era's high unemployment rates and severe poverty affected men more deeply than they did women. In fact, many argued that women *should* be at home, because they were "stealing" the jobs of large numbers of unemployed men. To this point, Eleanor Roosevelt presented a highly unpopular opinion:

> *The principle of denying work to any one who wants to work, married or single, is an obnoxious one. It is a dangerous and terrible thing to do. Frequently a married woman has parents or other dependents whom she must help and support, or she must supplement her husband's income to give her children the opportunities they need. Moreover, no one can judge the subjective value and necessity of work for another person.*[10]

Aside from the traditional First Lady duties of hostessing and maintaining household affairs—and in a divergence from the First Ladies who had come before her—Roosevelt wrote a daily column for the United Feature Syndicate from 1936 through 1962, and for *Ladies' Home Journal* from 1941 to 1949.[11] She also taught at the Todhunter School, which she co-owned, hosted radio broadcasts, and gave lectures. More important, she advocated for peace and for class, racial, and sexual equality during her years in the White House and throughout her later, very public life. She worked to aid suffering mining towns; held press conferences with female reporters during the 1930s, when she learned those women's jobs might be threatened by the Depression[12]; and wrote numberous books, including her autobiography and a collaboration with William DeWitt on the UN. Roosevelt was the most prominent progressive female voice of the '30s, and she continued advocating for her signature causes well into her eighties.

Eleanor significantly influenced domestic affairs, particularly as they pertained to women, and continued her political life, as well as enraging her detractors, long after FDR's death. A firm believer in understanding the world, not merely the United States, she met with Russian leader Nikita Khrushchev while the propaganda-laden Cold War was alive and well. Eleanor was one of the first delegates to the United Nations, and a representative for the Human Rights Commission, of which she became chair in 1947.[13] She also aided in drafting the "Universal Declaration of Human Rights and the Covenants."

Pop culture's rebellion is usually youthful, reinforcing the idea that at a certain point the questioning of authority will pass and opinions will change, and that this progression is merely an eroding sense of optimism. As Roosevelt demonstrated, women and people in general can revolt and evolve at any time during their lives. She was also a reminder that fearlessness has never been the sole province of men, nor of uninformed, inexperienced youth. Roosevelt was not someone "born with" a revolutionary spirit. She boldly transformed herself from a wife in the wings to a left-wing, sharp-tongued rebel.

Between 1945, when Eleanor packed up her things, and 1992, the First Lady's east wing of the White House was fairly quiet. Save for Jacqueline Kennedy—and celebrity clientele who have rehabilitated at the Betty Ford Clinic in California—First Ladies are not imprinted strongly on popular cultural consciousness. Perhaps that's why Hillary Clinton became such a legend in 1992. Like Roosevelt, Clinton was hounded by the press during her husband Bill's first presidential campaign for being, once again and sixty years later, "too involved," "too opinionated," and "power hungry."

As the Roosevelts did, the Clintons became a focus of the national press. Vastly different from (and younger than) the White House couples who oversaw the twelve years of Republican reign that preceded the Clintons, their arrival on the national political scene was more energizing than that of the usual staid candidates. Throughout Bill Clinton's terms in the White House, and particularly considering the fate of his presidency, the Clintons retained a hold on the culture at large, beyond the political sphere. In 1992, change was in the air: Third-wave feminism and leftist politics had reached a boiling point, and the stirrings of indie rock began to influence pop music. Politics were vibrant in youth and pop culture on the whole. As some of the most prominent figures in America, the Clintons were very visible signs of a much needed turning of the cultural tide.

A highly successful lawyer who specialized in family and children's issues throughout her career, Clinton wanted to continue her work during her husband's presidency. "I had begun to assemble my own staff as soon as Bill announced his candidacy," she wrote in her 2003 autobiography, *Living History*. "This was a departure from protocol, in which the candidate's staff controls his wife's schedule and message. I was different—something that would become increasingly apparent in the months ahead."[14] While the traditionally Democrat-blue coasts seemed electrified by the possibility of change, the press fanned the flames of moderates and conservatives, who weren't as enamored of Hillary's unapologetic, headstrong drive, knowledge of policy, and experience. After the media began to lambaste her for her candid remarks, Clinton adopted a more sedate stance.

Clinton also recalled a night of New Hampshire campaigning when her husband introduced her: "Recounting my two decades of work on children's issues, he joked that we had a new campaign slogan, 'Buy one, get one free.'"[15] The press pounced on it, as well as on two comments Hillary made that some people interpreted as demeaning to homemakers, throughout the campaign. Reactions to strong-minded women apparently hadn't changed much since 1933. As *The Philadelphia Inquirer* noted in early 1992, "You vote for Bill Clinton because you see him as a moderate, conciliatory leader, and you would also get Hillary Clinton with her hard-charging style and activist agenda."[16] By July, the same reporter noted Clinton's traditionally polished demeanor:

> *For reasons calculated or otherwise, most of Clinton's hard edges were chiseled away by the time she arrived at the convention. Her public schedule has focused on women's teas and lunches, where, with mock seriousness, she stumps for votes for her chocolate-chip cookie recipe. (She's in a Family Circle cookie contest with Barbara Bush.)*
>
> *The new image is straight out of a family values textbook—from political partner to dutiful wife and mother. She has posed for news photographs several times with her 12-year-old daughter, Chelsea.*[17]

Once Hillary had been "born again" as a contender for First Lady, the Republican camp scrambled to reposition her as careening on the outer reaches of the far left wing. Laughably, they went so far as to call her a "radical feminist"[18]—though she might identify as feminist, she has certainly never been radical. "Some of the attacks," she wrote in *Living History,* "whether demonizing me as a woman, mother, and wife or distorting my words and positions on issues, were politically motivated and designed to rein me in."[19] In some ways, the tactics worked. As election day loomed, the press noted the change in Hillary's presence over the course of the campaign; not only was she appearing to be more of a wife and mother, but she was also saying less.

Once she moved into the White House, however, she proved that she wasn't bereft of opinions. Hillary ushered in a new and refreshing role for the late-twentieth-century First Lady. After eight years of Nancy Reagan and four of Barbara Bush, she became a symbol of a more youthful White House, one that was at least voicing the concerns of the Left, which had been cast aside during the past twelve years of Republican rule. Throughout the terms of her husband's administration, Clinton became an ambassador for women's and children's issues around the world and within the nation—not a huge leap from what she had focused on throughout her law career. However, unlike Eleanor, who became more boldly articulate as FDR climbed from governorship to the presidency, Hillary was willing to soften herself for political gain—in effect, she self-censored to heighten the appeal of a potential Clinton administration in 1992, while at the same time using her alleged "rebellion" to rally for the more progressive women's vote.

During her presidential campaign in 2007 and 2008, news coverage of Clinton simultaneously scuttled aside cries of sexism, even while sources such as *The Washington Post* reported on the color of her pantsuits and pondered her decision to wear them while campaigning.[20] When she showed a hint of cleavage while addressing Congress in July 2007, major news sources, as well as the blogosphere, leaped to cover the item. And when Clinton welled up with emotion at a campaign event in Portsmouth, New Hampshire, in January 2008, in response to a question about how she's able to keep up with the rigorous pace of her campaign, she generated a media maelstrom—not to mention jokes about her finally showing her human side on the one hand and being a "crybaby" on the other. What some saw as inevitable weakness in women, others took as a cold and calculating manipulation of public opinion. The political cynicism of the general public and the press is wholly understandable, but would this be the strategy of a woman who's already seen firsthand how the media will skewer women for expressing either tears or anger? Doubtful. In a column in March 2008, columnist Maureen Dowd relayed a comment she'd heard about Hillary: "Hillary doesn't make it look like fun to be a woman. And her 'I-have-been-victimized' campaign is depressing."[21] After a tearful Hillary appeared all over the news, Dowd accused her of trying to wrangle straying female voters by crying in public.[22] Hillary was depressing because she ran a female-oriented campaign, manipulative because she expressed emotion, and a robot if she expressed none. Shrews can't win.

Individual responses to her political viewpoints aside, Clinton was scrutinized much more intently throughout her campaign for her wardrobe and her appearance than her opponents were, which occasionally forced the conversation away from the campaign (and toward the circus she and Barack Obama were mutually part of). It's the same reaction the press has had toward political women since Eleanor Roosevelt decided to play an active role in her husband's administration. With Clinton's feet now planted firmly in the establishment, rather than on its edges, her femininity—and, more significant, how it played into her political strategy—was once again under media surveillance. On a 2008 *Saturday Night Live* episode, *SNL* cast member and head writer Tina Fey proudly declared, "Bitch is the new black!" when she announced Clinton as her favorite candidate for president. Fey also happily self-identified as a bitch, but the fact is, Clinton did little during her campaign (and during her tenure as New York senator) to warrant the nickname, however tongue-in-cheek it may be. Whether it's the oft-used "bitch" or the played-out "shrew," opinionated women can't shirk the nickname.

> *All I'm trying to say is, that there are lots of things that a man can do, and in society's eyes, it's all hunky-dory. A woman does the same thing—the same, mind you—and she's an outcast.*[23]
> —Katharine Hepburn in *Adam's Rib*

Screen actress Katharine Hepburn was fast-talking, quick-witted, and high-spirited during the early part of her career in 1930s cinema. As an actress, Hepburn brought a refreshing distinctiveness to the screen. She is still wonderful to watch. Her straight-backed, arched-browed cautioning of leading men was empowering in and of itself; and her polished modern style, endlessly witty quips, and affected deep voice—not to mention characters that underscored her personality and rebellious image—continue to make for great entertainment. Hepburn also espoused nontraditional roles, such as tomboy Jo March in *Little Women*; a wisecracking debutante, disowned by her father when she decided to become an actress, in *Stage Door*; a woman disguised as a man in *Sylvia Scarlett*;[24] a fumbling yet very smart writer who tried to access more of her traditionally feminine side for her lover in *Woman of the Year*; a misbehaving society girl in *The Philadelphia Story*; and a feminist lawyer in *Adam's Rib*.

Hepburn's initial foray into film in 1932 ushered newness into Hollywood. Her personality shone through in her characters' wise wit, and her physical appearance wasn't that of the typical Hollywood beauty over which the public fawned. Her boyish figure and preference for pants onscreen caught the attention of the press in the 1930s, as did her clever, less traditionally feminine characters and the dialogue she delivered in a dry, rapid-fire monotone. Juxtaposed with the female characters around her, such as an actress prone to fainting, martyrdom, and eventually suicide in *Stage Door*, Hepburn's stubbornness and unconventional stoicism were amplified.

The headstrong Hepburn was quelled five years after her arrival in Hollywood, however. A 1937 publicity campaign threaded its way through film-industry publications that named some of the most rebellious women onscreen (along with Fred Astaire) as "box office poison," ostensibly for the largesse of their paychecks—but in light of the Production Code's hold over Hollywood, the fact that Hepburn, Bette Davis, Joan Crawford, Marlene Dietrich, and Mae West comprised the majority of the list seems suspicious.[25]

The admonishment of the ad campaign and media disapproval of Hepburn catalyzed her decision to take roles that were more

palatable for audiences than her raucous résumé of the 1930s.[26] The
'40s presented a Hepburn whose characters, while still divergent
from those of other female leads, were tamed by film's end. "Out of
the headstrong deviance of the 1930s," wrote Hepburn biographer
William Mann, "Kate emerged as the archetype of the strong yet
feminine woman, whose battle of the sexes was not really a threat to
the status quo but merely a search for love."[27] While Hepburn tried
to maintain control of her image—something a star like Marilyn was
never able to do—her '40s roles capitulated to the security of public
popularity. Still, she managed to surrender with her own sensibility
somewhat intact.

For example, *Adam's Rib* centered on the feminist cause, and
as Amanda Bonner Hepburn's fiery stance and confidence were
electrifying. She doggedly argued for women's rights throughout the
movie, and was vindicated as a feminist when an accused woman
was found not guilty. When Amanda's husband (Spencer Tracy) was
hired as the case's prosecutor, the film became an overt battle of
the sexes, with Hepburn on the side of women and feminists, and
Tracy struggling as her more traditional husband. By the end of the
film, Hepburn and Tracy had mended their embattled relationship,
and both pro- and antifeminist positions were justified. Hepburn's
feminism, elucidated so clearly throughout the film, eventually
compromised with a more conservative position, and her character's
commanding aspects were subdued. The subtle message was that
feminists merely "needed a good man" to get all that anger out of
their systems. Then again, seeing a feminist who neither went crazy
nor ended up dead or alone or murderously possessed was a nice
change of pace, too.

Hepburn appeared to turn the tables in life as much as she did on film. Perhaps because of the highly progressive environment in which she was raised, her most interesting radical act happened when she was a child, not yet a star: She shaved her head, wore boys' clothes, and went by the name Jimmy.[28] Many years later, Hepburn openly criticized HUAC's 1947 snooping in Hollywood, wearing a bright red dress to a political rally for a candidate with socialist leanings.[29] By the time *Adam's Rib* was released in 1949, Rosie the Riveter had retreated and support for working women had dissipated post–World War II, casting Hepburn's career-driven characters in sharp relief against the era's offscreen women, who were being shooed back into the kitchen.

Hepburn's roles still have more heft than those of many of her female peers—not to mention today's cadre of mostly dull leading ladies. Colleagues such as Joan Crawford and Bette Davis—who were never boring—often ended up in bizarre or cartoonishly deranged roles. Hepburn retained roles grounded in some semblance of reality, which were more relatable than the wide-eyed witches of later Crawford and Davis vehicles. In the end, most of Hepburn's movies were fun, energetic romps straying from the cinematic formula of the 1940s and—while they were still sealed with a promising kiss—clearly communicating progressive ideas, hammered into Hepburn's dialogue by a usually apolitical Hollywood.

*T*he "poisonous" Bette Davis and Joan Crawford were sharp-tongued and strong; they embodied a self-assured glamour more reminiscent of Mae West than of glamour girls such as Rita Hayworth or Marilyn Monroe. They both landed many successful, lauded roles in film: Bette Davis starred in *Dark Victory* and *Jezebel,* and Joan Crawford played the lead in *Mildred Pierce* and *Sudden Fear,* as well as appearing in *The Women,* a groundbreaking 1939 film that featured an entirely female cast.

As the women grew older and their careers took downturns after their buoyancy in the '30s, they were both cast endlessly as shrews in mostly low-budget and horror flicks, most memorably *What Ever Happened to Baby Jane?* (1962), the story of two sisters confined to their home and hopelessly dependent on and resentful of each other. Davis constantly relived her younger, successful years as an actress, and Joan Crawford played her long-suffering ill sister. The film has gained a campy cult following, but it often feels like a commentary on the two aging stars, creating spectacles of their worn celebrity and towering personalities. With overblown acting and exaggerated noir, the film featured campier versions of the catfights and drama that audiences found in the more serious movies at the zenith of Davis's and Crawford's careers. Even in Davis's earlier *All About Eve* (1950), her strong, sassy character was repeatedly foiled by a manipulating up-and-comer clawing to steal her spotlight. (Interestingly, the film was supposedly based on the career of Tallulah Bankhead, another hard-living, quick-quipping firebrand actress from the early twentieth century.) Davis prevailed, however; she was nominated for an Oscar, as was Anne Baxter, who played her conniving onscreen nemesis.

Following *Mildred Pierce,* which became one of Crawford's career highlights in 1945, she played a needy, insecure lover, Louise, who became so obsessed with trying to win back her lover, David, that she married the man David (and she) worked for and attempted to sabotage David's relationship with her stepdaughter. The 1947 film, *Possessed*, attributed her "possession"—an inability to see the truth clearly—to her former boss's suicide, for which she had convinced herself she was responsible. But the underlying intimation was that her rejection by David was what drove Louise to insanity. After all, it wasn't her female boss's name she muttered over and over again throughout the film. Crawford's earlier characters, such as Mildred Pierce—an abandoned wife who rebuilt her life by opening her own restaurant, became highly successful, and eventually triumphed over her murdering, manipulative daughter—were exonerated in the end. But only two years later, *Possessed* presented a much more aged Crawford, desperate and anxious to the point of murdering her former lover. Another shrew successfully tamed.

On the lighter side, comedienne Lucille Ball's character on *I Love Lucy* was also "tamed" at the close of every episode. *I Love Lucy* aired on television from 1951 through 1957, starred Lucille Ball and Desi Arnaz, and followed their life as a married couple in New York City. True to the decade, Lucy Ricardo was a housewife who became consumed with her husband's bandleader lifestyle, and often concocted harebrained schemes to test his loyalty and insert herself into his nightclub act (to no avail, of course). The dimwitted Lucy, though often hilarious, was always outsmarted by her husband in the end, who mocked her insecurities and obvious longing for a more stimulating life. When Lucy's plots backfired, Ricky's gentle, condescending admonishments would bring her back down to earth and restore her security. In other words, Lucy's "hysteria" was her irrational undoing, and only her husband could do away with it.

Lucille Ball's comic genius—she often played in drag—always outshined her outer stylishness and beauty, too, making it loud and clear, once again, that funny women can't be sexy. *I Love Lucy* also implied that women who are hopelessly insecure about their partners aren't smart or clearheaded. But Ball was certainly the best-known physical comedienne of the twentieth century. Aside from Carol Burnett, very few women are known for her brand of slapstick humor, even today.

Ball also attested to the misguidedness of the traditional male opinion that women are incapable of humor. As late as 2006, *Vanity Fair* columnist Christopher Hitchens argued that women's ability to reproduce somehow rendered us incapable of being truly funny. Hitchens' shaky theory perpetuates irreconcilable differences between the sexes, makes funny women less appealing to men; it also promotes the notions that women (who don't know humor from Adam) need an endless parade of rather dull "chick flicks"; that publishing must crank out predictable "chick lit"; and that men who find comediennes entertaining are emasculated. Female taste, therefore, continues to be less desirable to the culture at large—a pattern that ensures fewer mainstream opportunities for women in comedy, and for young women to discover female artists who are anything other than what men find appealing.

Lucille Ball (as well as with the dozens of funny women working today whom Hitchens ignored) may steadfastly refute the "women are humorless" idea, but her appeal came at the cost of depicting a woman lacking autonomy and a career of her own, and who appeared completely naive and in the dark at the close of each episode of *I Love Lucy*. Apparently, she also had no short-term memory; there was never a point when Lucy learned to trust her husband or figured out a way to successfully outsmart *him*. Arnaz was the fatherlike, finger-wagging, more powerful public figure, and Lucy the adoring, if not hapless, housewife. This dynamic seemed all the more superficial and degrading in light of the fact that in Arnaz's and Ball's real-life marriage, Ball was undeniably the more influential, iconic figure in popular culture.

*R*eal-life women rebels are always restricted more dramatically in life than they are in art. Without the power and privilege of Hollywood stacked in their favor, and without a neatly packaged plot wrap-up, the stakes are higher and the risks greater, and the payoff doesn't involve a long, recorded, transgressive legacy made to seem more significant than it actually is. Without scripts, directors, or finely honed dialogue to either tone them down or make them appear more polished than they are, truly marginalized women are so demonized by the public that they begin to appear much worse than their alleged crimes. They also tend to fade into relative cultural obscurity, while fictional rebels live on.

Angela Davis, a prominent 1960s black activist, author, and professor, lost her teaching job at UCLA in 1969 for admitting to her membership in the Communist Party—even though California court precedents stated specifically that membership in the party could not be enough to prohibit teaching.[30] Eventually, she was fired for her political activities outside of the classroom, rather than for the communist association that had initially put her in the public hot seat.[31] (Ronald Reagan, then the governor of California, was hell-bent on ousting her. He was also a "friendly witness" in Washington's search for Hollywood reds in 1947.[32])

Although Davis's public allegiance to the Communist Party was what introduced her to public consciousness, her significance is much greater than her party affiliation. Reactions to her political position reached far beyond the UCLA campus and the board of regents. Davis contended that after a court decision to prevent her from being fired, the threats against her dramatically increased. "Bomb threats were so frequent that after a while the campus police stopped checking under the hood of my car for explosives," Davis wrote in her autobiography. "Of necessity, I had to learn the procedure myself."[33] Davis was aware of her position as a scapegoat, and that her case and public persona were used as a warning to subversive groups.

> . . . I knew that all this publicity was not really aimed at me as an individual. Using me as an example, they wanted to discredit the Black Liberation Movement, the Left in general, and obviously also the Communist Party. I was only the occasion for their manipulations.[34]

Davis's powerful persona is difficult to convey. She's a combination of the pop-cultural definition of rebellion on the run and a real-life rebel who has retained a place in the public eye without being overtly sexual, violent, or cruel. Her image as a '60s radical is probably better known at this point than the details of her outlaw activities.

The image of her afro and raised fist is the most identifiable, as it links her to the Black Liberation Movement of the late '60s, when she was brought up on murder, kidnapping, and conspiracy charges in connection with a prisoner's botched courtroom escape and the murder of a judge.[35] She was also charged with supplying the guns for the courtroom-escape plan. Her case became international news when she went underground to escape the law in 1970 and was subsequently arrested in New York City after traveling across the country in disguise and relying on a network of friends and sympathizers in California, Detroit, Chicago, Miami, and New York. Davis was on the FBI's Most Wanted list that year. She was acquitted in 1972, but her time in jail was a transformative experience that committed her to the prisoners' rights movement, which she continues to advocate for today.

Davis was more likely to be punished than revolutionary white women who took similar kinds of brave political risks without publicly displaying any hesitation about doing so. When she ran from the law, Davis became an even more enigmatic character, mirroring the fictional wandering male rebel. As she herself has thoroughly stressed, though, she wasn't alone at all; rather, she became a symbol and a figurehead for collective revolutionary activity.

Davis's opposition was revolutionary, particularly because she was a radical black woman. And, in an era when civil rights and racial equality were the Black Liberation Movement's top priorities, her insistence on addressing women's inferior position in the Black Liberation Movement also put her at risk within her own community. Nevertheless, she appealed for women's equality within all facets of the radical Left, criticizing her peers' resistance to include Black women's liberation in the overall racial struggle:

I became acquainted very early with the widespread presence of an unfortunate syndrome among some Black male activists— namely to confuse their political activity with an assertion of their maleness. They saw—and some continue to see—Black manhood

*as something separate from Black womanhood. These men view
Black women as a threat to their attainment of manhood—
especially those Black women who take initiative and work to
become leaders in their own right.*[36]

This sexism infected all aspects of the Left; it was not unique
to black-radical circles. A lack of belief in women's ability to rebel
effectively, as well as a downplaying of the importance of women's
need for political change, was as much a social epidemic within
revolutionary circles as it was outside of them.

Since the '60s, Davis has written five books, including the
landmark feminist text *Women, Race & Class* (1982), which revo-
lutionized thought on systematic oppression in the United States.
Although Davis's work has become part of the modern theoretical
academic canon, her true cultural impact remains her earlier visionary ideas, her legendary legal showdown, and her continued insistence for justice.

Authors Alice Walker and Judy Blume both published controversial mainstream works, and suffered at the hands of censorship,
in the 1980s. (They certainly weren't the last authors to fan those
flames in the United States—since its 1997 debut, J. K. Rowling's
Harry Potter series has encountered blowback from the religious
Right for discussing witchcraft, and then for featuring homosexuality in 2007.) But ultimately, Walker's and Blume's intimate female
narratives became contemporary classics. These two writers have
become role models in contemporary culture, and their characters
(such as Blume's Margaret in *Are You There, God? It's Me, Margaret*

and Walker's Celie in *The Color Purple*) have become legendary as well. The works continue to impact popular culture: Recently, Blume was the subject of the 2007 anthology *Everything I Needed to Know About Being a Girl I Learned from Judy Blume,* and Walker's *The Color Purple* was adapted for the Broadway stage in 2005 and produced by Oprah Winfrey.

Blume, whose books were passed from hand to anxious hand—the covers of some ripped off, answering young women's unutterable questions—was a wildly popular young-adult author who addressed teenage issues such as puberty, body image, and sex in the 1970s and '80s. Generally, her work normalized teenage sexuality, including masturbation, same-sex attraction, and menstruation. Because of her blunt sexual content, Blume became the subject of controversy when the religious Right took issue with her books; as a result, many of them were banned sporadically throughout the '80s. Montgomery County, Maryland, declared her novel *Blubber* offensive *not* because it dealt directly with sexuality (it didn't), but because Blume didn't punish her characters for what some deemed morally questionable behavior (in this book's case, school bullying).

"I think it's far more important to present characters and situations and leave it open-ended," Blume commented at the time. "Yes, it's been banned in Montgomery County . . . because I didn't punish anyone for bad behavior. But that's not the way life is. So you have to learn your lessons another way, by becoming sensitive and by putting yourself in someone else's shoes."[37] In considering the issue again later—for it would rear its head again occasionally during the '80s—she said, "It's about control. And fear is contagious. I don't know why people think that if only they can control what their children read, they can control their children's minds. It doesn't work that way."[38]

Regardless of Maryland's argument for teaching personal responsibility, the main Blume hubbub—and probably the unspoken reason her other works were targeted as well—revolved around children's receiving sexual information through the filter of someone more lenient, liberal, or forgiving than their parents. If Blume hadn't treated sexuality in such a forward-thinking way—by standardizing what Christianity deemed sin-worthy and by not condemning teens for their feelings— she wouldn't have generated so much attention to begin with. Blume never apologized for the content of her books; she joined the board of the National Coalition Against Censorship instead. And in 2004, she received a *Poets & Writers* award for literary courage.[39]

As Blume was, author Alice Walker was attacked—for her Pulitzer Prize–winning, truth-telling novel *The Color Purple*. While the sexual abuse and homosexuality in her book were in question, she withstood criticism within the black community that was far more potent. Even though black women had criticized black males' sexism in the past, Walker was berated and boycotted for her negative portrayal of abusive black men. The book addressed rape, same-sex attraction and love, violence against women, domestic violence, and the economic and educational poverty of people of color in the early twentieth century. And although the book was as a compassionate testament to how oppression has blighted black men, Walker was obviously expected to either overtly forgive them for it or ignore it altogether.

When making the film version of the book, Walker worked with white male director Steven Spielberg, an approach for which she was criticized—even though her contract stated that at least half of the film's crew must be female, from the Third World, or black.[40] Contrary to the popular belief that she "sold out" for choosing a white director, Walker actively guaranteed that marginalized people would receive work on the set. Her motivation for writing the book was equally compassionate, if not more so. In explaining that reading material for slaves was limited to the Bible and pointing out the psychological damage such a singular viewpoint inflicted on the black race, she wrote: "We needed to see how we looked, I thought, behaving as if still under the spell of a religion that made it nearly impossible to love the female body that was our source.[41] Walker's ideas were disseminated widely in mainstream white culture, a fact that undoubtedly strengthened black people's negative reactions to her work. But even more heated, defensive responses sprouted around her depiction of women choosing to love each other instead of Mister, the man in the house. "There may be some people who are uncomfortable with the idea of women being lovers," she said in 1982. "But I feel they should outgrow that. Being able to love is more important than who you love. If you love yourself as a woman, what's to prevent you from loving another woman? I think many women feel a sense of liberation about that part of the story."[42] Would the novel have generated as much controversy if Walker had kept the love between Celie and Shug completely platonic, or if their onscreen kiss had never made it past the cutting room? If the ongoing backlash against gay content in literature—from *The Well of Loneliness* to Allen Ginsberg's *Howl* and even to *Harry Potter*—is any indication, signs point to no. At the time of the film's release, an editorial in *Carolina Peacemaker* waved away the notion of black lesbianism as a valid way of life, citing heterosexual love as more powerful. The editorial further accused *The Color Purple* of unrealistically portraying black lesbianism as a transcendent experience for some women.[43] Of course, skewed viewpoints about lesbianism's legitimacy are not exclusively the province of black men, but the editorial's author was clearly unwilling to acknowledge lesbianism as a natural drive, rather than as one wrought by social oppression.

In *The Same River Twice,* Walker described how the criticism of the novel affected her. "It was painful to realize that many men rarely consider reading what women write," she explained, "or bother to listen to what women are saying about how we feel. . . . That they see our stories as meaningless to them, or assume they are absent from them, or distorted. Or think they must own or control our expressions. And us."[44]

While Walker battled to make her point of view heard and delicately balance the dialogue within her own community with the objections of society at large, *The Color Purple* generated public debate and scorn because Walker was a woman criticizing men and making them appear simultaneously more oppressive and less oppressed than her female characters. Instead of being able to conduct a dialogue about her characters, the reality of life for women of color, or her Pulitzer, Walker was forced to devote all her energy to repeatedly defending her characters' choices and her own storytelling decisions. It's likely that the ensuing dialogue would most likely not have taken on so many layers and levels if Walker had backed down instead of defending herself. In fact, her strongest, frankest reactions were printed in the nation's publications of record, such as the following, from *The Washington Post*: "But why shouldn't I be tough on men?" she said in 1982. "This is a country in which a woman is raped every three minutes. Where one of three women will be raped during their lifetimes, and a quarter of those are children under twelve. . . . If I write books that men feel comfortable with, then Í have sold out. If I write books that whites feel comfortable with, I have sold out."[45]

Walker insisted on telling her side of the story—to an audience that was eager to pounce on arguments about race, class, and gender. And because women don't generally generate media attention when they censure men's movies for poor portrayals of women, this public firestorm was of particular importance to women artists.

It's not like I got up in the morning and said, "Okay, now let's start a new controversy." I don't do anything in order to cause trouble. It just so happens that what I do naturally causes trouble. And that's fine with me. I'm proud to be a troublemaker.[46]

—Sinéad O'Connor

*T*he bile that blind U.S. patriotism can produce was leveled in the '90s mostly at Irish pop singer Sinéad O'Connor, who became popular when she released her second album, *I Do Not Want What I Haven't Got,* in 1990. The video for the single "Nothing Compares 2 U," which introduced O'Connor to a mainstream audience courtesy of MTV, featured a shaved Sinéad in a black turtleneck, staring down the viewer unblinkingly. The image captivated American audiences, the song settled on the Top 40 charts for fifteen weeks,[47] and O'Connor was nominated for four Grammys.[48] Even before O'Connor became publicly angry and insolent, her image was startlingly different from pop stars', particularly female pop stars'. From skimpy, ultrafeminine clothing to manes of heavy-metal hair, women in videos were the polar opposite of Sinéad; as a result, the media copied and satirized O'Connor and her look. But incidents following the acclaim she received for *I Do Not Want What I Haven't Got* sent her reputation into the badlands.

First, O'Connor refused to play "The Star-Spangled Banner" before one of her concerts, leading Frank Sinatra to comment that she deserved a kick in the ass.[49] "I think of the lyrics of the song as being very dangerous," she told *Rolling Stone* in 1992. "I think if you are into censorship, you should censor *that,* frankly. 'Bombs bursting in air' and the 'rockets' red glare' isn't anything I'm interested in singing about. And yet N.W.A. piss everyone off singing about AK-47s."[50] Incorporating American gender bias into the mainstream dialogue, she also commented on the flurry of negative press she received: "The main reason [for the backlash] is that I'm a woman. If I were a young man and I was on the TV saying these things, I would not be as brutalized. Secondly, it's because I'm not a safe woman in any way. That's because of the way I look, of course . . . the shaved head. I can't be put in any category, and that freaks people out."[51]

O'Connor also refused to perform on *Saturday Night Live* when she discovered she would share the stage with Andrew Dice Clay, whose comedy relied on misogyny and homophobia for laughs. Finally, in another stint on a separate, 1992 episode of *Saturday Night Live*, O'Connor held up a photo of the pope, called the Catholic Church the "real enemy," and tore up the picture. It was the most publicized of her U.S. protests. She explained the act in 1992:

> *"I did it as a symbol of my rejection of what [the Catholic Church is] teaching people and of my belief that their influence in the*

world must be torn apart," she explained. "I accept that tearing the picture can be viewed as a negative attitude, but one has to do what one can do. If I hadn't torn the picture, we wouldn't be having this conversation. Now people will listen to what I'm saying and let me explain what I'm talking about."[52]

Not only did O'Connor become the center of a media storm for her transgressions, but NBC received three thousand complaints after the show aired. A ban of her albums followed, including a few group burnings of her work and a mobilization by the National Ethnic Coalition of Organizations, which pledged to donate $10 to anyone who sent in copies of her albums.[53] The brief bout with infamy cost O'Connor. Not one of her albums has sold as well in the United States as *I Do Not Want What I Haven't Got,* and while she remains popular and continues to write and perform, the critical acclaim she initially received has dwindled over the years. Although the controversy might not have completely tanked her success in the United States, one would think that if her lessened popularity were due only to poor sales or unsuccessful album releases, she would have gotten at least *some* mainstream attention for her acoustic cover of Nirvana's "All Apologies," which was released in 1994, the year Kurt Cobain died. Her so-called rage—as a woman standing up to the power structures oppressing her—was legitimate, but the flood of unfavorable exposure O'Connor received for challenging U.S. and religious traditions exposed our national lack of comfort with confrontation and our inability to stomach criticism; our lack of understanding of our position in the world; and our endless need to be considered "right."

Similar to the ongoing sneers Sinéad O'Connor can wrangle, Yoko Ono, performance and sound artist and wife of John Lennon, continues to incur blame and bitterness from Beatles fans—and not just for her abstract music, which is certainly an acquired taste. Yoko's real flaw, in the eyes of Beatles fans, was her supposed "control" over John Lennon. She's often blamed for breaking up the Beatles—which is actually an act that emasculates Lennon and his bandmates while shrewifying Ono. In reality, Ono and Lennon spoke out publicly and forcefully against the Vietnam War, and both were outspoken feminists. While they were busy scapegoating Yoko for the band's split, male Beatles fans may actually have been acting out of a (not-so-)latent discomfort with their idol John's new focus on women as an oppressed group—a viewpoint they probably viewed as Ono's influence, anyway. While Lennon's fans might have been keeping women out of "their" radical movements, he penned "Woman Is the Nigger of the World," released posthumously in 1986, and written and performed as early as 1972.

Fan hatred for Ono is clear. It's not a stretch to believe that Beatles fans who continue to demonize Ono do so because she was a woman affecting the political views of her husband—a man whom they deemed "cool," and a rebel fighting the good fight. And even though Lennon was naturally politically aligned with Ono, it was easier for fans to castigate her for espousing unpopular causes like feminism than it was to hold the beloved leader of an all-boy rock brigade responsible. If Ono had been a white American or European rather than Japanese, and traditionally feminine rather than rebellious about it; if she had kept her opinions to herself and had not been an expressive artist and an overt pacifist feminist—in effect, if she had remained mute—the disparagement she continues to endure probably would have been tempered. And Ono bravely soldiers on. Her latest full-length music release debuted in 2007, and owns her bad reputation instead of ignoring it. The album is unapologetically titled *Yes, I'm a Witch*.

Not only were Ono and O'Connor outsider women who, in O'Connor's words, were not "safe," they were both foreigners pointing the finger at a xenophobic country that was, and continues to be, overly threatened by criticism, and were thereby rejected by the mainstream and by hyperpatriotic segments of the American population.

Women don't necessarily need an American visa to be silenced, though. Onstage in London in 2003, the Dixie Chicks' lead singer, Natalie Maines, declared she was "ashamed the president of the United States is from Texas."[54] Like the knee-jerk reactions to O'Connor's behavior, the Chicks' albums were publicly trashed in Missouri,[55] and in Nashville, a call-in campaign forced their single off the air. Maines responded to the press with an apology but also stated, "I feel the president is ignoring the opinion of many in the U.S. and alienating the rest of the world. . . . My comments were made in frustration, and one of the privileges of being an American is you are free to voice your own point of view."[56]

Since 2001, many people have been censored by the press and unnecessarily boycotted or attacked by the public for expressing displeasure with U.S. military action or the president, but it was disappointing that Maines apologized. When Maines made her anti-Bush statement, the Dixie Chicks were positioned at number one on the Billboard country album chart, and had been Grammy nominees that year.[57] Their album also ended the year at the top spot for an album by a group or a duo on Billboard's Top 200 (probably due to the controversy, not to the apology). Maines's mea culpa was obviously a scramble to maintain sales and was probably motivated by media machines such as Sony, the group's label, or by a boycott from radio behemoth Clear Channel, to keep record sales afloat. The Dixie Chicks could likely have avoided an explicit apology and still profited; after all, by that point, their careers had clearly benefited from the controversy by attracting an expanded fan base outside of country music. But attacks on Maines dominated the media and tamed her as a result.

A few months later, the Chicks decided to embrace their new outlaw position, posing for an *Entertainment Weekly* cover emblazoned with "traitors," "big mouth," and "Saddam's angels," among other terms. It might be a relief to see women reveling in their rebel personae, but the Dixie Chicks' pride was tainted by Maines's earlier apology. The Chicks' hesitant embrace of their relatively new outsider status still feels disingenuous, and they were clearly steered by public reactions and corporate strategy.

A woman with a concise argument and her own voice is still considered dangerous enough to be treasonous, subject to attack and harassment, and thoroughly disciplined. The repeated taming of the shrews in our society limits how powerful female rebellion can be, and rather than valuing (or at least listening to) dissenting voices, the public and press generally home in on an outspoken woman's perceived weaknesses and hammer away at her until she becomes culturally irrelevant, changes her ways, shuts her mouth, or appears insane enough for her opinions to be turned into a cultural joke. The overall message, in yet another predictable reaction to female rebellion, is that opinionated women will be culturally ostracized (or, in Lucy's case, admonished) for opposing *anything* that warrants being picked apart or deconstructed.

When pop-culture rebellion intersects with real rebellious acts that truly defy the status quo, it dilutes them. Because our society is more accustomed to watered-down versions of rebels that we see in the movies or on TV, more conservative audiences tend to quickly cry "traitor" about, or simply silence, true revolutionaries seeking lasting change. Thankfully, rebellion can't ever be completely, permanently contained. That lack of containment and the struggle against silence are precisely what we should celebrate dissenting women for, rather than discouraging it by penalizing them. If we had more lasting images of subversive—and angrily so—women who haven't been met with silence or punishment or demands for apologies, as well as more women willing to take the heat head-on, we wouldn't have such an overwhelmingly negative reaction to women when they do speak out. And shrews nationwide would never have to worry again.

chapter 6

Angels, Aliens, and
Ass Kicking

I always wanted [Buffy the Vampire Slayer] to be an icon. I wanted
her to be a hero that existed in people's minds the way Wonder
Woman or Spider-Man does, you know? I wanted her to be a doll
or an action figure. I wanted Barbie with Kung Fu grip![1]
        —Joss Whedon, creator of *Buffy the Vampire Slayer*

Kicking female kung-fu masters, heroines harnessing superpowers, and women performing daring feats are more common in
today's action and sci-fi movies and television shows than ever before. Storm and Jean Gray grace the *X-Men* film series; Halle Berry
starred as Catwoman; *Buffy the Vampire Slayer, The X Files,* and *Xena:
Warrior Princess* had long and healthy runs on TV; *Alias* was a cult

hit; and Sarah Connor, the protagonist of the *Terminator* film series, picked up her own television series, *Terminator: The Sarah Connor Chronicles,* in 2008. However, despite superheroines' and action heroines' current prevalence, they are still relative newcomers to movie and TV screens.

Male action and sci-fi heroes have dominated both genres since their beginnings. The most profitable and long-lasting films and television programs focus more on men than on women: The original *Star Trek* series certainly had female cast members, but the most enduring characters (William Shatner and Leonard Nimoy) and the majority of the crew were male. There were also more prominent male stars on *Star Trek: The Next Generation,* such as Patrick Stewart and Wil Wheaton. The many movies and incarnations of James Bond, which are now classics, featured women in sexually compromising and seductive positions. *Star Wars* and *Jaws,* the first two blockbuster adventure films, broke box-office records. Roy Scheider and Richard Dreyfuss defeated the killer shark in *Jaws.* Princess Leia had a major part in *Star Wars,* but Luke Skywalker's maturity and development were the focus of the first three films George Lucas released in the '70s.

In the '80s, action films like *Raiders of the Lost Ark* and *Indiana Jones and the Temple of Doom,* starring Harrison Ford, were high-grossing hits, as were macho movies like *Die Hard, Lethal Weapon, 48 Hours,* and *Rambo.* More recently, in the *Lord of the Rings* trilogy (which also broke box-office records), adventurous bravery and wizardry were almost exclusively the province of men (or any variety of nonhuman males). In *Spider-Man,* Peter Parker's heroic acts were motivated by his strong sense of personal responsibility and by his high school friend Mary Jane, who always needed rescuing from male villains. At least the *Harry Potter* series, which has also struck box-office gold since the first film's release in 2001, features the smart, practical, and capable Hermione.

Action and sci-fi heroines, like male action heroes, are mainly variations on standard characters and story lines. There's the big-budget, blockbuster sci-fi heroine, such as Ripley in *Alien* and Trinity in the *Matrix* trilogy; the superheroine based on comic-book characters, like Wonder Woman and the female mutants of *The X-Men;* and the action heroine who is faced with overwhelming physical demands and often lacks the overt glamour of many blockbuster female leads, such as Pam Grier in *Coffy* or Uma Thurman in *Kill Bill.*

Typically, action films offer the extreme version of each gender. Male heroes tend to have steady emotions, even when they're in agonizing pain; they're usually muscular, carrying tremendous guns and heaps of ammo; and they exhibit no hesitation or humility when it's time to fight the enemy. Women have long been saved by the action hero, and the rescue sparks a love affair between them. Ladies-in-waiting have traditionally underscored the hero's masculinity. Action heroines have dramatically changed the formula of action adventures by presenting women who can save themselves and who exhibit traits similar to the hypermasculine action hero's. But the action genre's gender extremes sometimes highlight the heroine's femininity too, whether through her costume or through other, subtler means.

Action and adventure films also present fantastical versions of human strength: Even in more reality-based action films, men and women alike survive leaps from towering skyscraper to towering skyscraper, twelve gunshots, or falls from a hundred feet, or perform masterful kung fu while flying through the air, to name just a few feats. However, there is a catalog of action heroes whose capabilities come from within, rather than from superpowers like those of Superman, Spider-Man, or Wonder Woman. Surviving males, like those in *Die Hard, Lethal Weapon,* the *Bourne* and James Bond series, *Independence Day, Enemy of the State, Speed, Enter the Dragon, Star Wars, Raiders of the Lost Ark,* and *Rambo,* portray the everyman who overcomes intimidating and life-threatening odds. Their strength comes directly from their own, very human powers—not to mention an extreme amount of ammunition or martial-arts skills.

The women who can overcome those same odds without being imparted robotics or superpowers, or coming from another planet, are few and farther between. Some that have include Angelina Jolie in *Mr. and Mrs. Smith,* the Bride in *Kill Bill,* Demi Moore in *G.I. Jane,* Jodie Foster in *Panic Room* and *The Brave One,* '70s blaxploitation heroine Pam Grier, Charlie's Angels, Thelma and Louise, Princess Leia, and the heroines of disaster films like *Twister.* But far more action-adventure heroines use superpowers and robotics—powers that don't require the "everyday" woman to be thrown into circumstances in which she must use her own strength to pull her through. In the cases in which women do rely on their strength, they're usually answering to men or working for the government, such as Scully on *The X Files* or Sydney on the television show *Alias.*

In some cases, as with superheroines like Wonder Woman, being female still precludes, or informs, acting the hero. Where characters of depth and brawn are presented in relatively realistic packaging, the themes of motherhood and gender often inform the film's story line and the characters' motivations, as in *Alien* and *Kill Bill.* Maybe it's too early in the female-action-hero legacy to avoid dealing with issues of gender, and maybe gender should be welcomed as a new direction for action films. But aside from reinforcing glorified masculine stereotypes (which borrow heavily from the male-rebel archetype), male action heroes do not become embroiled in fights rooted in their experiences as men; they wave guns to emphasize their masculinity instead. Female action stars, conversely, are expected to wield those same guns, seduce audiences, defeat villains, make statements about gender, and retain physical perfection and a decent makeup job while doing it. Twice the job for half the credit, indeed. For now, depictions of women as pure action heroines are still sporadic at best, and make the females who embody these roles rebellious and fairly unique. Their characters are subjected not only to alien life forms and enemies of all kinds, but also to gender bias in ways male action heroes never would be.

The first time women action heroes cropped up with more than passing frequency in U.S. pop culture was on television in the mid-1970s. While '70s sitcoms handled contemporary issues like single motherhood and career-driven women, prime-time programming cranked out female characters with superheroic bravery, too. The Bionic Woman, a character in the hit show *The Six Million Dollar Man,* gained a spin-off series of her own in 1976. The series was also remade for television in 2007. Both Jaime Sommers (the Bionic Woman) and Steve Austin (the Six Million Dollar Man) were humans implanted with robotic, superhuman strength and ability. Jaime, a former professional athlete and schoolteacher, leapt like Wonder Woman, but her strength didn't rely on external props like the lasso and wrist cuffs Wonder Woman used. Jaime was human and acquired her powers after being severely injured, while Wonder Woman was from Amazonian Paradise Island and had been alive for more than two thousand years. In the scope of superheroines, Jaime Sommers was a more realistic, everyday woman than Wonder Woman. Though aided by implants, the Bionic Woman appeared to be jumping, crushing, fighting, and running at top speed all on her own, a quality that made her bold feats all the more real to young audiences. Furthermore, the Bionic Woman wasn't forced to wear the go-go shorts that compatriots like Wonder Woman donned; her uniform was a loose-fitting pantsuit.

Bionic Woman was a short-lived hit, lasting only from 1976 to 1978, but her image long surpassed the series' run. As for the newer version of the series, even *Entertainment Weekly* opined, "*Bionic Woman* is a flowery-feminist show whose go-girl premise depends on some dude asserting control over a young woman's body without her permission."[2] The same could be said of the original, which also frequently relied on Jaime's relationship with Steve Austin to generate plotlines. Although Jaime might have implicitly served men, she was much more autonomous than other prime-time women battling villains.

Enter *Wonder Woman*. Other shows featuring the superheroine had appeared on television already—a cartoon on the early-'70s animated series *Super Friends* and the 1977 *All-New Superfriends Hour*—as well as in a limp 1974 made-for-television movie starring actress Cathy Lee Crosby.[3] None of these earlier images are as memorable as that of Lynda Carter, the television series' live-action Wonder Woman—a series that fiddled with the nuances of the early, patriotic themes of the comic, shifting her 1940s, World War II patriotic duties into present-day situations. Steve Trevor, the man she was sent to protect from malevolence and to whom she was still hopelessly loyal, now worked for the government in a vague "security"-type capacity. The show was a tribute to Wonder Woman's strength: She performed leaps and captures, wrangled the truth from deceitful villains, and dodged bullets. She was graceful and gracious as well, and on occasion easily carried an unconscious or injured Steve in her arms, as superheroes have always done with females in distress. Carter's costume and physical image took a page from the comic book: Her athletic, healthy body sported the gold-eagle bustier and star-covered briefs.

Like *Bionic Woman, Wonder Woman*'s presence on television was brief—it only aired from 1976 to 1979. The superwomen of the '70s were fun and strong, but none of the shows invested in high-quality programming. While the special effects were, understandably, limited by the decade's television technology and budgets, the shows' plotlines were also usually thin, and the acting was often subpar.

The quality wasn't what resonated with young girls, though. Along with a slew of merchandise marketing for both series, the images lasted much longer than the actual programs because they captured young girls' active imaginations, giving those who weren't comic-book fans pop culture–based action-adventure role models of their own. While Mattel marketed its traditional line of Barbie dolls, Kenner released a Bionic Woman doll (complete with robotic implants in the arm) and Mego sold a line of Wonder Woman action figures, offering girls who favored both dolls and superheroines a host of possibilities for play outside of Barbie's fashion, homemaking, and romance-oriented pursuits.

For all their positive points, the 1970s prime-time heroines were sometimes still objectified. Naturally, wardrobe choices in the superheroine realm were an extension of a stylistic history long practiced in comic-book pages. The original characters were created in a genre whose audience was composed overwhelmingly of boys, a fact evidenced by the great number of male heroes, versus the handful of females. Superheroes were, of course, forced to don tights and Speedo-esque briefs, and, like Batman and Robin, have long been the butt of jokes about homoeroticism. Females, in turn, were inarguably drawn by men and for men, to represent the male ideal of the female body.

Today, little has changed about the comic-book aesthetic: Female heroes are still drawn with disproportionate chest sizes and infinitesimal waists for the benefit of their audience, even in recent covers of *Wonder Woman*. Hollywood has followed comic books' suit, and the standard female action hero wears what has become typical superheroine garb: bikinilike briefs and bustiers that convey an air of sexual suggestion.

But the combination of smart and sexy isn't all bad or damaging. Superheroines aren't submissive, and the tide has turned so that heroines across genres are doing the saving as often as they are being saved. It's the costumes' roots that are problematic, as they made female action heroes of the earlier twentieth century much more vulnerable to voyeurism, especially since women and girls were not dressing skimpily in the 1940s, '50s, or much of the 1960s—until the advent of the miniskirt. While some costumes, such as those in the *Catwoman* movie, are more explicitly sexual than others, they follow a stylistic formula originally marketed to young boys. Where male heroes have become symbols of perfect masculinity—handsome, suave, strong, immortal or nearly indestructible—heroines emerge as "perfect" females, complete with sculpted bodies, camera-ready faces, mostly agreeable natures, and revealing costumes, as well as the necessary ethical code and an instinct for heroism. We've witnessed the evolution of women in action and superhero films from damsels in distress to heroines fighting for justice or life, and now heroines who no longer rely on sex appeal or traditional costumes pack more of a punch for female audiences by adding an element of realism, as *The Matrix*'s Trinity, Ellen Ripley in the *Alien* series, *The Terminator*'s Sarah Connor, and suburban high schooler Buffy the Vampire Slayer do.

Sometimes fantastic heroine beauty or physical perfection comes in another package altogether. In 1976, the TV series *Charlie's Angels* premiered; it ran through 1981. The show featured three women who began in the police force but found themselves relegated to working as crossing guards and phone operators, so they opted instead to become private detectives. Unfortunately, the show's political overtones ended there. The Angels were working, single women who were dedicated entirely to their jobs. But throw in a slew of suggestive undercover outfits topped off by blindingly shiny hair, and the women were primarily fulfilling the 1970s Aaron Spelling formula for success: Women who were easy on the eyes, plus a plot light enough on content to focus on their sexiness. As a cultural image, *Charlie's Angels* has renewed its icon status with younger generations, thanks to the 2000 film version of the series and its less successful sequel in 2003, but the original concept, arriving at the height of the women's movement, offered its characters little room for autonomy by planting them firmly under the thumb of Charlie, their mysterious boss.

In the opening sequence, Charlie introduced their story by saying, "Once upon a time, three little girls went to the police academy." The effect of the line was quickly reversed when the three gorgeous Angels graced the opening sequence, sitting in hot tubs, strutting in bikinis, and flipping their astoundingly perfect hair. While they always managed to outsmart villains and solve crimes, their under-cover disguises as secretaries, magician's assistants, or models often played to male fantasy. Kris (played by Cheryl Ladd) once went un-dercover as a pigtailed "dumb blond" drenched in light-pink clothing. First-season star Farrah Fawcett also went on to become one of the most popular sex symbols of the 1970s.

As for the show's action, the women were often held captive or trapped in precarious situations. They ran *a lot,* mostly feebly, and chased, tripped, or pushed criminals, rather than kicking them directly to the ground and pinning them there. The amount and type of action on *Charlie's Angels* were indicative of the 1970s' signature lack of television subtlety, but the Angels' often weak physical attempts also highlight how far the mainstream action heroine has come—from high heels and perfect lip gloss to one who regularly kung fus, kickboxes, or body-slams her way to safety.

In some ways, the film version of *Charlie's Angels* mocked the absurd blend of three glamorous women, delicately fighting crime without mussing their hairstyles, and plotlines that indulged in serious themes, such as an episode in which television's Angels uncovered a forced pregnancy and black-market baby ring. While other films, such as the *Starsky & Hutch* remake, are overt send-ups of the original series, *Charlie's Angels* didn't satirize the centerfold sexiness of the original. The film modernized the three women, who were experts in disguise, detonations, and martial arts, providing much more interesting action sequences than the pantsuited, feathered-haired maidens found on television. But the TV series' saving grace, the fact that romantic interests took a back seat to the women's jobs, was casually brushed aside in the film. Instead, the movie's subplots revolved around the women's relationships: Lucy Liu's Alex Munday struggled to keep her profession a secret from her action-actor boyfriend; Cameron Diaz's spirited and endlessly dopey Natalie fell in love; and Drew Barrymore's character was introduced to the audience as she woke up in bed after a one-night stand, and was eventually kidnapped by the film's villain after she had slept with him.

The movie's rapid pacing, nonstop soundtrack, and highly complex action sequences made it easy to watch without attending to its underlying messages, but scenes in which the women were clearly sexualized above all else undermined their empowered qualities. More than anything, the newer crop of Angels was willing, able, and fun—an extension of the light characters on the series. But despite all the movie's upgraded special effects and extended fight sequences, double entendres and dance sequences that emphasized the Angels' sexuality made them come across more as "girls gone wild" than as killing machines.

As the *Charlie's Angels* television series began to fizzle, sci-fi warrior Ellen Ripley showed up to replace it. Ridley Scott's *Alien*, one of the first films of the 1970s to bring women's physical strength to the screen, combined the suspense of the new blockbuster action films such as *Jaws*, the sci-fi craze triggered by *Star Wars*, and the independent women of films like *Alice Doesn't Live Here Anymore*. Cinema of the late '60s and '70s also offered up now-classic fare featuring women at the epicenter of horror, such as *Rosemary's Baby*, *The Exorcist*, and *Carrie*. Yet horror films tended to focus on women with bodily or psychic connections to the supernatural—long the fate of female characters since the witch hunts of the Middle Ages and the 1600s, and throughout the course of modern literature. While the films are amusing and suspenseful, there's certainly nothing new or inherently empowering about watching women embody evil or house demons.

Ridley Scott, a director with a more progressive vision of the action heroine than most of his peers, has presented several strong female leads: In addition to *Alien*, he directed *G.I. Jane* and *Thelma & Louise*. Released in 1979, on the heels of the '70s feminist revolution, *Alien* was no *Barbarella*-type camp; it boasted a then-high budget of approximately $11 million and high-quality filmmaking and special effects. Far from being an Angel, Ellen Ripley was a serious action heroine in a movie with a respectable, suspenseful, and meaningful story line. Finally.

Alien followed seven crew members on a futuristic space mission, on which they discovered a malicious alien life form that attached itself to human hosts and killed them to reproduce. As the ship came under siege from an alien life form and the crewmembers were picked off one by one as they hunted the lurking enemy, Ripley was left alone to escape the monster.

Sigourney Weaver's Ripley sweated and swore and battled the alien attack until the final minutes of the film. Unlike so many women in the suspense and horror genres, Ripley faced her fear, was saved only by herself, and never expressed a desire to be rescued. While the less glamorous road was well traveled by female actresses in the 1970s, Ellen Ripley's look was tougher than the fairly standard sans-makeup Hollywood image. It was also striking to see both female crew members—Ripley and her colleague Lambert—free of the sci-fi space skirt that was prevalent on the first *Star Trek* series, which had premiered in 1966. Ripley was muscular and toned. She was a strong female with a deep voice who never hesitated to state her opinions or appear forceful with a mostly male crew. When she tried to articulate her plan for how to rid the ship of aliens and was interrupted by a crew member, she yelled, "Will you listen to me, Parker? Shut up!"[4] Ripley then spat that she wanted to "blow [the alien] right the fuck into space."[5] As she safely watched the spaceship *Nostromo* explode from the shuttle to which Ripley had escaped, the heroine muttered bitterly, "I hate you, you son of a bitch."[6] She was a far cry from affable vixens with blinding smiles and long-lashed, glittering eyes. Instead, *Alien* featured females who never took on the characteristics of either decorative or emotionally unstable women.

It's also interesting to note who survived the alien war longest. Caine, Ash, and Dallas—the white men on board—were killed first; two white women and one black man survived longer. The characters that are typically considered the most "expendable" victims in mainstream horror and suspense films were given in *Alien* more of an opportunity to develop and prove their heroism.

Ripley was essentially the ultimate female action hero, free from the humiliation of becoming completely sexual—until the very last scene, that is, in which she stripped down to her underwear once she had made it from the self-detonating ship to a safer shuttle. Rendered entirely vulnerable once she had undressed, she then discovered that the alien was on the shuttle. Because Ripley had worn crew gear throughout the film, the transition from hiding her body to displaying it completely was startling. The moment was ultimately suspenseful, but it also gave men the opportunity to see Ripley as physically defenseless and appealing, and it nullified some of her more gender-neutral qualities. It's almost as if Scott knew a male audience would need sexual vulnerability to keep Ripley "feminine" and audiences comfortable. Why else would she have packed a bikini-brief set for a long spaceship job?

The success of *Alien,* which grossed more than $70 million at the box office, inspired a series of three more films, beginning with *Aliens* in 1986. James Cameron occupied the director's chair, and the era was different. Both of those circumstances conspired to bring longer shoot-'em-up sequences and lighter banter to the film, typical of the propensity of 1980s' action films toward slimmer plotlines, mediocre acting, and dialogue that stated the obvious. In some ways, *Aliens* took on more characteristics of the action genre than of sci-fi. Ripley, like the rest of the film, was tougher and more determined than she was in *Alien.* As in the first film, she battled a resistant crew and eventually led a mission on which she was initially an outsider.

Ripley sported an even shorter hairstyle and remained mostly makeup-free. But Cameron also, unfortunately, retained Scott's original costume choice: Ripley appeared in her underwear not once in the film, but twice. Twice—because it was a sequel? The repetition of this image revealed what male audiences—or Cameron, at least— found legendary about their heroine. Still, Cameron ultimately didn't shortchange Ripley; women's appearances were changing in Hollywood in the '80s, once again becoming overly made up (in such films as *Working Girl*) or overtly sexual (as in *Flashdance's* burlesque imagery), but Cameron didn't force Ripley (or his other action heroine in *The Terminator*) to revert to a glossed-over, more conventionally feminine look.

In both *Alien* and *Aliens,* references to gender were laced into the storylines. Ripley's disrobing aside, the first film can be read as a story about the new woman breaking away from a traditional female role. Mother, the *Nostromo's* talking computer, represented the old guard, the earlier generation, or the systematic oppression of women as a whole. Ripley also fought forced fertilization by an alien and escaped into uncharted territory—much like the feminist and working-woman revolution out of which *Alien* arose. In the sequel, Ripley took on maternal qualities in her relationship with rescued survivor Newt, a young girl left behind in an invaded human colony. Newt and Ripley's relationship inched closer to a mother/daughter one when, in a hackneyed parent/child scenario, Ripley put Newt to bed. The film's climactic rescue planted Ripley and Newt in a nest of alien eggs, face to face with the mother alien as she laid them. The mother tore herself from birthing to chase Ripley after she destroyed the nest. And in the final showdown, Ripley fought the mother alien and prevailed once again, only to climb back into that bikini underwear, as if she had to sustain objectification by men to be seen as both a victorious warrior heroine and a woman. Still, Ripley remains the least decorous or traditionally feminine sci-fi idol of the 1970s and '80s. Even the gun-waving Princess Leia—also a less conventional leading lady—had to negotiate a ridiculously draped robe (while her fellow resistance fighters wore leggings) and a heavy, intricate, albeit iconic, hairstyle.

James Cameron also directed the first two films of the *Terminator* series that began in 1984. Both movies became quintessential Hollywood blockbusters. *The Terminator* featured Arnold Schwarzenegger as a robot sent from the future to kill Sarah Connor. In the first *Terminator,* the role of the heroine was closer to that of a horror-movie victim turned conqueror: Arnold was a monster sent to destroy Sarah, and she fought him only at the end of the movie, after her male protector had been killed. Linda Hamilton, who played Sarah Connor in the first two *Terminator* films, was never a helpless victim; she participated actively in chase scenes and showdowns. However, she was also not the iconic figure in either film—as in horror movies in which an antihero corners a female lead, the film's entertainment value lay in Arnold Schwarzenegger. Although Sarah defeated him in the end, the monster was notorious and got to deliver memorable punch lines such as "I'll be back."

The enigmatic monster is a regular theme of horror stories from *Frankenstein* on, but in the '70s and '80s, villains such as Jack Torrance in *The Shining* and Freddy Krueger in *Nightmare on Elm Street* terrorized women who fought back, only to have the men's gleeful viciousness be remembered as the movies' real enjoyment. As a heroine, Sarah Connor suffered the same fate. The final duel in *The Terminator* forced her to kill the machine only when she had no other choice. Her coup de grâce consisted of pushing a button to crush the Terminator with machinery—a less-than-heroic device for an action flick's epic conclusion.

By the series' second installment, *Terminator 2: Judgment Day*, James Cameron brought Arnold back as a terminating robot reprogrammed for good, not evil. Once again, the Terminator was sent back to the past, this time to protect Sarah and her son, John, from T-1000, an evil, upgraded Terminator. In *Terminator 2,* Sarah Connor was more physically toned and less feminine-looking. After wearing pink throughout the first film, she sported tank tops in the sequel.

She'd amassed an arsenal of weapons to combat Terminators and had sharpened the ax she'd grind—she was singularly focused on preparing for the Terminator's return.

Everything in the second film was upgraded: The effects employed the best of digital technology, the acting and dialogue were improved, and Arnold became even more comedic in his new protector role. Rather than crushing the new Terminator with machinery (as she did in the first film), Sarah wielded a massive gun to do the job. In the sequel's final showdown, Sarah played a more active and eager part in offing the robot, blasting away at T-1000 repeatedly. Still, in the end it was Arnold who finally destroyed the threat.

Sarah Connor was an energetic and strong action heroine. But she had male guardians in both films—Kyle Reese in the first film, and Arnold in the second—who ended up doing most of the work. By the time *T3: Rise of the Machines* was released in 2003, Sarah Connor was gone, and so was James Cameron. The film revolved around an adult John Connor, paired with Claire Danes as the more delicate Kate Brewster, whose bravery paled in comparison with Sarah's. The Terminator was female, blond, beautiful, and as nasty and violent as her predecessors. Neither the film itself, nor T-X, the female robot, became as renowned as the first two *Terminator* films did.

While Ripley battled aliens in outer space and Sarah Connor fought futuristic enemies, *The X Files'* Dana Scully investigated supernatural activities on Earth. The television series ran from 1993 to 2002 and was made into a feature-length film in 1998—and again in 2008. Gillian Anderson's Dana Scully was not your average heroine, either. One of a duo of FBI agents who handled X files—FBI investigations dealing with the supernatural—Scully was thoughtful, knowledgeable, and the less frivolous of the two agents. Costar David Duchovny played the intuitive, occasionally squeamish foil to Scully's more hardboiled investigator and scientist. Scully was articulate and mostly calm, a straight-faced detective and sassy scientist all at once. Other heroines have had to slip in and out of glamorous clothing, but Scully's signature style comprised dark-colored suits, a completely realistic wardrobe choice for an FBI agent. While her intelligence was extraordinary, she had no superhuman strength and no "powers" to keep her from appearing as an ordinary woman dealing with extraordinary (or extraterrestrial) circumstances.

The Matrix trilogy, a series of sci-fi films released between 1999 and 2003, featured Trinity as the action heroine. Played by Carrie-Anne Moss, Trinity was always a hard-driving, serious woman with the same physical capabilities as her male costars Keanu Reeves and Laurence Fishburne. The Matrix was heavily stylized, and the stars' cool was emphasized through their clothing, their speech, and their behavior. All three deadpanned their way through the films, and Trinity was just as knowledgeable as, if not more so than, Neo (played by Reeves). The Matrix's heroic team members were able to download programs that allowed them to perform superhuman physical feats in the artificial world of the Matrix, but their success and survival still depended upon their instincts and smarts, and Trinity was one of the most accomplished resistance fighters. While her clothing hinted at femininity in some scenes, Trinity retained her ultracollected exterior throughout the trilogy, remaining completely stoic through long fight sequences and highly exaggerated gun battles. Prior to her assaults, she often delivered the type of one-liners that are usually doled out by male action heroes like Schwarzenegger and Bruce Willis.

Avoiding the gender extremes that traditional action and adventure movies feature, Trinity and Neo were similarly androgynous: They both wore sunglasses and almost identical clothing; demonstrated comparable attitudes; and had the same skin, hair color, and hairstyle. As leading love interests and side-by-side fighters, Trinity and Neo displayed physical and emotional parallels that dissolved classic trappings of gender in the *Matrix* films and that are a cinematic rarity. Indeed, beyond Trinity's romantic interest in Neo, which was certainly not a main plot fixture in the trilogy, her gender didn't come into play.

The *X-Men*, both as a comic and as a film series, combined forward-thinking ideologies similar to those of *The Matrix*. Sexual and racial equality played important roles in the superhero-driven, good versus evil storylines. The film trilogy, a blockbuster film series that began in 2000 and ended in 2006, portrayed a group of mutant humans, feared and being hunted by the public and the U.S. government. The X-Men's mutations, which often took the form of superhuman qualities or skills, were considered undesirable by the human population. The films revolve around alienation and acceptance, and the rebel outcasts are both the prey of authority and the force of general "good" in the films. As in many sci-fi-oriented premises, the females fought alongside their male counterparts and had equal powers and status. The film series featured an ensemble cast that included female characters Jean Grey (Famke Janssen), Storm (Halle Berry), Rogue (Anna Paquin), and Mystique (Rebecca Romijn). And though the trilogy's gender roles were no less complex than its notions of good and evil, the characters periodically fell victim to stereotyping.

All three films focus in part on the struggles of Jean Grey, a doctor with telekinetic powers. Grey was the ultimate heroine in one film, the force of destruction in another. As her alter-ego Phoenix in *X-Men: The Last Stand*, she initially exhibited her deadly power as sexual, seducing men in the midst of her chaos. Her complex character vacillated between good and wildly bad, calm and complete calamity. While Grey was an effective leading blockbuster heroine, her destructive and forceful qualities were kept in check by the men who feared her. When such qualities were unleashed upon the world, it was a male character (Magneto) who encouraged her appetite for evil, and a male character (Wolverine) who had to kill her to save the planet. Jean Grey's cohorts, Storm and Rogue, also flaunted heroic traits, albeit in more traditional ways. Storm controlled weather systems to combat her enemies, sometimes draped in vinyl and costumes intimating bondage. Her ability to be a leader was one of her character's main strengths, although her role was less engaging than the women surrounding her. Rogue, obsessed with worry that she'd hurt those who touched her because of her power to generate extreme heat, found herself constantly conflicted by the sexual and physical struggles that came along with her mutation. A runaway whose look was more reminiscent of a teen rocker than a superhero, Rogue could have been the rebel of the X-Men film series; her sexuality brimmed at the forefront of her struggle and made her more of a typical leading female in film. By the end of the final film, Rogue decided to renounce her mutant abilities and become human in order to pursue her romantic happy ending.

Mystique was a mutant who could take the exact shape, voice, and image of anyone she chose. Fearlessly, she was able to slide beyond the boundaries of the complex moralities the trilogy presented, sometimes performing heroic feats and other times inflicting harm. She was ultimately loyal to Magneto, however, and her lack of empathy toward humans made her seem overwhelmingly defiant and angry. In the end, Mystique embodied the hardened evil-female role.

While women were integral to plot development and action sequences alike in this trilogy, the male characters' powers were more overtly aggressive and physical. Cyclops shot lasers, for instance, and Wolverine fought with knives. The women's powers were more mystical and abstract, and more aligned with the supernatural, pushing up against the territory that witches and occult film heroines occupy.

Despite this, in all three films it's ultimately the women who save the world. When Rogue and her male mutant peers escaped an attack on Professor X's school, it was Rogue who insisted they return to save Wolverine. Mystique gained entry to the lair of a character attempting to orchestrate war between mutants and humans. In *X2: X-Men United*, Jean Grey made the consummate sacrifice by giving up her life to save her fellow X-Men. While women making sacrifices isn't unusual on film or in reality, the theme of women as the ultimate heroes of a coed ensemble set this trilogies apart, which is ironic given the series' chosen name: X-Men.

Other female action films have revolved around gender as well, such as Ridley Scott's 1997 film *G.I. Jane,* about the first female Navy Seal's struggle against military sexism. A bald Demi Moore starred as Jordan O'Neill, the embattled Seal who withstood the verbal and physical harassment of her commanding officer and fellow soldiers, as well as false claims that she was gay. *G.I. Jane* isn't a widely remembered film, but it added to Scott's catalog of strong female leads and showcased Moore's physical strength and determination. In addressing sexism directly, it also infused what would have been an otherwise standard plotline with political and social significance. Not only did the film provide serious tests of Moore's and her character's physical prowess, it also illustrated women's potential for having powerful convictions and a desire to escape the confines of socially defined femininity, as was the case in a scene in which Moore shaved her head, voluntarily abandoning vanity in an effort to gain acceptance from her male fellow soldiers. Once again, Scott focused on a fierce woman overcoming serious career and personal hurdles—and this time, she was doing so on Earth. Like *Thelma & Louise* (and unlike most action films), *G.I. Jane* was written by a woman, Danielle Alexander.

Unfortunately, *G.I. Jane*'s groundbreaking visual aesthetic was never granted to Sydney, the leading character in the prime-time series *Alias*. Jennifer Garner starred in the cult hit, which ran from 2001 to 2006. Sydney, a double agent for the CIA, was a kind of female James Bond. Armed with various gadgets and dropped into outrageous espionage situations in cities around the world, she defused bombs, picked locks, and always cornered, if not pummeled, her enemies. She was a highly intelligent, multilingual, courageous character with emotional depth and humanity. She was also unflinchingly daring, and emerged victoriously from dangerous scenarios.

However, Sydney also slipped in and out of costumes and situations that repeatedly objectified her. Although sequences following her sexier scenes usually contained a physical fight or a hot-and-bothered nemesis surrendering information, the moments that eroticized Sydney were longer, often panning the length of her body slowly, and relied on the typical formula for sex-object shots in film, such as slow motion, blowing hair, or the spy girl's emerging soaking wet from a pool. Sex also permeated the *Alias* atmosphere when Sydney disguised herself as a dominatrix in a red leather bustier and confidently descended a staircase at an S&M club in Berlin. In order to wrangle information from a potential informer, she bound him and took risqué photos of them together to use as blackmail material. In another episode, Sydney modeled lingerie, subject to a sequence of slow-motion shots of her in different outfits, walking the length of a hallway and waving a riding crop. As she pounced on her target, she spat out a complaint about how uncomfortable it is to wear lingerie. But the ensuing fight sequences and her acknowledgment of her discomfort rang hollow after repeated escapades that purposely planted her in those types of situations.

"Garner has the extraordinary confidence to allow Abrams and Co. [the show's creator] to use her like a doll," wrote *Entertainment Weekly* in 2002. "She gives over her long face and lanky body to any wig, any lipstick hue, any outfit, and becomes a startlingly alert woman whose thinking is always a half step ahead of her enemies, her allies, and us."[7] Sydney *was* doll-like: The show's dark aesthetic relied on her wigs and clothing to provide a splash of color in certain scenes, emphasizing her looks above what was going on around her. Her ever-changing appearance became as intriguing as some story lines, and after a few episodes, anticipating her wardrobe and wig changes became an aspect of viewers' engagement in the show.

There's little doubt that her character's decorative qualities played into *Alias*'s popularity. While her real-life persona is distinct from her character's, Jennifer Garner became a successful sex symbol and was named the "hottest woman" of 2002 by girlie mag *Maxim,* which was certainly influenced by her *Alias* scenes. No matter how strong Sydney was, the show's music-video montages and shots of her body presented mixed messages about her objectification, positioning her image uncomfortably between serious spy and predictable eye candy.

Action heroines have generally been required to embody both sex and street smarts, and while much of the 1970s passed before Hollywood began inserting women into more action-oriented, autonomous, and heroic roles, some blaxploitation films, such as Pam Grier's movies of the early '70s, gave women onscreen mobility and complexity much sooner. Blaxploitation movies' smaller budgets and their creation outside of the Hollywood system meant filmmakers didn't have the same easy access to glossy, high-quality special effects as Hollywood action films did. Blaxploitation films' guerilla nature worked in their favor: The genre wasn't subject to content and dialogue restrictions or concerned with big-studio fears of offending or alienating mainstream audiences. As a result, the films were able to speak to and for the black community by addressing social issues and the power structures plaguing ghettos and big cities in the 1970s. Blaxploitation is really the only surviving pop culture vehicle outside of literature containing explicit messages about black oppression and urban decay previous to rap's rise in the 1980s. As a genre, it was able to go farther than television shows addressing social issues such as *All in the Family* or *Good Times*, both of which acknowledged and sometimes openly discussed the issues that plagued the decade, but being prime-time television, could only go so far without alienating their wider audience.

Actress Pam Grier became blaxploitation's female archetype, starring memorably in the vigilante vehicles *Coffy* and *Foxy Brown,* released a year apart, in 1973 and 1974. Director Jack Hill featured a stylish and sensual Grier avenging drug and prostitution exploitation in urban areas. Beyond being sexy and fashionable, Grier's characters operated on their own terms, reacting to the ways in which drugs and prostitution affected their lives. She took on systems of oppression single-handedly and engaged in vigilantism—the only option, she believed, for battling corrupt authorities.

While the struggle of being a woman, particularly a black woman, was threaded throughout the plots of both films, Grier's characters were subject to sexism. Director Hill took advantage of scenes in which Grier appeared physically threatened to bare her breast or rip her clothes revealingly, and shot those scenarios from voyeuristic angles that lingered on her exposed body. While women can relate to the brutality with which Grier's characters sought revenge after such moments, they are clearly shot to hold the attention of viewers with other, more prurient interests.

The sly Foxy was an interesting blend of femininity and ferocity: She was topless numerous times throughout *Coffy,* yet she fought for justice in the black community. She also avenged her own rape and captivity by killing her rapist and another man who fed her heroin. When Foxy's boyfriend was killed, she discovered that the guilty party was the head of a prostitution ring, slipped into it, and ended up publicly humiliating a judge who hired her. She also liberated another captive prostitute and sent her off to Seattle to rejoin her husband and child. The gun-toting, enraged Coffy was identified as a "liberated woman" by her politician lover, and deftly used her sexual power to seduce her captors and disentangle herself from threatening situations. Coffy and Foxy both used sex to ensnare unsavory men; the pimps and johns they encountered were usually killed or injured—but only after some kind of sexual encounter.

The messages of Foxy and Coffy weren't always clear, especially considering the films' random portrayals of lesbianism. An odd scene was thrown into the middle of *Foxy Brown,* in which Claudia, the prostitute Foxy was trying to rescue, ended up at a gay bar populated by humorless lesbians whom Foxy fought off in a bar brawl. It was a completely gratuitous degradation of lesbians—as was a scene in *Coffy* in which Coffy visited a junkie prostitute, seeking information about a pimp and dealer. The prostitute's girlfriend, a commanding, demanding butch, came home to find a threatening Coffy holding her girlfriend down. As Coffy slipped away from the situation, she giggled as she heard the beginning of a domestic dispute.

But the women always did get their revenge. Foxy's and Coffy's missions were complete when they had destroyed men who either brutalized them (Foxy) or used them (Coffy). Foxy dealt castration to a white dealer in *Foxy Brown*—employing a method historically, brutally used against the black male population. The iconic look of black pride, the afro, which appeared in both *Coffy* and *Foxy Brown,* was an expression of liberation—and acted as a stash for Grier's characters' weapons: It hid a gun in *Foxy Brown,* and razor blades and a small pin used to kill a gangster. The afro not only recalled black liberation in blaxploitation; it was a symbol of vigilante power as well. The cultural significance of a black woman playing a part that wasn't a nurse or a maid was different enough. On the heels of the civil rights movement and black liberation, a sensual black woman's avenging her community's oppression took subversion one step further, and her castrating and killing white men made the film more deeply revolutionary. Although sexism was linked to exploitation in both films, the number of nude scenes distracted from messages of male blame by providing audiences with erotic suggestiveness, which may be one reason the films weren't taken more seriously.

Foxy Brown and *Coffy* were transformed from B-movie fare into fearless films through the use of justice-seeking characters and fairly radical political dialogue, featuring issues and images Hollywood has never presented. Pam Grier's characters also came out of the films alive and intact, having succeeded in carrying out all of their plans for revenge. Unlike in *Charlie's Angels*, which premiered in prime time two years after *Foxy Brown*, Grier had no controlling, faceless boss steering her. Her own conscience and decision making propelled her into her role as autonomous renegade. Pam Grier's characters might have had help, but they plotted vengeance alone.

Grier's films also provided a clear message about exactly how the black community was being held down, and by whom, and glorified working for righteousness outside a corrupt system. Viewing Foxy through the lens of 1970s abandonment of inner-city black communities can make her seem an inspiring action heroine, one who certainly helped lay the groundwork for actresses to come

*T*hirty years after *Foxy Brown*'s debut arrived *Kill Bill*, Quentin Tarantino's two-volume epic depicting the vengeful lone survivor of a wedding-rehearsal massacre. *Kill Bill*'s iconic status is, admittedly, questionable due to its recent release, but history has shown that Tarantino films quickly become cult classics. *Kill Bill* was loaded with new takes on action-heroine and rebel imagery. In typical Tarantino fashion, it paid stylistic homage to two very male genres: outlaw/cowboy sagas and '70s kung-fu films. It featured leading males from the kung-fu and action genres (actors Sonny Chiba and David Carradine) and transplanted women into a colorful, updated interpretation of otherwise rote formulas. The assassins who worked for Bill were also all female, and all engaged in lengthy, ultraviolent showdowns with the Bride, played by Uma Thurman.

In the tradition of the nameless, mysterious rebel, the avenging character was identified only as "the Bride" in the first volume's credits, along with her assassin alias, Black Mamba. The loner Bride always fought back, never cried, and eventually trumped her attackers, who sometimes arrived in assembly-line fashion, allowing the Bride nothing more than a breath between full-on kung-fu fights. Overblown, shocking violence is another Tarantino tradition, which he usually handles cartoonishly. *Kill Bill*, though, could be highly disturbing and was controversial for some feminist audiences.

Tarantino's glorified antiheroes exist amid rich, unexpected, and colorful visual aesthetics, with smooth camera movement and unusual angles to match his soundtracks, which are informed by the blaxploitation, kung-fu, and action genres. He spared none of his signature style for *Kill Bill*'s female assassins, making them the true equivalent of his cache of killer men. The first volume of the film exaggerated its female characters' cool attitude, especially during O-Ren Ishii's walk through the House of Blue Leaves. She strutted, framed by her gangster minions, expressionless, unfazed, and stylized. As with so many male mobsters before her, the owners of the establishment bowed as she passed by. The Bride swept through swordfights with O-Ren Ishii's gang, the Crazy 88, without a hint of emotion, other than an occasional reaction to pain. And the final face-off between O-Ren Ishii and the Bride was a classically constructed outlaw confrontation: The two women were left alone to duke it out once everyone else had fled or been killed.

While the Bride's toughness matched that of female action hero Trinity's, it also used gender to motivate her (and to drive almost all of the film's other women to violence). The Bride's raison d'être was motherhood; at the end of the film, when Beatrix (the Bride's real name) showed up to kill Bill and found her long-lost daughter living with him, she was instantly transformed into a feminine figure: Having worn jeans and boots and occasionally outlaw leather throughout both films, here she wore a lace-trimmed tank top and a skirt. The abrupt wardrobe change, particularly on a woman who was about to enact her ultimate revenge fantasy, suggested that she was "tamed" by her maternal nature, or that the filmmaker guessed that motherhood and outlaw leather don't mix. For all her killer instincts, in the end Beatrix became the polar opposite of the traditional male rebel: She ran toward domesticity, not away from it.

Tarantino has written interesting, complex, and active female characters into other action films, such as *True Romance, Pulp Fiction,* and *Natural Born Killers,*[8] but these women often serve as plot foils— another bias plaguing films about male rebels. Virtually every female in *Pulp Fiction* wasted men's precious time: Uma Thurman's Mia overdosed; Fabienne (Maria de Medeiros) limited her boyfriend's valuable time to escape—by *crying,* no less; and Honey Bunny (Amanda Plummer) was a seemingly cold-hearted criminal who had a breakdown in the middle of a restaurant holdup. In both *Natural Born Killers* and *True Romance,* the lead women—Juliette Lewis and Patricia Arquette, respectively—were in typically victimizing situations of abuse and prostitution, and both were rescued by male lovers.

Given all the action heroines bogged down by various gender biases, whether through story lines or objectification, a series like *Buffy the Vampire Slayer,* which was stripped of gender stereotyping, cast the predictable gender traits of other action heroines in sharp relief. The program, which aired from 1997 to 2003, was highly successful with young audiences—it helped to increase the WB's advertising revenue 137 percent between 1997 and 1999—and it continues to have a cult following today.[9]

As a self-identified feminist, *Buffy* creator Joss Whedon has stated that he purposely created a character that melded a superhero's strength with a feminist awareness. "[O]ne of the reasons I've always been attracted to female heroines," he explained, "is that I have always been interested in the people nobody takes seriously, having been one the greater part of my life."[10] Buffy, played by Sarah Michelle Gellar, a high school student who fought vampires lurking in her school, wore typical high-school-girl gear—mostly pants, at that—and was not routinely sexualized throughout the series. The characters surrounding her included equally natural-looking (and acting), socially awkward, smart, and sarcastic friends. While muting the sexual potential for a plot rife with possibilities for it, Buffy battled like a warrior and stood tough throughout long fight sequences and standoffs with various creatures from the underworld. Buffy also dealt with being an outcast because of superpowers that made her vastly different from her high school classmates and from the typical suburban town in which she lived. The show displayed the inevitable awkwardness of being a high school student and the confusion of being a girl growing into a woman, never mind one with a tremendous responsibility to protect humans from the vampires stalking them. In the way she assumed responsibility, Buffy bore some resemblance to the iconic, youthful Spider-Man, another teen outcast burdened with extraordinary powers.

Other characters were equally unconventional. Willow, Buffy's witch sidekick, had lesbian relationships that normalized homosexuality and made the show's same-sex portrayals more than voyeuristic—a novelty on mainstream television marketed to teenagers. Angel, a romantic interest who caused Buffy great turmoil (he was a vampire), provided eye candy for female and gay male viewers alike. In being subjected to domination and bondage by both high school girls and female vampires, Angel became an unpredictably objectified teen idol, and offered adolescents a more commanding, less explored side of female sexuality.[11]

The show had an extensive run, continues to have a rabid fan base, and was financially successful. Despite the reflex of both television and Hollywood to produce more of what has already been proven popular, most other television producers didn't attempt to recreate Buffy, a unique, brave, victorious, extremely popular character who remained free of the ever-present obligation to be seductive that plagues other female TV characters, even adolescent ones. Only the series *Charmed* attempted to follow in Buffy's footsteps, but the show featured three women already objectified in mainstream culture, Alyssa Milano, Shannon Dougherty, and Rose McGowan. The young women on *Charmed* all possessed secret powers and regularly fought and outsmarted demons, but they were also hyperfeminine and upheld television's ideal of youthful beauty. The show was often entertaining, but neither the fairly flat characters nor the plotlines were as overtly smart or quirky as those found on *Buffy*.

Above all, the action heroine who can provide an adrenaline rush for female audiences requires a sense of real independence. Even the superheroes are usually tied down: Wonder Woman's television persona was beholden to Steve Trevor, the Bionic Woman was on-again, off-again with Steve Austin, and the Angels were, from the outset, characterized as Charlie's property. *Alias's* Sydney was voyeuristic fare too often to appear in control. Characters like the Bride, Foxy, Coffy, and Ripley, however, acted on their own, made their own decisions, and generally hatched their own plans, whether they let the audience in on those schemes or not. The Bride traveled around the world, training, stalking, and avenging, and never revealed her plan for revenge until it unfolded onscreen. Sarah Connor was beholden to decisions she would make in the future, thereby working for a larger cause she hadn't even experienced yet. Buffy was responsible for keeping her town, school, and personal life from inevitable harm, while Ripley rebelled against the organizations she was hired to protect and hurled herself wordlessly into outer space. The more heroines are unfettered by the presence of bosses or protectors, and the more they trust their own instincts and intellect to guide them, the more adventuresome and admirable they can seem to other women—especially to women seeking new directions. After all, if the heroine can't fly, the least she can do is fly by the seat of her go-go shorts.

Hollywood has finally allowed fighting, active, physically and emotionally strong women to be included in its definition of what's sexy. As the cadre of action heroines grows, the depth and variety of action films can provide women with affirming moments, even if those movies aren't always as empowering from start to finish as *Alien* is. Girls seeking modern rebels have a wealth of opportunities to discover female role models who have interests other than marriage and are engaged in behavior other than merely reacting to leading men. Aside from the sexuality that insists on planting itself in the midst of otherwise adrenaline-fueled story lines, maybe respecting women's ability to be believable action heroes is victory enough—at least for the time being.

chapter 7
Uneasy Riders

We have the facility to judge each other by entirely different criteria than [those that are] imposed upon us by the superstructure of society. We have a view which reaches beyond profit margins into poetry, and a vocabulary to articulate the difference.

Thanks for including me, Ms., really. But just promise me one thing; if I drop dead tomorrow, tell me my grave stone won't read:

ani d.

CEO.

Please let it read:

songwriter

musicmaker

storyteller

freak.[1]

—Ani DiFranco, in a 1997 open letter to *Ms.*, after the magazine
stressed her financial victories over her artistic ones

So far, overblown media hype and drama and no-holds-barred
sexual content are key components of twenty-first-century
culture. Given our instant access to information, female rebelliousness
is relatively abundant and easy to find, but with these privileges
come the burdens of the century's other phenomena—including
reality television's scattered personalities and an increasing trend
toward using celebrities' personal lives for entertainment. As a result,
female rebellion is often overshadowed by the foibles of pop culture's
damaged women.

As personalized technology, such as iPods and TiVo, increasingly
allows us to customize our exposure to news and entertainment, the
degree to which we share collective cultural experiences lessens. As a
result, which celebrities and rebels will survive beyond this generation
to become lasting icons becomes less clear. What we individually
consider rebellion impacts us as much or as little as we dictate. Our
tailored approach to media facilitates our ignoring any loathsome
or discomforting ideas, people, opinions, images, or events on any
given day, so we can remain safely within our comfort zone and avoid
anything new, different, or challenging.

The Internet's ability to provide anonymous spaces means we
can vicariously create an air of rebellion without actually living it,
and without actually interacting with other insubordinate women.
Based sheerly on the level of fiction we can conjure, anyone can

create a courageous online persona. Our own personal rebellions can be shunted into a space that's separate from our reality. On the upside, constructed, enigmatic online identities mean that the traditional trappings of a female icon aren't necessarily at play. But they also mean that we can't always rely on rebellion in cyberspace for inspiration—when women's cultural value is still contingent upon physical beauty, the rejection of beauty standards remains a potent aspect of female revolt.

The more time we spend communicating online in intimate, individual, anonymous ways with equally anonymous audiences, the less we intimately engage in reality-based revolt. As a result, the bravery and confrontation that were once integral parts of everyday rebellion in our real lives aren't necessary in our virtual ones. Then again, young women with digital access can also easily find other women who are upending the world, and can create revolutions of their own.

*T*here is no clear-cut recipe for creating an icon today. Eight years into the twenty-first century, questionable and somewhat lasting infamy has been bestowed upon the subjects of reality television; a hotel-chain heiress; celebrities' children; mostly mediocre actresses; and pop stars dropping glossy, overproduced songs and videos into a largely predictable catalog of contemporary music. Even women's popular books now fall into the vapid category of "chick lit," and superficially depict the lives of career-oriented, fashion-forward young women, as in the best-selling 2003 novel *The Devil Wears Prada*. The media and its consumers have become enraptured by indulgent young women who have achieved fame for nothing more than the shock value of their drug- and sex-related exploits.

Britney Spears, Paris Hilton, Lindsay Lohan, Kate Moss, and Angelina Jolie are a few of the handful of women repeatedly deemed newsworthy by network and entertainment outlets alike. Highly trafficked blogs driven by celebrity gossip, like Perezhilton.com, Tmz.com, and the Gawker Media group have become increasingly popular over the last few years, too, and add to the glut of daily news stories and silly scoops about celebrity women. The networks went as berserk as gossip blogs did when Paris Hilton was facing jail time for violating her 2007 court-ordered probation for drinking and driving. Even CNN's stale old television talk-show host Larry King dedicated a program to the argument over whether Hilton should serve time. CNN also reported live from the courthouse when Britney Spears was expected to attend a custody court hearing in 2007. A flood of reporters from around the world hounded Angelina Jolie when she went into labor in Namibia in 2006. Aside from Jolie—who works with the United Nations for the rights of global refugees—the women gaining the attention of the world are mostly priority news items for having breakdowns and various mental illnesses, eating disorders, and addictions. While we may dismiss these stories as insignificant, their impact on pop culture certainly is not.

For youthful women seeking something more meaningful than gossip, there aren't accessible, alternative images that attain the same high level of "importance" in the news as the lives of Hilton, Spears, and the like. The isolation a woman often experiences during her teen years as she searches for deeper meaning and intellectual engagement can increase when the adult and cultural worlds around her are thoroughly obsessed with exactly the same concerns as the stereotypical teenage girl is: diets, shopping, and boys. What younger women do see, without extended life experience to teach them otherwise, is a world where women's instability, blatant sexuality, self-destruction, and greed become qualities to be rewarded with adulation or media exposure. This kind of veneration inevitably affirms the message that our greatest mistakes and weaknesses—rather than our strengths, victories, and personal vision—are what generate the most attention and keep tongues wagging.

On the flip side, we do have women-owned, women-run, substantive, and easily accessible magazines, such as Bitch, BUST, and Ms. And some blogs, such as Gawker Media's Jezebel, cover fashion and celebrity news with a healthy balance of dry wit and feminism. Defiant Jezebel representatives went so far as to pass out "gift bags" to attendees of Fashion Week in September 2007—barf bags emblazoned with the Jezebel logo. The bags' contents acknowledged the modeling industry's rampant eating-disorder problem by including tongue depressors, mints, and ex-lax.[2]

Feministing.com is another online forum for hip, young-feminist discussion. Some movements within hip-hop also speak out against sexism (namely, MySistahs and Take Back the Music), and writers such as T. Denean Sharpley-Whiting and Joan Morgan explore and express the culture's effect on young women. There is a host of prolific female experimental musicians, as well as irreverent, ever-evolving songwriters such as P. J. Harvey and outspoken, insistent ones such as Kathleen Hanna (both of whom are now major-label acts); Missy Elliot, with her inventive hip-hop; and Londoner M.I.A, who creates world politics–focused pop. Strong-voiced, unique, passionate writers, such as Michelle Tea, Suheir Hammad, Sister Spit's spoken-word performers, and Zadie Smith, are abundant. And women like Mary

Gaitskill, Joan Didion, and Toni Morrison demonstrate continuing passion for and celebration of female difference.

And while the overriding politics of the last eight years of conservative reign in the United States has divided the country over hot-button moral issues and war, the nation is teeming with rebellious and outspoken females, even if they aren't as prominent as the shallow, consumerist, or self-destructive women over whom the media fawns. Among these are peace activist Rachel Corrie, killed in Palestine in 2003; Jill Carroll, the compassionate American journalist who was kidnapped in Iraq in 2006; and organizations such as Women for Women International. Progressive Afghani, Iranian, and Saudi women risk their lives for equality. Gender rebels nationwide and around the world are living open and full lives, and activists are fighting for civil protection and liberties for the gay, lesbian, bisexual, and transgendered communities.

Girls are fed traditional teen escapades on film, and the press delighted in its 2007 and 2008 press coverage of Britney Spears' meltdown. Britney's widely documented head shaving in 2007 could have signified a rejection of the schoolgirl/sex-kitten image she had projected for so long. But her unpredictable behavior following that act, such as alleged threats of suicide and her inability to care properly for her children, nullified the possibility that bald Britney might become a more powerful statement than bombshell Britney.

The media has happily engaged in such feeding frenzies in recent years, relying on unwound women like Spears for sales. The turmoil has apparently worked for audiences, too: Celebrity magazines alone—such as *OK!, In Touch, Life & Style,* and *Us Weekly*—which are all marketed more to women than to men—experienced an overall circulation upswing in 2006 and 2007, even as print media underwent a general decline.[3] When sales figures keep climbing, stories on women's deterioration become an increasingly valuable commodity to be swapped, marketed, and mocked in the media.

So, what do the covers, which far more people than the magazines' readers see, say? In the first two months of 2008 alone, magazine covers one-upped each other in their teasers on the latest in the Britney scandal. *In Touch* wondered if Britney was "delusional," and ran a separate cover of her emblazoned with the quote "I'm Not Crazy!" *Life & Style* went even further when one cover promised details on Britney's "multiple personalities," and *Star* magazine was eager to brand Britney "Insane!" in the same month.

Singer Amy Winehouse, who has considerably more talent and depth to offer than most haunted Hollywood-gossip fodder, bounced in and out of rehab for the latter half of 2007 and into 2008. Photos exhibiting a rail-thin, pale, drooling, and allegedly high Winehouse got major exposure in her native England and in U.S. gossip weeklies and blogs. At the same time, teenage girls began donning their own interpretations of Winehouse's fantastically exaggerated beehive and '60s-inspired eyeliner. With her ever-present dramatic makeup and teased hair, Winehouse is the physical opposite of the pop-star parade of cosmetic perfection, and her singing and musical styles are strikingly different from most of today's pop. Borrowing from '60s soul, she reflects more self-deprecation, anger, and blunt language than most other mainstream songwriters—even if she still pines for love and men. And while Winehouse was rewarded for her musical artistry with five Grammys in early 2008, her very public and voracious drug addiction often overshadows her work. The media's focus on her bad habits detracts from our ability to enjoy her irreverence, which has become defined by her indulgences instead of her individuality, her uncommon and striking physical appearance, and her refusal of mainstream beauty standards that still hold true for other pop stars. Without an addiction and an on-again, off-again marriage, Winehouse might represent the success of the tough bad girl with a tender side—the kind of girl many of us secretly admired and imitated (or were) when we were growing up.

If there aren't drug habits to report on, there's always sex. Thanks to Paris Hilton's massive leap to fame following million-dollar profits for a sex tape leaked in 2004, the shock value attached to unbridled sexuality now extends well beyond the submissive, available standard Marilyn set in the 1950s. Many young girls today believe that being hedonistic and blunt about casual sex is sexy, newsworthy, daring, and fun. As Ariel Levy documented in *Female Chauvinist Pigs,* young, mostly heterosexual women have begun, in larger numbers, to burst into the boys-will-be-boys club, rather than venturing down new, more interesting paths celebrating sexuality on their own terms. Trips to strip clubs and brazen declarations of a love of pornography meant to be marketed to men are now considered "cool" activities for young women. Indulgence through shopping, and exhibitionism and lesbian acts intended to attract male attention, have all become markers of a new kind of resistance for young women. But the new, aggressive version of mainstream female sexuality merely reinforces what men want, rather than making girls more autonomous. Sexually voracious young women are resisting the rebellion that helped them get where they are—

feminism's strong rejection of the typical "sexy" standard and of female behavior meant only to provoke male attention.

Marriage and motherhood have also somehow slipped into a pattern of seeming to oppose the status quo while actually reinforcing it. Today, the right to work that made rebels out of 1970s feminists is rejected by increasing numbers of women who choose to buck careers and retreat to the home front. While the number of marriages has decreased over the last few years in the United States[4]—intimating less traditional views about familial structures and marriage in general, and a shift in domestic roles—moms' attitudes toward work have changed. The number of working mothers who favor working full-time has fallen eleven points, while the number of at-home mothers who would want full-time work has dropped eight points since 1997.[5] Furthermore, the number of at-home mothers who prefer not to work climbed nine points in ten years.[6] A Pew Research Center survey conducted in 2007 found that 81 percent of women surveyed felt their relationships with their children and partners were more fulfilling than anything else in their lives. The same survey revealed a job or career to be the least important factor in their personal fulfillment.[7] Of course, choosing domestic life over a career is just as legitimate a choice as the option of staying single or focusing on a career. It's just confounding that the more choice we are granted, the quicker some women revert to tradition.

With more women opting for the domestic life that our feminist foremothers rejected, household bliss is emphasized. Women have long been told that our wedding day is the most important day of our life, and cable television presently runs programs, like *Bridezillas* and others, in which weddings happily wrap up a series of errors connected with them. *Bridezillas* delights in women's stress and selfishness leading up to their wedding days, justifying temper tantrums and the singular focus on wedding planning. Bridal programming, along with the aggressive marketing of engagement rings and wedding-related romantic comedies such as *Bridget Jones's Diary, Monster-in-Law, Wedding Crashers,* and *Meet the Parents* still posits a wedding as one of the only versions of personal success. In reality, wedding mania seems to increase every year. According to TheWeddingReport.com, approximately $65 billion was spent on U.S. weddings in 2007.[8] Because this industry is so profitable, advertisements are fraught with aggressive, repetitive messages for (mostly female) young audiences and viewers throughout the year. No matter how much choice we're offered, we're bombarded with the role we're told we've always wanted to play, and that is supposedly most satisfying for young women. Clearly, returning to traditional ways of living rather than redefining them isn't rebellious at all—particularly when doing so upholds the same dogma that more conservative camps reinforce.

Single women on television might prevail, though. In 2001, *Six Feet Under* premiered on HBO; it ran from 2001 to 2005. The hit series followed the members of the Fisher family, who owned a funeral home and were dealing with the death of their father. It also featured smart women with fully visible dark sides: Brenda Chenowith, a highly intelligent, independent woman with a penchant for self-destructive behavior; Claire Fisher, an outcast, artistic young adult struggling with her search for self; and Claire's mother, Ruth, who was discovering who she was after a lifetime of being a wife and mother, were three of the ensemble's leading characters. Another vibrant and outspoken addition toward the end of the series was Bettina, played by Kathy Bates. Bettina became Ruth's wisecracking partner in crime, teaching the more retiring Ruth how to shoplift, indulge herself, and seek adventure. The series highlighted women who continually questioned their own choices, took and left lovers, followed their own instincts (sometimes grappling with unfavorable outcomes), and didn't conform to Hollywood conventions of beauty or behavior. It also portrayed complicated relationships that didn't always end happily or cleanly; during the series finale, Ruth finally derived more fulfillment from her female friends than from men. Unfortunately, Brenda's later life turned out to revolve around her damaged brother—but then again, the plot didn't depend much on happy endings. Claire eventually did find love, but only after she sought her own fulfilling path.

The single most influential show marketed to women since its debut in 1998 is HBO's *Sex and the City*. The show's reruns are heavily syndicated, and it has profited heavily from DVD sales. With opening weekend profits higher than $56 million for the 2008 feature film, *Sex and the City* shows strong signs of remaining in the iconic-female annals.

Sex and the City was undeniably entertaining, but not consistently rebellious. It did, however, uniquely depict the lives of four professional women in Manhattan and their dating travails without implying that they were pathetic for being single. They also weren't portrayed as anomalies anxiously jumping at the first available date. Each woman embodied a single-female stereotype: an oversexed, singularly focused older woman; a more repressed, baby- and marriage-obsessed WASP; a hardened, intellectual, feminist lawyer; and a supposedly quirkier, inquisitive writer. Quick wit, quality writing, fairly good production quality, and a candid approach to once-taboo topics such as oral sex, nonmonogamy, same-sex relationships, and abortion made the show a nationwide hit. But the main characters' lifestyles were also as luxurious as the fashion magazines from which their outfits were selected. All four women were glamorous, decked in designer duds, and fairly privileged; they shopped and ate out and exclaimed loudly over one another's ridiculously expensive shoes.

While *Sex and the City* broadened representations of women's sexuality to some degree and compassionately articulated some of the struggles single womanhood involves, it also reinforced the idea of female revolt as singularly sexual. The most outrageous, bold, and defiant character, Samantha, based her rebellion on completely sexual terms. While fun to watch, Samantha was typically thin and blond, and overly concerned with physical appearance. She could magically redirect almost every conversation to sex—which wasn't all *that* different from the cultural reflex of earlier decades to equate women's badness with sexual activity, no matter how bluntly she could put a man down, or how quickly she could kick him out of bed.

The consumer culture and compulsive shopping habits that supposedly define the Western woman were also tied into the *Sex and the City* phenomenon. Soon after the show debuted, magazines such as the consumer-goods publication *Lucky* appeared; it hit newsstands in December 2000 and now boasts a circulation of 1.1 million.[9] Between women's magazines like *Lucky* and cable's reality-TV programming featuring makeovers, fashion, models, and hairstyles, the majority of the products being marketed to women—

and to which women are responding in large numbers—contribute intensely to a message that we're willing to spend anything on fashion and cosmetic surgery, two indulgences that rely heavily on female insecurity. Programming and advertising dollars directed at female audiences in the twenty-first century reveal how our culture still perceives women: as self-, food-, and diet-obsessed impulsive spenders who would rather be shopping than doing almost anything else—unless a woman follows in Samantha's footsteps, in which case sex is a priority over sample sales.

Women can find some inspiration in *Sex and the City* and its stars. The show constantly prioritized female friendship over romantic relationships, was light on infighting and female competition, depicted personal fulfillment detached from male approval, and revealed at least three of the four women as being more concerned with self-discovery and experience than with babymaking and marriage. However, Charlotte, the character who was alternately elated and miserable, depending on her marital status and how close she was to having a picture-perfect, upper-class life, tempered the message of the other three women. The addition of a character like her also increased the show's accessibility for viewers feeling pressured to fulfill traditional female roles. But Miranda, Samantha, and Carrie searched for love and satisfaction on their own terms, and Carrie's final voice-over during the series finale stressed, " . . . [T]he most exciting, challenging, and significant relationship of all is the one you have with yourself. And if you find someone to love the you you love, well, that's just fabulous."[10] While that statement doesn't necessarily overshadow the series' consumer-driven, aspirational aspects, the program at least ended with a message that was more interesting, engaging, and empowering than the romantically based "happy endings" to which women are usually subjected.

While the fashion industry sells women on buying luxury goods, styles associated with rebellion for much of the post–World War II twentieth century went commercial, and then, more recently, beyond commercial to high fashion. Clothing bearing skulls, crossbones, and tattoo designs, and motorcycle gear such as leather jackets and biker boots, is sold in department stores and by higher-end sportswear designers like Ed Hardy. The continuous mass marketing of the punk aesthetic, music, clothing, and attitude means that those former indicators of real rebellion are now status symbols and sales tools—hollow echoes—especially when they're overpriced and intertwined with designer logos and names. Rebellion no longer represents the individuality once associated with the rocker or biker look—it stands for having spending money.

The advertising industry finds rebellion fashionable, too, using it to equate individualism with consumer decision making. There's the Secret campaign that has revamped its old "Strong Enough for a Man, but Made for a Woman" motto to the faux-feminist tagline, "Strong Enough for a Woman," appropriating women's empowerment to hawk deodorant. Chevy's "American Revolution" campaign has reduced revolt to the act of the company producing a truck, and the consumer purchasing one. Brands attempt guerilla marketing through interactive online messages meant to connect customers with brands that pass for original. Levi's launched a 2007-2008 design competition to create a new pair of jeans, and Dove sponsored a contest challenging consumers to develop a new commercial in 2008.

The do-it-yourself ethos long associated with underground music and art now has corporate cachet. Even *Easy Rider*'s Dennis Hopper has traded in his chopper and his love beads to endorse the investment firm Ameriprise.

With recently successful popular female singers like Amy Winehouse, Fergie, Beyoncé Knowles, Gwen Stefani, Pink, Rihanna, and Mariah Carey, the pop-music industry has not marketed real rebellion since hip-hop and alternative music in the early 1990s, followed by the late-'90s (albeit questionable) shift toward loner males with axes to grind, like Eminem. Hip-hop has transitioned from boasting about killer rhymes to bragging about expensive toys. The more corporate and mass marketed rock, hip-hop, and pop become, the less likely we are to find a subversive figure in the bunch whose controversial qualities aren't rooted in self-indulgence.

As madness, marriage, addiction, and exploitative hedonism dominate the news, images of female rebellion become lost once again in society's reinforcement of traditional womanhood. Women are still characterized as fragile, unstable, and in need of rescue—the polar opposite of the male rebels who fascinate our culture. The same media outlets that feed on Britney's insanity and Paris's sexual activities scramble to make nice with the public when women spontaneously slip up on their own. Jane Fonda's and Janet Jackson's recent media gaffes, which both involved the female body, were perceived as inappropriate enough to create media spectacles out of minor incidents. Whether the moment was accidental or planned, a seconds-long shot of a blurry nipple (which was shielded) during the 2004 Super Bowl half-time show made a pariah out of performer Janet Jackson—even though the program's expensive beer commercials probably revealed more of the female form than she did. Jane Fonda sparked a day or two of press coverage and public outrage in February 2008 when she mentioned a monologue, entitled "Cunt," from *The Vagina Monologues* during a conversation on NBC's *Today*. Thankfully, when Fonda apologized for using the word, she noted how "silly" it was that people were offended by it. (A quick perusal of coverage of Fonda's on-air comment also revealed remarks from furious readers still crying foul over her 1972 trip to Hanoi.)

These spontaneous blunders underscored society's discomfort when women's bodies are referenced or revealed independent of the media's or the public's preapproval. The "offenders" were forced to apologize for not adhering to cultural expectations of decency, even when the incidents were mistakes, and even when the media chooses to sell and document far more unsavory female behavior. Once again, though, there's a silver lining: The extreme reactions that Fonda and Jackson provoked mean that rebellion today can be as simple as slipping a moment of chaos into the media's overly palatable, tentative, and hypersensitive programming.

A facade of insurgence is also well worn in the political arena. In a fervent backlash against the Clintons' eight years in the White House, members of the right wing, and particularly the latest Bush administration, have been exuding a false sense of rebelliousness to boost their popularity, play "tough guys," and present their maverick images as refreshing and new. Bush's down-home persona—underscored by his Crawford, Texas, ranch, cowboy boots, swagger, and smirking speech—pushed an agenda making an aggressive case for war while repeatedly telling the press that the administration had little interest in swaying Americans politically. The Right also used the same kind of manipulative tactics to invigorate evangelical voters and slow cultural progress—and feminist progress, including abortion rights and safer-sex education—and a host of civil-rights platforms stagnated in the process.

In adapting the characteristics of the rebel while not evidencing anything close to actual rebellion, the Right became another unfortunate and misleading face of current cultural uprising. On the other hand, real rebellion was repeatedly squelched. There was the backlash following Natalie Maines's criticism of the president, and when more unwelcome resistance to the administration's stance arrived, as Kanye West stated on a live, televised fundraiser in the wake of Hurricane Katrina, "George Bush doesn't care about black people," the press pounced. (A quickly repentant NBC cut West's remark from the show before it aired in the Pacific time zone.[11]) Both West and the Dixie Chicks are minority rebels who, against the backdrop of a culture fearful of appearing unpatriotic, were truly courageous in risking their hard-won popularity to take their individual stands.

But still, the forces of pop culture predominantly take the low road. Five reality television programs made the top-ten list of most-watched shows of the 2006–07 prime-time television season.[12] Their presence on that list emphasized the popularity of programming that privileges spectacle above all else, usually through coverage of unstable, competitive women. In fictional prime-time television ventures, *Desperate Housewives* was the buzz of its debut season in 2004, winning six Emmys for its over-the-top satire of disturbed suburban domesticity. In recent years, television has added some female characters and programs that focus on women who balance out the notorious and devious housewives: The highly popular *Grey's Anatomy* features the sarcasm and passion of Christina Yang (played by Sandra Oh), and crime and detective shows such as *Law & Order* and *CSI* include career-driven, intelligent leading females. *Ugly Betty* studies the travails of a young, down-to-earth girl working in fashion; a clairvoyant (played by Patricia Arquette) solves crimes on *Medium*; Holly Hunter stars as a self-destructive detective in *Saving Grace*; and Kyra Sedgwick is hardened investigator Brenda Johnson in *The Closer*.

Both *Weeds* and *The L Word* contain fairly complex elements of gendered rebellion (along with a mixed bag of other messages). *Weeds* tells the story of Nancy Botwin (played by Mary-Louise Parker), a suburban housewife and mother, who, when her husband dies young, is so desperate for money that she transforms herself from a conventional middle-class woman into a drug dealer—and evolves into a tough-minded businesswoman during the series. *Weeds* also provides running commentary on the conformity of middle- to upper-class suburban living in the United States. Nancy is surrounded by narcissistic neighbors, such as the nasty and competitive Celia Hodes (played by Elizabeth Perkins) and Kevin Nealon's Doug Wilson, Nancy's brazen accountant and customer. Nancy's subversions are often similar to Foxy Brown's or Coffy's—she escapes various situations by seducing predatory men or competing drug dealers. Nancy does what she needs to do to survive, but sometimes what she needs to do borders on being a gratuitous plot twist. Still, Nancy is an interesting character whose morality isn't black-and-white; she's tough and resourceful when necessary, and proudly rejects the conventionality of her wealthy community.

The L Word focuses on a circle of lesbian friends in West Hollywood. An early advertising campaign for the show touted the rather
witty and telling tagline, "Same Sex, Different City." No wonder—
over the last five seasons, the characters have become increasingly
glamorous, and the show has become more consumerist in the same
way *Sex and the City* did. Viewers can log on to Showtime's website
to find out how to purchase the designer clothes *The L Word*'s stars
wear, and the show has run sweepstakes for shopping sprees. But *The
L Word* has also addressed artistic censorship surrounding religious
conservatism, sexual experimentation, gender experimentation, bira-
cialism, bisexuality, coming out, same-sex familial partnerships, and
gender discrimination in the workplace. It's featured lesser-known
female musical acts, like Peaches and Tegan and Sara, and has hired
female directors, such as Mary Harron, who directed *I Shot Andy Warhol* and *The Notorious Bettie Page*.

In appearance, most of the women on *The L Word* reinforce traditional media-derived beauty standards, pursue mainstream careers,
and dress in conventionally sexy ways. Still, subversiveness is present:
The two most outwardly rebellious characters, Shane and Max, wear T-
shirts and jeans and are more androgynous than the rest of the show's
cast. Max's story line concerns the evolution of his gender identity, and
Shane is rigorously nonmonogamous; her history includes her mas-
querading as a male hustler. Another character, Jenny, who moves to
Hollywood at the outset of the series, begins cheating on her fiancé with
a woman, comes out as a lesbian, and ends up staying in Hollywood
on her own. Later in the series, a career soldier undergoes a "don't ask,
don't tell" investigation, comes out of the military closet, and quits the
army to be with the woman she loves. Another episode features Glo-

ria Steinem discussing lesbianism over coffee with the cast. And Kit, a character played by Pam Grier, is the cast's token straight woman, but even she experiments with lesbian relationships. The show's overall approach to sexuality is unexpected, yet relaxed and fluid.

There have been many groundbreaking moments on *The L Word*, as well as clear, open discussions of feminism, power dynamics, and class differences; however, the show also continues to glorify wealth, fashion, and glamour. While this tendency could be construed as revolutionary, considering stereotypical conceptions of lesbians as allegedly unattractive and almost always masculine, it promotes the same materialism that mainstream marketing to women targets. Because the show's creators keep the cast almost exclusively feminine, they also sustain the marginalization of butch lesbians and miss a golden opportunity to defy mainstream myths that such women are transgressive.

Hollywood may not have budged much, but female filmmakers, artists, and performers of all kinds express diverse perspectives on women's lives. With access to the proper avenues and a little ingenuity, women can uncover myriad ways in which to dig new forms of revolution out of the cultural sludge. The crux of our challenge to claim rebellion for ourselves and make it new, different, and prominent is our rejection of the hero worship associated with traditional rebel males.

Scratching the surface of pop culture to find more interesting and high-profile women with the potential to outlast their own generation is demanding. Even '80s rockers such as Debbie Harry, Joan Jett, and Cyndi Lauper, who once seemed assured of their longevity, have faded into semi-obscurity or musical pigeonholes. Courtney Love, one of the most outspoken female musicians of the last fifteen years, has shed her run-down, feminist-rocker image for designer clothes and a rigorous overhaul via cosmetic surgery. Her recent behavior slots her more in the category of Lohan or Moss; she's a far cry from her earlier antiestablishment self.

Not that other musicians haven't picked up the torch; there are plenty of talented, underappreciated women in indie rock, noise, punk, and hip-hop. Even pop singer Pink released the angry and thoughtful song "Dear Mr. President" in 2006. And the Gossip's large frontwoman, Beth Ditto, posed nude for the cover of *NME* in 2007. Acts of insubordination are going on everywhere—we just need to celebrate them publicly.

The musician closest to establishing a lasting image of the modern woman rebel is Ani DiFranco, a career singer-songwriter whose catalog has evolved along with her subject matter and sound. From her first independent release in 1990 to her nineteenth in 2007, DiFranco has told the changing story of being a woman in America—and a realistic, grounded woman at that. Since the early days of her career, DiFranco has sung about sexual violence, feminism, abortion, labor, the working class, her own definition of and struggles with love, her bisexuality, and being an indie artist pursued and misunderstood by mainstream record labels and the press, all within the context of her own life. She also infuses her music with thoughtful and empowering content for women without leaning on constructed, traditional sexuality to hold her audience's attention. Her feminism is mostly humorous, too: She criticizes the patriarchal structure in a much more accessible and lively way than most feminist rhetoric does, and in the process battles the cliché of the humorless, single-minded feminist.

DiFranco's guitar is staccato and sharp—it doesn't smoothly and calmly lull listeners through a song—and her voice warbles and yells and then whispers, in no predictable pattern, as if she is trying to chase and pin down her gleeful, chaotic strumming.

DiFranco's poetry, as unpretentious as her political content, remains steeped in the everyday. In early work, such as "Fixing Her Hair," DiFranco sings about a long-locked friend shaking her tresses in the mirror. A bald Ani observes with haunting portent the root of her friend's happiness, an abusive man. "Imperfectly," on the surface, tells the story of the narrator crashing her friend's car. Against the backdrop of a banged-up pickup truck, the lyrics urge listeners to joyfully accept physical imperfections. DiFranco's politically grand thoughts trickle underneath the mundane ones, and neither type revolves solely around love and loss.

DiFranco's work represents a digression from both the folk music of the '60s (which on the surface was typically hard pressed to elicit a giggle) and punk rock (which usually channeled either absurdity or rage). Somewhere between punk and folk, she has embraced individuality, transcending the stifling political correctness that marked the '90s. Accomplishing what is often seen as an impossible task, she has also become an icon of both the business and artistic worlds. Her ability to maintain indie credibility and her political and social consciousness while building her fan base and a self-sustaining business is unprecedented, particularly for female musicians.

For a long time, DiFranco's life consisted mostly of touring and performing, at first by herself. In some ways, her story represents the perfect culmination of Kerouac's longed-for freedom, and the vindication of a woman trapped by the political climate, such as Billie Holiday. With a zest for living that oozes from her work and not merely her public image, DiFranco humbly embodies many characteristics of the traditional loner rebel, all the while incorporating progressive politics and an insistence on being herself into her professional life, her participation in the press, and her work. As she described in a 2003 interview:

> *So even when I'm writing about a love affair or something very private as part of my experience as a young woman in the world, I think of it as very political stuff. I'm aware of it as being so. But now that I'm, whatever, 32 or something, it's like it's my problem. My government, my country, and the current political international crises are my problems because I'm an adult American. I find that, unwittingly sometimes, I feel more connected to the superstructures of society. We're born into these systems, but we're very much outside them when we're young. It's like it's not our society. We have no power. We're only learning, really, how it works and what our role in it is. I'm writing about big-P politics for the first time, just because it's more a part of my life now. Suddenly I'm a voting adult and it's my job to fix it.*[13]

Beyond musical aesthetics, which are always subjective, DiFranco's career choices, deep sense of personal responsibility, and willingness to speak her mind and retain relative control of her public image can be inspirational. DiFranco is a reminder that women can continually question their life choices and unapologetically change their minds, as well as define their own version of success. She wouldn't say being a female rebel is easy, but she helps us believe it's conceivable. The possibility of leading a successful and happy life on one's own terms, as a public and proud woman, is the most important concept to take away from DiFranco's work.

Even with careers as impressive as DiFranco's, there's no easy way to tell which women's stories or images will become signature symbols of this decade's pop culture. I'd like to think that what we'll cherish is not the "downward-spiral" trends, but the rebel who rises above the compulsion to make a nervous breakdown a public spectacle. A rebel girl today is someone who can remain down to earth in the midst of a culture that is injected with monumental doses of narcissism. Maybe, by eschewing beauty standards and designer fashion, she opts out of the stereotype of the greedy, vain, diamond-encrusted, starving woman. This rebel girl goes against the grain and she knows why—she can articulate it in her own voice, tossing aside the tired clichés of sexual exhibitionism, addiction, and insanity as tactics for making herself known. The rebel girl defines "sexy" for herself. She does not carry $500 handbags. She will never invest her hard-earned money in stomach stapling or Botox.

She eats carbs, throws away her scale, and honors women in ways other than those promoted by the rabid paparazzi. She doesn't hesitate to travel alone, keenly understands that having children isn't the only way to have a fulfilling experience as a woman, and will thoroughly assess marriage before entering into it. The rebel girl supports like-minded women and creates space for difference, rather than perpetuating the competitive female self-loathing brought on by an endless parade of advertising. She recognizes that feminism's causes and concerns are hardly passé. She knows that there are rebels out there who are infinitely more interesting than Jack Kerouac, James Dean, or Neal Cassady.

She understands that sometimes the rebel girl has not been born a girl or should have been born a boy, and will protect others' right to be their outcast selves without having to endure discrimination. Beyond the haze of her computer screen, she is her uncontrived, possibly contentious, honest and shameless self in reality. Her language may be sarcastic and biting, and is always open and delivered with a dash of joy. As is true of so many rebel girls before her, her value will be acknowledged only when time has caught up with or even surpassed her, but the real rebel girl does it anyway, out of love for living out loud.

Women's history of rebellion on our own terms, the kind that can send Kerouac packing, includes a century's worth of female rebels. Maybe that means we can fight, kick, sing, teach, write, argue, organize, inspire, create, paint, sculpt, swagger, and praise each other loudly, to ensure that examples of rebellion remain present and prevalent for later generations of restless, curious young women. Since pop culture has never gotten it quite right, the solution is to question what we can, and to set healthy, creative, brave, constructive examples. The answer, you see, is actually quite plain: The next rebel is you.

conclusion

Cultural icons are steeped in the mythology that's been created
around them. In both fiction and reality, pop culture's most
venerated images also represent, and buy into, the most limiting
aspects of traditional gender roles. For men, being "bad" is lauded,
becomes literary legend, and is propped up by Hollywood's history
of male antiheroes. "Bad," in all of its gradations and variances—
abandonment, occasional apathy, unhappiness, violence, even the
tough guy with a heart of gold—has shaped society's more typical
conceptions of rebel behavior.

Obviously, our culture rarely celebrates similarly rebellious
behavior in women and rebels of color. Pop culture's portrayal of
female icons has historically downplayed the badness nestled in

good girls, as well as the goodness buried in bad girls. For women, the term "bad" has a host of decidedly unadmired connotations, brought into play to criticize women the minute they decide to sidestep established feminine expectations and demonstrate a sense of autonomy, or display the curiosity and restlessness that make male icons seductive. Unlike for men, what's truly been defined as "bad" for women is adventure, cunning, waywardness, anger, biting wit, failure to uphold our gender's physical expectations, strong opinions, or too much passion. Representations of our rebellion have been restricted or misconstrued. Our boredom or dissatisfaction with, or our dislike for, pop culture is hardly a surprise, given that we're presented with such one-dimensional women—we've spent our lives surrounded by insufficient examples of inspiration.

When I started to think about writing this book, I was plagued by the question of why certain curious young girls—including me—picked up Kerouac as an introduction to American countercultural writing. *On the Road* sat on the bookshelf of virtually every young woman I knew—but it wasn't born of a counterculture that honored or even acknowledged us as people capable of committing acts of actual rebellion. The aesthetic continues to be riveting—but the women the Beats worshipped? They were fence posts, rest stops, support beams. They weren't Beat. They didn't *move*.

However, women have always moved in the same revolutionary ways as legendary men do—we've just had more to push against along the way. We've faced much stricter criteria for what makes us worthy of hero worship; misconceptions about what being a "real woman" means; and the overwhelming cultural demand that we travel the same, predictable roads of womanhood that existed before us.

Whether we've found positive images of our rebellion has depended upon whether it was trendy or marketable for women at the time, and on the media's fickle coverage of our movements.

In pop culture or real life, the minute a woman peers outside of the very small box she's been placed in, she's elicited reactions that aren't always positive. For women living in the public eye, sidestepping traditional gender roles —no matter how much they were adored—has always been a gamble. They might be branded forever for a slip-up or for saying something unpopular. Sometimes they're pitied or become a spectacle, such as when Janis Joplin became infamous for her self-destructive behavior, rather than for the talent that originally brought her to the fore. A public misstep might also end in a trial. Most of the time, rebellious women have been the targets of criticism, or have become invisible or forgotten once they refuse to act as women are expected to act.

The history of our behavior and how it is perceived can therefore be read through how we treat and interpret our cultural idols. What we've chosen to remember and revere also informs pop culture's fictional rebels, such as characters gone mad from oppression, like Thelma and Louise; the long-repeated stereotype of the furrowed-browed, sex-starved, man-hating feminist; or the characters depicted by writers like Alice Walker and Sylvia Plath. Our renowned figures in fiction, film, and television also perpetuate our expectations of women in reality: Monroe was forced to recycle her ditzy-blond role in one film after another, thereby feeding her public persona and dumb-blond jokes. The eternally smiling, waiting, youthful, and seductive pinup in Bettie Page's photos imparted just as much fiction about women's sexuality. The exaggerated, singular aggression of the sexually liberated Samantha Jones; the willing, loyal, always beautiful Angels; and Wonder Woman, ever ready to come to the rescue—such fantasies create higher, distorted expectations of us in reality.

But all these women need is a little depth, or a little perspective, to represent something more valuable to us. Then we can finally see ourselves beneath the veneer of surface goodness, badness, self-destruction, submissiveness, naiveté, blind anger, silent suffering, self-righteousness, violence, or witlessness.

Having been raised on pop culture, and having roundly rejected the whole behemoth as I got older, I have always been cynical about what someone like Marilyn Monroe could possibly teach me. But my cynicism has given way to admiration, considering how much more monstrous already oppressive standards were for women living public lives back then, when a large majority of the American public was dismayed by them or misinterpreted them. How strange it must have been to be assessed by total strangers in public, and by reporters in print, as suffragists were. How challenging it must have been for artists to conceive rebellious characters, like Woolf's Orlando, when they resided only in thin air.

The bias must have been maddening, too—to have burned with passion, on the level of Billie Holiday or Angela Davis or Alice Walker, and to then have walked into public spaces and had your opinions blasted immediately, both because you were a woman and because you were black in a culture in which preexisting beliefs and history kept you from being taken seriously, or even listened to at all. How irritating—to put it mildly—to try to speak to end a war or gain voting rights, only to be mocked or ignored. How enraging to be a feminist woman in love with a famous musician and forever blamed for the destruction of his most successful artistic achievement. And how discouraging to be so beautiful, so brilliant at the blond-bombshell caricature, that being taken seriously as an actress lands you right back in the same part over and over again—so much so that you're constantly expected to play the role to the hilt in your personal life.

Being a woman in the public eye and defining one's own terms of living are defiant (and tiring) enough to be admirable; these acts alone involve more rebellion than the entire white-male-rebel canon. In identifying deeper aspects of our icons' subversive qualities, we make room for and legitimize our own behavior—even our less desirable, selfish, mean streak—in our public or private life.

No matter how our culture at large might balk at, ignore, minimize, or erase the sassiest and strongest types of irreverent women, we need to make their existence known. Their example can pick us up by the collar when we're slumped over, make our hearts swell, and keep us going—headstrong, strong-willed, courageous, and swaggering off into the next sunset. We need female role models who haven't caved and who think—if only for respite from a culture currently overloaded with hypersexualized, overly self-indulgent women. Clever and demanding women who look different, sound different, contribute something, and press onward are necessary, at the very least, for us to sharpen our own tools of resistance—however light or heavy, blunt or sharp—and define what we want and how we are going to get it. Instead, pop culture, inadvertently or not, has a history of teaching women to devalue the power of other women's presence by celebrating the uninspired, completely predictable elements of femininity, when what we should be worshipping is the utter liberation that comes from tossing aside cultural demands.

The most important—and mostly absent—aspect of rebellion in our iconic women is a realistic sense of depth: courage and righteousness leavened with humor; sexuality balanced with discernment and self-care. We've been largely bereft of heroines who draw on their own innate strength and resourcefulness, outspoken women who have transcended their shyness, or ordinary females with greatness glimmering underneath their surface.

We are infinitely complicated women. Our images require as many layers as we ourselves contain.

Notes

INTRODUCTION

1. *Breakfast at Tiffany's,* directed by Blake Edwards (1961; Los Angeles: Paramount Home Video, 1999).
2. Plummer, *The Holy Goof,* 75.
3. Kerouac Archives, New York Public Library, "Beatific Soul," viewed November 2007 and March 2008; Charters, *Kerouac: A Biography,* 76.

CHAPTER 1: THE REBEL CURVE

1. *The Wild One,* DVD, directed by Laszlo Benedek (1953; Culver City, CA: Columbia TriStar, 1999).
2. *Raging Bull,* DVD, directed by Martin Scorsese (1980; Los Angeles: MGM/UA Home Entertainment, 2000).

3. Gunderson, "'Massacre' Sales Top 1 Million."

4. Lee, *Virginia Woolf*, 520.

5. Marlon Brando played the crooning gambler-turned-lover Sky Masterson in *Guys and Dolls*.

6. *The Wild One*.

7. Lyman, "Marlon Brando, Oscar-Winning Actor, Is Dead at 80."

8. Crowther, "'Streetcar Named Desire,' With Vivian Leigh, Has Premier at the Warner Theatre."

9. Lelyveld, "Jack Kerouac, Novelist, Dead; Father of the Beat Generation."

10. Charters, *Kerouac: A Biography*, 349.

11. Kerouac, *On the Road*, 133 (original emphasis).

12. di Prima, *Recollections of My Life as a Woman: The New York Years*, 102–03.

13. Charters, *Kerouac: A Biography*, 350.

14. Plummer, *The Holy Goof*, 42; Charters, *Kerouac*, 74.

15. Kerouac, *On the Road*, 42.

16. Charters, *Kerouac: A Biography*, 349.

17. Kerouac, "Article on Youth Movements."

18. Bangs, *Psychotic Reactions and Carburetor Dung* (New York: Random House, 1987), 216 (original emphasis).

19. Whitburn, *Billboard Top 10 Singles Charts*, 7–10.

20. Editors, "James Dean, Film Actor, Killed in Crash of Auto."

21. Fujiwara, "The Rebel."

22. Biskind, "The Enemy Within," in *Seeing Is Believing*, 200–02.

23. Kael, "Marlon Brando: An American Hero."

24. Biskind, *Easy Riders, Raging Bulls*, 45.

25. Ibid., 63.

26. Ibid., 64.

27. Davis, *Angela Davis: An Autobiography*, 182.

28. *Easy Rider*, DVD, directed by Dennis Hopper (1969; Culver City, CA: Columbia TriStar Home Video, 2002).

29. *On the Waterfront*, DVD, directed by Elia Kazan, (1954; Culver City, CA: Columbia TriStar Home Video, 2002).

30. Guralnick, *The Rolling Stone Illustrated History of Rock and Roll*, 20–21.

31. Ibid., 32.

32. Plummer, *The Holy Goof*, 6.

33. Charters, *Kerouac: A Biography*, 275.

34. DePaulo, "The Strange, Still Mysterious Death of Marilyn Monroe."

CHAPTER 2: CRIME AND PUNISHMENT

1. Echols, *Scars of Sweet Paradise*, 311.

2. Woolf, *A Room of One's Own*, 49.

3. Ibid., 76.

4. Lee, *Virginia Woolf*, 3.

5. Woolf, *The Diary of Virginia Woolf*, 3.

6. Ibid., 91.

7. Woolf, *Orlando*, 158.

8. Editors, "Suicide Note."

9. Repetitive themes of nature and time are repeatedly proven in Hermione Lee's *Virginia Woolf*.

10. Ted Hughes also published an intimate account of his relationship with Plath in a volume of poetry called *Birthday Letters*, which was published in 1998.

11. Pollitt, "A Look at the Poems."

12. Plath, *The Unabridged Journals of Sylvia Plath*, 98.

13. Frances McCullough foreword, *The Bell Jar*, viii.

14. Plath, *The Bell Jar*, 77.

15. Ibid., 69.

16. Ibid., 85.

17. Locke, "The Last Word: Beside the Bell Jar."

18. Duffy, "Lady Lazarus."

19. Plath, *The Bell Jar*, 243.

20. Aurelia Plath in Ames, Lois, "A Biographical Note," *The Bell Jar*, 262.

21. Karen Kukil foreword, *The Unabridged Journals of Sylvia Plath*, ix; Ted Hughes destroyed Plath's final journal entries.

22. Plath, *The Unabridged Journals of Sylvia Plath*, 391.

23. Editors, "Holiday Movies: The Dark Side of Christmas."

24. Eugenides, *Middlesex*, 221–22.

25. Ibid., 243.

26. Ibid., 518.

27. Clarke, *Billie Holiday: Wishing on the Moon*, 96.

28. Dufty and Holiday, *Lady Sings the Blues*, 79; Clarke, *Billie Holiday: Wishing on the Moon*, 140; Holiday went on tour with Artie Shaw in 1938, not in 1937.

29. Dufty and Holiday, *Lady Sings the Blues*, 84.

30. Ibid., 83.

31. Clarke, *Billie Holiday: Wishing on the Moon*, 128.

32. Dufty and Holiday, *Lady Sings the Blues*, 68.

33. Ibid., 86.

34. Davis, *Blues Legacies and Black Feminism*, 184.

35. Clarke, *Billie Holiday: Wishing on the Moon*, 168; the song was eventually recorded by Commodore Records, whose records were pressed by Columbia.

36. Mae Weiss, interviewed in Clarke, *Billie Holiday: Wishing on the Moon*, 140.

37. Barney Josephson, interviewed in Clarke, *Billie Holiday: Wishing on the Moon*, 161.

38. Clarke, *Billie Holiday: Wishing on the Moon*, 153; Davis, *Blues Legacies and Black Feminism*, 176.

39. Clarke, *Billie Holiday: Wishing on the Moon*, 176, 225, 346.

40. David Ritz foreword, *Lady Sings the Blues*, xv.

41. Editors, "Alone with the Blues."

42. Palmer, "Big Mama Thornton Plays Rare Club Appearance."

43. Echols, *Scars of Sweet Paradise*, 223.

44. Ibid., 179.

45. Ibid., 290.

46. Dick Cavett and Janis Joplin, *The Dick Cavett Show*, June 25, 1970.

47. Editors, "Culture."

48. Editors, "The 50 Worst Things Ever to Happen to Music."

49. Editors, "Blues for Janis."

50. "Strange Record"; sixty years later, in 1999, *Time* magazine named "Strange Fruit" the best song of the twentieth century, in "The Best of the Century."

51. Ellen Willis, "Janis Joplin," in *The Rolling Stone Illustrated History of Rock & Roll*, 385.

52. Clarke, *Billie Holiday: Wishing on the Moon*, 264.

53. *The Children's Hour*, directed by William Wyler (1961; Los Angeles: The Mirisch Company/United Artists).

54. Editors, "Woman Who Posed as a Man Is Found Slain with Two Others."

55. Friedman Law Offices, "Brandon: An American Tragedy."

56. Maslin, "1999: The Year in Review—Film; Discovering Fresh Ways to See and Sell."

57. Editors, "Transgendered Community Remembers Death That Sparked a Movement."

58. Davis, "1993 Part 1."

59. Editors, "Inmate Recants in 'Boys Don't Cry' Case."

60. Editors, "Transgendered Community Remembers Murder."

61. Smothers, "Woman Is Arrested in Series of Killings in Florida."

62. Editors, "Woman Who Posed as a Man Is Found Slain with Two Others."

63. Hawthorne and Kapler, "Aileen Wuornos Led Rough Life on Road."

64. Siskind, *Easy Riders, Raging Bulls,* 38.

65. LaSalle, *Complicated Women,* 190.

66. Ibid., 200.

67. Ibid., 190–91.

68. Seiler, "Psssttt! Chicago Has a Secret Past!"

69. Ibid.

CHAPTER 3: CHERRY BOMBS

1. Mae West, "Things I'll Never Do—by Mae West," in Louvish, *Mae West: 'It Ain't No Sin,'* xi.

2. Marilyn Monroe, in Meryman, "Marilyn Lets Her Hair Down About Being Famous."

3. CMG Worldwide, www.marilynmonroe.com. Monroe's website is run by CMG Worldwide, a group that also manages the estates of Bettie Page, Marlon Brando, Billie Holiday, and James Dean, among others: www.cmgworldwide.com/clients.html.

4. Rose, Hau, and Schupak, "Top-Earning Dead Celebrities."

5. CMG Worldwide, www.marilynmonroe.com/about/facts.html.

6. Monroe in Meryman, "Marilyn Lets Her Hair Down About Being Famous."

7. Sarah Churchwell's *The Many Lives of Marilyn Monroe* depicts in detail the ways in which the major biographies about Monroe diverge, and the images created in their wake.

8. Capote, "A Beautiful Child," in *Music for Chameleons: New Writings by Truman Capote,* 230.

9. Mailer, *Marilyn, a Biography,* 138.

10. Whitey Snyder in Clark, *The Prince, the Showgirl and Me,* 74.

11. Goodman, Ezra, "To Aristophenes & Back," *Time,* May 14, 1956.

12. *Gentlemen Prefer Blondes,* DVD, directed by Howard Hawks (1953; 20th Century Fox Home Entertainment, 2001).

13. Clark, *The Prince, the Showgirl and Me,* 71.

14. Billy Wilder in Luce, "What Really Killed Marilyn."

15. Clark, *The Prince, the Showgirl, and Me,* 40.

16. Churchwell, *The Many Lives of Marilyn Monroe,* 337.

17. Ibid., 4.

18. Luce, "What Really Killed Marilyn."

19. Mailer, *Marilyn: A Biography,* 133.

20. Clark, *The Prince, the Showgirl and Me,* 87.

21. Ibid., 141.

22. DePaulo, "The Strange, Still Mysterious Death of Marilyn Monroe."

23. Sahagun, "She's Known for her Body of Work. Pin-up Girl from '50s Found Fame, Naturally."

24. Harlan Ellison, "The Queen of Guilty Pleasures," in Foster, *The Real Bettie Page,* x.

25. Cook, "My Story—The Missing Years."

26. Ibid.

27. Foster, *The Real Bettie Page,* 39.

28. Cook, "My Story—The Missing Years."

29. Foster, 57.

30. Ibid., 45.

31. Ibid., 89.

32. Cook, "My Story—The Missing Years."

33. Ibid.

34. Ibid.

35. Foster, *The Real Bettie Page,* 73.

36. Foster, *The Real Bettie Page,* 13; Luce, "What Really Killed Marilyn."

37. Foster, *The Real Bettie Page,* 22.

38. Ibid., 29.

39. Luce, "What Really Killed Marilyn."

40. Ibid.

41. Marilyn Monroe, in Meryman, "Marilyn Lets Her Hair Down About Being Famous."

42. Monroe, in Luce, "What Really Killed Marilyn."

43. Cook, "My Story—The Missing Years."

44. Leland and Malone, "The Selling of Sex" (brackets added).

45. Givens, "Madonnarama."

46. Bosley Crowther, in James, "Audrey Hepburn, Actress, Is Dead at 63."

47. Billy Wilder, in James, "Audrey Hepburn, Actress, Is Dead at 63."

48. Audrey Hepburn, in "Black Is Back, à la Hepburn."

49. Editors, "Audrey Hepburn's Little Black Dress Sells for a Fortune."

50. *Breakfast at Tiffany's.*

51. Kael, "Fatal Attraction."

52. Ibid., 377.

53. Schissel, *Three Plays by Mae West,* 204.

54. Ibid., 20.

55. Ibid., 23.

56. Ibid., 23.

57. Ibid., 7.

58. Mae West in Schissel, 75.

59. Louvish, *Mae West: 'It Ain't No Sin,'* 197.

60. Ibid., 208.

61. LaSalle, *Complicated Women*, 78–9.

62. Louvish, *Mae West: 'It Ain't No Sin,'* 213–14.

63. Ibid., 267.

64. Ibid., 455–59.

65. Ibid., 73–4.

66. Good, "Ill Na Nas, Goddesses, and Drama Mamas," in *The Vibe History of Hip Hop*, 373.

67. Ibid., 377.

CHAPTER 4: THE POLITICAL GETS PERSONAL

1. Editors, "The Revolution," in Sherr, *Failure Is Impossible*, 155.

2. Emmeline Pankhurst, "When Civil War Is Waged by Women," in *Feminism: The Essential Historical Writings*, ed. Miriam Schneir (New York: Vintage Books, 1994), 300.

3. Seneca Falls Convention, "A Declaration of Sentiments and Resolutions," in *Feminism: The Essential Historical Writings*, 76–77.

4. Sherr, *Failure Is Impossible*, 107-108.

5. Ibid., 165.

6. Ibid., xii.

7. Ibid., 142–43.

8. Ibid., 145.

9. Ibid., 145–46.

10. Ibid., 146.

11. Ibid., 148.

12. Ibid., 12–13.

13. Ibid., 4.

14. Daniels, *Wonder Woman*, 11–12.

15. William Moulton Marston, in Daniels, *Wonder Woman*, 23.

16. Library of Congress, "Rosie the Riveter: Real Women Workers in World War II."

17. Friedan, "The Mistaken Choice," in *The Feminine Mystique*, 273-274.

18. Unknown, in Steinem, *Outrageous Acts and Everyday Rebellions*, 9.

19. Robison, Jennifer. "Feminism: What's in a Name?"

20. Editors, "The New Feminists: Revolt Against 'Sexism.'"

21. Steinem, *Outrageous Acts and Everyday Rebellions*, 4.

22. Pat Robertson, in Associated Press, "Pat Robertson Warns Pa. Town of Disaster."

23. Steinem, *Outrageous Acts and Everyday Rebellions*, 384.

24. Brownmiller, *In Our Time*, 94.

25. Fonda, *My Life So Far*, 414.

26. Whitburn, Joel, The Billboard Book of Top 40 Hits (New York: Billboard Books, 2000), 521.

27. Ibid., 434-435.

28. Ibid., 249-250.

29. Ibid., 236-237.

30. Fonda, *My Life So Far*, 195.

31. Ibid., 274.

32. Associated Press, "'Worth It,' Says Fonda Spitter."

33. Fonda, *My Life So Far*, 318.

34. Editors, "Jane Fonda Accuses Nixon."

35. Editors, "House Committee Refuses to Subpoena Jane Fonda."

36. Editors, "'70 Effort by Hoover to Discredit Jane Fonda Described in Memo."

37. Sheehy, "Women and Leadership: Jane Fonda."

38. Cindy Sheehan in Barsamian, "The Cindy Sheehan Interview."

39. Cindy Sheehan in Ensler, "My Son Brought Me Here."

40. Cindy Sheehan in Barsamian, "The Cindy Sheehan Interview."

41. Ripley, "A Mother and the President."

42. Ensler, "My Son Brought Me Here."

43. Ripley, "A Mother and the President."

CHAPTER 5: THE TAMING OF THE SHREW

1. Roosevelt, *The Autobiography of Eleanor Roosevelt,* 416.

2. Hager, "Candidates for the Post of First Lady."

3. Adams, "To the Woman in Politics Comes Also a New Deal."

4. Roosevelt, *The Autobiography of Eleanor Roosevelt,* 66.

5. Ibid., 68.

6. Ibid., 163.

7. Editors, "Eleanor Everywhere."

8. Roosevelt, *The Autobiography of Eleanor Roosevelt,* 279.

9. Ibid., 132

10. Barnard, "Mrs. Roosevelt in the Classroom."

11. Roosevelt, *The Autobiography of Eleanor Roosevelt,* 197–98. See also "Eleanor Roosevelt: First Lady of the World," http://www.fdrlibrary.marist.edu/ERBIO.html.

12. Ibid., 171.

13. Ibid., 315–16.

14. Clinton, *Living History,* 103.

15. Ibid., 105.

16. Voboril, "Elect Him, You Get Hillary."

17. Voboril, "Mother Hillary Gets a New Image."

18. Green, "With the Bushes' Go-Ahead, the GOP Goes After Hillary."

19. Clinton, *Living History,* 110.

20. Givhan, "Wearing the Pants."

21. Dowd, "Duel of Historical Guilts."

22. Dowd, "Can Hillary Cry Her Way Back to the White House?"

23. *Adam's Rib*, directed by George Cukor (1949; Burbank, CA: Warner Home Video, 2000).

24. Mann, *Kate: The Woman Who Was Hepburn*, 235.

25. McLellan, *The Girls*, 231.

26. Mann's biography explores this point at length in *Kate: The Woman Who Was Hepburn*, particularly in "Silencing the Most Articulate Voice," 344–364.

27. Ibid., 306.

28. Ibid., 36–37.

29. Ibid., 344–345.

30. Editors, "The Case of Angela the Red."

31. Davis, *Angela Davis*, 273.

32. Mann, *Kate: The Woman Who Was Hepburn*, 358.

33. Davis, *Angela Davis*, 220.

34. Ibid., 25.

35. Ibid., 26.

36. Ibid., 161.

37. Judy Blume in Dillin, "Judy Blume."

38. Blume, in Levy, "Judy Blume Honored for Literary Courage."

39. Levy, "Judy Blume Honored for Literary Courage."

40. Susan Dworkin, "The Strange and Wonderful Story of the Making of The Color Purple,'" *Ms.* magazine, December 1985; reprinted in Walker, *The Same River Twice*, 176.

41. Walker, *The Same River Twice*, 170.

42. Walker, in Rosenfeld, "Profiles in Purple & Black."

43. Tony Brown, "Blacks Need to Love One Another," *Carolina Peacemaker*; reprinted in Walker, *The Same River Twice*, 224.

44. Walker, *The Same River Twice,* 39.

45. Walker, in Rosenfeld, "Profiles in Purple & Black."

46. Sinéad O'Connor, in Wild, "Sinéad O'Connor."

47. Whitburn, *The Billboard Book of Top 40 Hits,* 466.

48. Wild, "Sinead O'Connor."

49. Light, "Sinéad Speaks."

50. O'Connor, in Wild, "Sinead O'Connor."

51. O'Connor, in Simpson, "People Need a Short, Sharp Shock" (brackets added).

52. Ibid.

53. Editors, "Tearing Up Late-Night TV."

54. Natalie Maines, in Reuters, "Dixie Chicks Pulled from Air After Bashing Bush."

55. Reuters, "Dixie Chicks Pulled from Air After Bashing Bush."

56. Maines, in Zacharek, "Bush, Shame and the Dixie Chicks."

57. Reuters, "Dixie Chicks Pulled from Air After Bashing Bush."

CHAPTER 6: ANGELS, ALIENS, AND ASS KICKING

1. Joss Whedon, in Ervin-Gore, "Joss Whedon."

2. Flynn, "Bionic Woman."

3. Daniels, *Wonder Woman,* 134–37.

4. *Alien,* DVD, directed by Ridley Scott (1979; Los Angeles: 20th Century Fox Home Entertainment, 2004).

5. *Alien.*

6. *Alien.*

7. Tucker, "Alias."

8. Tarantino wrote the scripts for *True Romance* and *Natural Born Killers,* but Tony Scott and Oliver Stone, respectively, directed them.

9. Mary Celeste Kearney, "The Changing Face of Teen Television, Or Why We All Love *Buffy*" in Levine and Parks, *Undead TV,* 38.

10. Whedon, in Ervin-Gore, "Joss Whedon."

11. McCracken, Allison. "At Stake: Angel's Body, Fantasy Masculinity, and Queer Desire in Teen Television," in Levine and Parks, *Undead TV*, 118, 124.

CHAPTER 7: UNEASY RIDERS

1. DiFranco, "Open Letter to *Ms.* Magazine" (brackets added).

2. Editors, "Fashion Week Make You Want to Hurl? We're Here to Help."

3. Pérez-Peña, "Celebrity Magazines Gain, but Not Industry Circulation."

4. Centers for Disease Control, *National Vital Statistics Reports*.

5. Pew Research Center, "Fewer Mothers Prefer Full-Time Work: From 1997–2007."

6. Ibid.

7. Pew Research Center, "As Marriage and Parenthood Drift Apart, Public Is Concerned about Social Impact."

8. Wedding Report, "Wedding Cost and Spending."

9. *Lucky Magazine* fact sheet.

10. "An American Girl in Paris: Part Deux," *Sex and the City,* season 6, episode 94, directed by Tim Van Patten (2004; Culver City, CA: Darren Star Productions, Home Box Office, Sex and the City Productions).

11. De Moraes, "Kanye West's Torrent of Criticism."

12. Editors, "2006–07 Primetime Wrap."

13. DiFranco, in Lanzendorfer, "I'm a Voting Adult and It's My Job to Fix It."

works cited

Biskind, Peter. *Easy Riders, Raging Bulls: How the Sex-Drugs-and-Rock 'n' Roll Generation Saved Hollywood.* New York: Touchstone, 1998.

Brownmiller, Susan. *In Our Time: Memoir of a Revolution.* New York: Dell, 1999.

Charters, Ann. *Kerouac: A Biography.* New York: St. Martin's Griffin, 1994.

Churchwell, Sarah. *The Many Lives of Marilyn Monroe.* New York: Metropolitan Books, Henry Holt & Company, 2004.

Clark, Colin. *The Prince, the Showgirl and Me: Six Months on the Set with Marilyn and Olivier.* New York: St. Martin's Press, 1996.

Clarke, Donald. *Billie Holiday: Wishing on the Moon.* Cambridge, MA: Da Capo, 2000.

Clinton, Hillary. *Living History*. New York: Simon & Schuster, 2003.

Daniels, Les. *Wonder Woman: The Complete History*. San Francisco: Chronicle Books, 2000.

Davis, Angela. *Angela Davis: An Autobiography*. New York: International Publishers, 1989.

———. *Blues Legacies and Black Feminism*. New York: Vintage, 1999.

DeCurtis, Anthony, James Henke, and Holly George-Warren, eds. *The Rolling Stone Illustrated History of Rock and Roll: The Definitive History of the Most Important Artists and Their Music*. New York: Random House, 1992.

di Prima, Diane. *Recollections of My Life as a Woman: The New York Years*. New York: Penguin, 2001.

Dufty, William, and Billie Holiday. *Lady Sings the Blues*. New York: Harlem Moon, 2006.

Echols, Alice. *Scars of Sweet Paradise: The Life and Times of Janis Joplin*. New York: Henry Holt and Company, 1999.

Eugenides, Jeffrey. *Middlesex*. New York: Picador, 2002.

Fonda, Jane. *My Life So Far*. New York: Random House, 2006.

Foster, Richard. *The Real Bettie Page: The Truth About the Queen of the Pinups*. New York: Citadel Press, 1997.

Kerouac, Jack. *On the Road*. New York: Penguin, 1976.

LaSalle, Mick. *Complicated Women: Sex and Power in Pre-Code Hollywood*. New York: Thomas Dunne Books, 2000.

Lee, Hermione. *Virginia Woolf. New York: Vintage Books, 1999.*

Levine, Elana, and Lisa Parks, eds. *Undead TV: Essays on Buffy the Vampire Slayer. North Carolina: Duke University Press, 2007.*

Louvish, Simon. *Mae West: "It Ain't No Sin." New York: Thomas Dunne Books, 2005.*

Mailer, Norman. *Marilyn, a Biography. New York: Grosset & Dunlap, 1981.*

Mann, William J. *Kate: The Woman Who Was Hepburn. New York: Picador, 2006.*

McLellan, Diana. *The Girls: Sappho Goes to Hollywood. New York: L.A. Weekly Books, St. Martin's Griffin, 2000.*

Plath, Sylvia. *The Bell Jar. New York: Perennial, 1999.*

———. *The Unabridged Journals of Sylvia Plath. New York: Anchor, 2000.*

Plummer, William. *The Holy Goof. New York: Thunder's Mouth Press, 2004.*

Roosevelt, Eleanor. *The Autobiography of Eleanor Roosevelt. Cambridge, MA: Da Capo Press, 1992.*

Schneir, Miriam, ed. *Feminism: The Essential Historical Writings. New York: Vintage Books, 1994.*

Sherr, Lynn. *Failure Is Impossible: Susan B. Anthony in Her Own Words. New York: Times Books, 1995.*

Steinem, Gloria. *Outrageous Acts and Everyday Rebellions. New York: Signet, 1983.*

Walker, Alice. *The Same River Twice*. New York: Scribner, 1996.

West, Mae, and Lillian Schlissel, ed. *Three Plays by Mae West*. New York: Routledge, 1997.

Whitburn, Joel. *Billboard Top 10 Singles Charts 1955–2000*. Menomonee Falls, WI: Record Research, 2001.

———. *The Billboard Book of Top 40 Hits 1955–2000*. Menomonee Falls, WI: Record Research, 2000.

Woolf, Virginia. *A Room of One's Own*. Orlando, FL: Harvest, 1989.

———. *Orlando*. Orlando, FL: Harcourt, edition unknown (originally published 1928).

———. *The Diary of Virginia Woolf: Volume 4, 1931–1935*. Orlando, FL: Harvest, 1983.

ARTICLES AND CHAPTERS

"The 50 Worst Things Ever to Happen to Music." *Blender*, April 2006. www.blender.com/guide/articles.aspx?id=1913.

"'70 Effort by Hoover to Discredit Jane Fonda Described in Memo." *New York Times*, December 16, 1975.

"2006–07 Primetime Wrap." *Hollywood Reporter*, May 25, 2007. www.hollywoodreporter.com/.

Adams, Mildred. "To the Woman in Politics Comes Also a New Deal." *New York Times*, April 30, 1933.

"Alone with the Blues." *Time*, August 27, 1973.

Associated Press. *"Holiday Movies: The Dark Side of Christmas."* *www.ap.org,* October 17, 2003.

———. *"Pat Robertson Warns Pa. Town of Disaster."* *Washington Post,* November 11, 2005. *www.washingtonpost.com/.*

———. *"'Worth It,' Says Fonda Spitter."* *CBS News,* April 21, 2005. *www.cbsnews.com/.*

"Audrey Hepburn's Little Black Dress Sells for a Fortune." *Hellomagazine.com,* December 6, 2006. *www.hellomagazine.com/celebrities/2006.*

Bangs, Lester. *"Where Were You When Elvis Died?"* In *Psychotic Reactions and Carburetor Dung.* New York: Random House, 1987.

Barnard, Eunice Fuller. *"Mrs. Roosevelt in the Classroom."* *New York Times,* December 4, 1932.

Barsamian, David. *"The Cindy Sheehan Interview."* *Progressive,* March 2006. *www.progressive.org/mag_intv0306.*

"The Best of the Century." *Time,* December 31, 1999.

Biskind, Peter. *"The Enemy Within."* In *Seeing Is Believing: How Hollywood Taught Us to Stop Worrying and Love the Fifties.* New York: Henry Holt and Company, 1983.

"Black is back, à la Hepburn." *International Herald Tribune,* October 1, 2006. *www.iht.com/articles/2006.*

"Blues for Janis." *Time,* October 19, 1970.

Capote, Truman. *"A Beautiful Child."* In *Music for Chameleons: New Writings by Truman Capote.* New York: Random House, 1980.

"The Case of Angela the Red." Time, October 17, 1969.

Centers for Disease Control. *National Vital Statistics Reports.* CDC.gov, July 21, 2006. *www.cdc.gov/nchs.*

CMG Worldwide, *www.marilynmonroe.com.*

Cook, Kevin. *"My Story—The Missing Years."* Playboy, March 17, 1998.

Crowther, Bosley. *"'Streetcar Named Desire,' With Vivian Leigh, Has Premier at the Warner Theatre."* New York Times, September 20, 1951.

"Culture." Time, January 30, 1989.

Davis, Kaley. *"1993 Part 1."* Stranger, June 21, 2007.

De Moraes, Lisa. *"Kanye West's Torrent of Criticism."* Washington Post, September 3, 2005.

DePaulo, Lisa. *"The Strange, Still Mysterious Death of Marilyn Monroe."* Playboy, December 13, 2005.

DiFranco, Ani. *"Open Letter to Ms. Magazine."* November 5, 1997. *www.columbia.edu/~marg/ani/letter.html.*

Dillin, Gay Andrews. *"Judy Blume."* Christian Science Monitor, December 29, 1981.

Dowd, Maureen. *"Duel of Historical Guilts."* New York Times, March 5, 2008.

———. *"Can Hillary Cry Her Way Back to the White House?"* New York Times, January 9, 2008.

Duffy, Martha. *"Lady Lazarus." Time, June 21,1971.*

"Eleanor Everywhere." Time, November 20, 1933.

Ensler, Eve. *"My Son Brought Me Here." O: The Oprah Magazine, 1 November 1, 2005.*

Flynn, Gillian. *"Bionic Woman." Entertainment Weekly, September 26, 2007. www.ew.com/.*

Ervin-Gore, Shawna. *"Joss Whedon." Dark Horse Comics, date unknown. www.darkhorse.com/news/interviews.*

"Fashion Week Make You Want to Hurl? We're Here to Help." Jezebel, September 6, 2007. http://jezebel.com/gossip.

Franklin Delano Roosevelt Museum. *"Eleanor Roosevelt: First Lady of the World." http://www.fdrlibrary.marist.edu/ERBIO.html.*

Friedan, Betty. *"The Mistaken Choice." In The Feminine Mystique. New York: W.W. Norton, 1997.*

Friedman, Herb. *"Brandon: An American Tragedy." Friedman Law Offices, date unknown. www.friedmanlaw.com/.*

Fujiwara, Chris. *"The Rebel." Boston Globe, October 30, 2005. www.boston.com/news/globe/ideas/articles/2005/10/30/the_rebel/.*

Givens, Ron. *"Madonnarama." Entertainment Weekly, May 11, 1990. www.ew.com/.*

Givhan, Robin. *"Wearing the Pants." Washington Post, December 9, 2007.*

Good, Karen R. *"Ill Na Nas, Goddesses, and Drama Mamas."* In *The Vibe History of Hip Hop*, ed. Alan Light. New York: Three Rivers Press, 1999.

Goodman, Ezra. *"Aristophenes & Back."* Time, May 14, 1956.

Green, Charles. *"With the Bushes' Go-Ahead, the GOP Goes After Hillary."* Philadelphia Inquirer, August 20, 1992.

Gundersen, Edna. *"'Massacre' Sales Top 1 Million."* USA Today, March 9, 200 www.usatoday.com/life/music.

Hager, Alice Rogers. *"Candidates for the Post of First Lady."* New York Times, October 2, 1932.

Hawthorne, Michael, and Robert Kapler. *"Aileen Wuornos Led Rough Life on Road."* Daytona News Journal, February 10, 1991. www.news-journalonline.com/special.

"House Committee Refuses to Subpoena Jane Fonda." New York Times, August 11, 1972.

"Inmate Recants in 'Boys Don't Cry' Case." CNN.com, September 20, 2007. www.cnn.com/.

James, Caryn. *"Audrey Hepburn, Actress, is Dead at 63."* New York Times, January 21, 1993.

"James Dean, Film Actor, Killed in Crash of Auto." New York Times, October 1, 1955.

"Jane Fonda Accuses Nixon." New York Times, July 25, 1972.

Kael, Pauline. *"Fatal Attraction."* In *Hooked*. New York: E. P. Dutton, 1989.

———. "Marlon Brando: An American Hero." Atlantic Monthly, March 1966. www.theatlantic.com/.

Kerouac, Jack. "Article on Youth Movements." Kerouac Archives, New York Public Library, 1949. Viewed November 2007 and March 2008.

Lanzendorfer, Joy. "I'm a Voting Adult and It's My Job to Fix It." Salon, June 10, 2003. http://dir.salon.com/.

Leland, John and Maggie Malone. "The Selling of Sex." Newsweek, volume 120, issue 18.

Lelyveld, Joseph. "Jack Kerouac, Novelist, Dead; Father of the Beat Generation." New York Times, October 22, 1969.

Levy, Kelly. "Judy Blume Honored for Literary Courage." USA Today, February 26, 2004.

Library of Congress. "Rosie the Riveter: Real Women Workers in World War II." www.loc.gov/rr/program/journey/rosie-transcript.html.

Light, Alan. "Sinéad Speaks." Rolling Stone, October 29, 1992.

Locke, Richard. "The Last Word: Beside the Bell Jar." New York Times, June 20, 1971.

Luce, Clare Booth. "What Really Killed Marilyn." Life, August 7, 1964.

Lucky magazine fact sheet, www.luckymag.com/services/presscenter/pressreleases/FactSheet.

Lyman, Rick. "Marlon Brando, Oscar-Winning Actor, is Dead at 80." New York Times, July 2, 2004.

Maslin, Janet. "1999: The Year in Review—Film; Discovering Fresh Ways to See and Sell." New York Times, December 26, 1999.

Meryman, Richard. "Marilyn Lets Her Hair Down About Being Famous." Life, August 3, 1962.

"The New Woman, 1972." Time, March 20, 1972.

"The New Feminists: Revolt Against 'Sexism.'" Time, November 21, 1969.

Palmer, Robert. "Big Mama Thornton Plays Rare Club Appearance." New York Times, July 4, 1980.

Peña-Pérez, Richard. "Celebrity Magazines Gain, but Not Industry Circulation." New York Times, August 14, 2007.

Pew Research Center. "As Marriage and Parenthood Drift Apart, Public Is Concerned about Social Impact." Pew Research Center, July 1, 2007. http://pewresearch.org/pubs/526/marriage-parenthood.

Pew Research Center. "Fewer Mothers Prefer Full-Time Work: From 1997-2007." Pew Research Center, July 12, 2007. http://pewresearch.org/pubs/536/workingwomen.

Pollitt, Katha. "A Look at the Poems." New York Times, May 20, 1979.

Reuters. "Dixie Chicks Pulled from Air After Bashing Bush." CNN.com, March 14, 2003. www.cnn.com/.

Ripley, Amanda. "A Mother and the President." Time, August 15, 2005. www.time.com/time/magazine.

Robison, Jennifer. "Feminism: What's in a Name?" Gallup.com, September 3, 2002. www.gallup.com/poll/6715/Feminism-Whats-Name.aspx.

Rosenfeld, Megan. *"Profiles in Purple & Black."* Washington Post, October 15, 1982.

Rose, Lacey, Louis Hau, and Amanda Schupak. *"Top-Earning Dead Celebrities."* Forbes.com, October 24, 3006. www.forbes.com/.

Sahagun, Louis. *"She's Known for her Body of Work: Pin-up Girl from '50s Found Fame, Naturally."* Los Angeles Times, March 11, 2006.

Seiler, Andy. *"Psssttt! Chicago Has a Secret Past!"* USA Today, March 24, 2003. www.usatoday.com/life/movies.

Sheehy, Gail. *"Women and Leadership: Jane Fonda."* New York Times, January 10, 1980.

Simpson, Janice C. *"People Need a Short, Sharp Shock."* Time, November 9, 1992.

Smothers, Ronald. *"Woman is Arrested in Series of Killings in Florida."* New York Times, January 18, 1991.

"Strange Record." Time, June 12, 1939.

"Suicide Note." Time, May 5, 1941.

"Tearing Up Late-Night TV." Newsweek, October 19, 1992.

"Transgendered Community Remembers Death That Sparked a Movement." CNN.com, December 28, 2003. www.cnn.com/.

"Transgendered Community Remembers Murder." USA Today, December 28, 2003. www.usatoday.com/news/nation.

Tucker, Ken. *"Alias."* Entertainment Weekly, October 18, 2002. www.ew.com/.

Voboril, Mary. *"Elect Him, You Get Hillary."* Philadelphia Inquirer, May 4, 1992.

————. "Mother Hillary Gets a New Image." *Philadelphia Inquirer*, July 17, 1992.

Wedding Report. "Wedding Cost and Spending." *The Wedding Report.* *www.theweddingreport.com/.*

Wild, D. "Sinéad O'Connor." *Rolling Stone*, March 7, 1991.

"Woman Who Posed as a Man Is Found Slain with Two Others." *New York Times*, January 4, 1994.

Zachareck, Stephanie. "Bush, Shame and the Dixie Chicks." *Salon*, March 18, 2003. *http://dir.salon.com/.*

SELECT MULTIMEDIA

Adam's Rib. Directed by George Cukor. 1949. Burbank, CA: Warner Home Video, 2000.

Alien. DVD. Directed by Ridley Scott. 1979. Los Angeles: 20th Century Fox Home Entertainment, 2004.

Aliens. DVD. Directed by James Cameron. 1986. Los Angeles: 20th Century Fox Home Entertainment, 1999.

Boys Don't Cry. DVD. Directed by Kimberley Peirce. 1999. Los Angeles: 20th Century Fox Home Entertainment, 2000.

Breakfast at Tiffany's. DVD. Directed by Blake Edwards. 1961. Los Angeles: Paramount Home Video, 1999.

Buffy the Vampire Slayer. season 3, disc 1. DVD. Various directors. 1998. Los Angeles: 20th Century Fox Home Entertainment, 2006.

The Children's Hour. DVD. Directed by William Wyler. 1961. Los Angeles: MGM Home Entertainment, 2002.

Charlie's Angels. *Directed by Joseph McGinty Mitchell. 2000. Culver City, CA: Columbia TriStar Home Video.*

Charlie's Angels, season 2. *DVD. Various directors. 2004.*

Coffy. *DVD. Directed by Jack Hill. 1973. Los Angeles: MGM Home Entertainment, 2001.*

Cool Hand Luke. *DVD. Directed by Stuart Rosenberg. 1967. Burbank, CA: Warner Home Video, 1997.*

Dirty Harry. *DVD. Directed by Don Siegel. 1971. Burbank, CA: Warner Home Video, 1999.*

East of Eden. *DVD. Directed by Elia Kazan. 1955. Burbank, CA: Warner Home Video, 2005.*

Easy Rider. *DVD. Directed by Dennis Hopper. 1969. Culver City, CA: Columbia TriStar Home Video, 2002.*

Five Easy Pieces. *DVD. Directed by Bob Rafelson. 1970. Culver City, CA: Sony Pictures Home Entertainment, 1999.*

Foxy Brown. *DVD. Directed by Jack Hill. 1974. Los Angeles: MGM Home Entertainment, 2001.*

Gentlemen Prefer Blondes. *DVD. Directed by Howard Hawks. 1953. Los Angeles: 20th Century Fox Home Entertainment, 2001.*

How to Marry a Millionaire. *DVD. Directed by Jean Negulesco. 1953. Los Angeles: 20th Century Fox Home Entertainment, 2001.*

Kill Bill: Volume I. *DVD. Directed by Quentin Tarantino. 2003. Burbank, CA: Miramax Home Entertainment, 2004.*

Kill Bill: Volume II. *DVD. Directed by Quentin Tarantino. 2004. Burbank, CA: Miramax Home Entertainment, 2004.*

Lara Croft: Tomb Raider. *DVD. Directed by Simon West. 2001. Los Angeles: Paramount Home Video, 2003.*

Monster. *DVD. Directed by Patty Jenkins. 2003. Culver City, CA: Columbia TriStar Home Entertainment, 2004.*

On the Waterfront. *DVD. Directed by Elia Kazan. 1954. Culver City, CA: Columbia TriStar Home Video, 2002.*

Possessed. *DVD. Directed by Curtis Bernhardt, 1947. Burbank, CA: Warner Home Video, 2005.*

Raging Bull. *DVD. Directed by Martin Scorsese. 1980. Los Angeles: MGM/UA Home Entertainment, 2000.*

Rebel Without a Cause. *DVD. Directed by Nicholas Ray. 1955. Burbank, CA: Warner Home Video, 1999.*

The Rose. *DVD. Directed by Mark Rydell. 1979. Los Angeles: 20th Century Fox Home Entertainment, 2003.*

The Seven-Year Itch. *DVD. Directed by Billy Wilder. 1955. Los Angeles: 20th Century Fox Home Entertainment, 2001.*

Silkwood. *DVD. Directed by Mike Nichols. 1983. Los Angeles: MGM Home Entertainment, 2003.*

Some Like It Hot. *DVD. Directed by Billy Wilder. 1959. Los Angeles: MGM Home Entertainment, 2001.*

A Streetcar Named Desire. DVD. Directed by Elia Kazan. 1951. Burbank, CA: Warner Home Video, 1997.

Sudden Fear. DVD. Directed by David Miller. 1952. Chatsworth, CA: Image Entertainment, 2003.

Taxi Driver. DVD. Directed by Martin Scorsese. 1976. Culver City, CA: ColumbiaTriStar Home Video, 1999.

Thelma & Louise. DVD. Directed by Ridley Scott. 1991. Los Angeles: 20th Century Fox Home Entertainment, 2007.

The Wild One. DVD. Directed by Laszlo Benedek. 1953. Culver City, CA: Columbia TriStar, 1999.

Wonder Woman, season 2: disc 1. DVD. Various directors. 1977. Burbank, CA: Warner Brothers Home Video, 2005.

X-Men, 2000, Bryan Singer, director, Twentieth Century-Fox Film Corporation; 20th Century Fox Home Entertainment, 2000.

X-2: X-Men United, 2003, Bryan Singer, director, Twentieth Century-Fox Film Corporation, 20th Century Fox Home Entertainment, 2003.

X-Men: The Last Stand, 2006, Brett Ratner, director, Twentieth Century-Fox Film Corporation; 20th Century Fox Home Entertainment, 2006.

Release dates, names of production studios, and occasionally actor and character names, as well as Academy Awards information, were obtained through the Internet Movie Database (www.imdb.com and www.imdbpro.com) and the Academy Awards Database, www.oscars.org/awardsdatabase, located on the Academy of Motion Picture Arts and Sciences website.

Acknowledgments

Many thanks and much love to my parents, Jack and Jackie Raha, who understand my rebellion as a path to self-discovery and my own worldview, and who provide a comforting "room of my own" when I need it.

I'm grateful to my editors, Anne L. Connolly and Brooke Warner, for making thoughtful suggestions, hearing me out, hashing it out, and allowing me to write about intriguing women, and to the whole staff at Seal Press and Perseus Books for believing in women and for working for us. Thanks to Annie Tucker for a meticulous, massive, and consistently impressive copyedit, as well as to Tabitha Lahr for photo research and a beautiful book design, and for picking up the slack when I couldn't.

I owe a debt of gratitude and love to the following people: Lorraine Raha and Eoin Milligan, and Jackie, Matthew, Jacqueline, and Gabriella Gaynor. To my funny, fiery, fabulous extended family, for positive support and comfort: Theresa Gagliano, Mike and Linda Raha, Stephanie Raha and Frank Sweeney, Cynthia Raha; and to my godparents, Anthony and Camille Gagliano, who might not have understood their rebel goddaughter but made the choice to love her anyway. To all members—far, wide, and extended—of the Gagliano, Raha, and Tomaccio clans and their families.

To my chosen family, the Ithacans, for years of rebel bliss and political discussions: Peter Pagano, Brian Greyard, Carly Guarino, Todd Skoglund, and every last one of you.

To new and renewed friends in Philly, for welcoming me, building me a new home, understanding when I had to hibernate, and putting up with a year of running rebel commentary: Sarah Amazeen, CA Conrad, Erin Davis, Elise Hacking, Lael Hesley, Sharon Linsenbach, JT Ramsay, my partner in crime Nikki Roszko; and to the activists, poets, and musicians of Philly, who never fail to amaze and inspire me.

To Susan Pearce, for seventeen years of friendship and fun, and to both Susan and Nicky Garrett, for opening their home to me and providing me with a writer's retreat beyond compare.

To Diane di Prima, for encouraging me to dive blindfolded into the fire.

For their continued support, thanks to Michelle Timmons, Marti Zimlin-Hurwitz, Johna DePasquale, Keri, Rob, and Griffin Kaminskey, Brennan, Kyra, and Holden Condo, and the East 3rd noise crew, especially Steve Lowenthal. To Alex Roszko, for endless surprises, beautiful food, and most importantly, love.

Finally, none of this would have happened without *Los Pitufos,* who provided epic dinners, *cacho,* gut-splitting laughter, late-night rant sessions, road trips, Phillies games, original music and the magic that is Powderfinger, cigarettes, wine, and general debauchery: Mike Balotti, Dan Collins, Mark Eckel, and AnaCe Velasquez. *Los Pitufos son mi corazón.*

photo credits

© Lael Hesley

About the Author

Maria Raha is the author of *Cinderella's Big Score: Women of the Punk and Indie Underground.* Her nonfiction work has also appeared in *Young Wives' Tales: New Adventures in Love and Partnership* (Seal Press, 2001) and *The W Effect: Bush's War on Women* (Feminist Press, 2004). She is the managing editor of *Swingset* and a contributor to *Bitch: Feminist Response to Pop Culture,* among other publications. Maria currently resides in Philadelphia.

selected Titles From seal press

For more than thirty years, Seal Press has published groundbreaking books. By women. For women. Visit our website at www.sealpress.com. Check out the Seal Press blog at www.sealpress.com/blog.

Cinderella's Big Score: Women of the Punk and Indie Underground, by Maria Raha. $17.95, 1-58005-116-2. A tribute to the transgressive women of the underground music scene, who not only rocked as hard as the boys, but also tested the limits of what is culturally acceptable—even in the anarchic world of punk.

Feminism and Pop Culture: Seal Studies, by Andi Zeisler. $12.95, 1-58005-237-1. Andi Zeisler, cofounder of *Bitch Magazine,* traces the impact of feminism on pop culture (and vice versa) from the 1940s to today.

Word Warriors: 35 Women Leaders in the Spoken Word Revolution, edited by Alix Olson, foreword by Eve Ensler. $15.95, 1-58005-221-5. This groundbreaking collection of poems and essays, the first all-women spoken word anthology, features the most influential female spoken word artists in the movement.

What Would Murphy Brown Do? How the Women of Prime Time Changed Our Lives, by Allison Klein. $16.95, 1-58005-171-5. From workplace politics to single motherhood to designer heels in the city, revisit TV's favorite—and most influential—women of the 1970s through today who stood up and held their own.

Pissed Off: On Women and Anger, by Spike Gillespie. $14.95, 1-58005-162-6. An amped-up and personal self-help book that encourages women to go ahead and use that middle finger without being closed off to the notion of forgiveness.

Body Outlaws: Rewriting the Rules of Beauty and Body Image, edited by Ophira Edut, foreword by Rebecca Walker. $15.95, 1-58005-108-1. Filled with honesty and humor, this groundbreaking anthology offers stories by women who have chosen to ignore, subvert, or redefine the dominant beauty standard in order to feel at home in their bodies.